Also by David Falkner

Sadaharu Oh: A Zen Way of Baseball
(with Sadaharu Oh)

THE SHORT SEASON

THE SHORT
SEASON

THE HARD WORK AND
HIGH TIMES OF BASEBALL
IN THE SPRING

David Falkner

Times
BOOKS

Library of Congress Cataloging-in-Publication Data

Falkner, David.
The short season.

1. Chicago Cubs (Baseball team)   2. Baseball—
Training.   I. Title.
GV875.C6F35   1986   796.357'64'0977311   85-40830
ISBN 0-8129-1266-7

*Grateful acknowledgment is made to the following for permission to
reprint previously published material:*
Alfred A. Knopf, Inc.: excerpt from "Anecdote of the Jar" by Wallace
Stevens. Copyright 1923 and renewed 1951 by Wallace Stevens.
Reprinted from *The Collected Poems of Wallace Stevens* by Wallace
Stevens, by permission of Alfred A. Knopf, Inc.

Harvard University Press: Poem #67, by Emily Dickinson. Reprinted
by permission of the publishers and Trustees of Amherst College from
The Poems of Emily Dickinson, edited by Thomas H. Johnson,
Cambridge, Mass.: The Belknap Press of Harvard University Press,
Copyright 1951, © 1955, 1979, 1983 by the President and Fellows of
Harvard College.

Alexander R. James: excerpt from *What Maisie Knew* by Henry James.
Reprinted by permission of Alexander R. James, Literary Executor,
Glandore, Co. Cork.

To the memory of
Benjamin H. Siff

Acknowledgments

A ny book done out in the open and which involves a large
cast of characters is inevitably a cooperative effort. In this
case, my principal thanks go to the players, coaches, managers,
executives, and fans who let me drop into their lives for a while.
I owe particular thanks to several people who made the way
easier for me. Tom Heitz of the Baseball Library at Cooperstown and Joe Reichler of Major League Baseball Productions
made research a pleasure, not a chore; Jim Henneman of the
Baltimore Sun introduced me to Miami, gave me a place to stay,
and shared with me a couple of unforgettable shrimp recipes
along with his extensive knowledge of the game. Bob Brown,
the publicity director of the Orioles, offered help and friendship—beyond any reasonable call of duty. I owe thanks, too, to
Dick Bresciani of the Red Sox, Joe Safety and Lou D'Ermilio of
the Yankees, Dan Ewald of the Tigers, Howard Starkman of the
Blue Jays, and to media directors on other teams who made my
comings and goings trouble-free. I was also greatly aided by
Andrew Siff, my nephew and research associate, whose baseball
acumen has already qualified him for a Häagen-Dazs ice cream
franchise. I benefited from the insights, advice, and friendship
of Ron Shapiro, Lee Lowenfish, David Black, and Peter

Skolnick—each of whom helped in ways that were individual and caring. I am indebted to my wife and family for a daily support and wisdom that cannot be adequately named here but that had everything to do with my being able to start and finish this book.

Contents

CONTENTS

PART ONE

EARLY
ARRIVALS

CHAPTER ONE

Sunrise in the Desert

Driving east on Highway 10, a few miles beyond the city limits of Phoenix, a green road sign leads a traveler toward the Superstition Highway. You take this road with the unsettling name for a time, and you are aware that all the while you are ringed by flame-shaped mountains called, not surprisingly, The Superstitions. Of course there is a story behind the naming of these hills—but for now, no matter. We Americans are creatures of the present and, in the present, in this soft spring desert air of 1985, The Superstitions mark the latitude and longitude of the Chicago Cubs' dream for a world championship. As all die-hard Cub fans, and most casual baseball fans know, the Cubs have not had a world championship since the gaudy year of 1908, two years before the death of Tolstoy. For the Cubs to have surrounded their dream with these hills is peculiar enough. Yet they have taken unto themselves the added burdens of a spring training ground named after an extinct Indian tribe—the Ho Ho Kam—and a picturesque ballpark located directly across the street from a cemetery, with its distant view of The Superstitions. How do the bearers of such burdens view such thinking?

"That's a lotta crap!" says Jim Frey, manager of The Superstitions' darlings—and one of the game's genuinely decent men. The San Diego Padres, victorious over the Cubs in the 1984 playoffs, were all the haunting he needed to guarantee a tortured winter and the concomitant yearning for something new in the spring of 1985.

"What a pile that one is!" growled Dallas Green. Green is six feet five inches, a booming presence in the manner of John Wayne. Wrigley Field without lights, state legislatures, and local lunatics, not the haunting of mountains and old Indian tribes and neighboring cemeteries, are the real hobgoblins of his spring. Winning is not a mystical idea, any more than damming the Colorado or riding into Dodge City and restoring law and order.

"Haven't Cub fans, over the years," I lamely persisted, "actually built up a small industry around losing?"

For Dallas Green, this question was slow-pitch softball to a home run hitter. "Well," he said, "we're gonna knock that industry the hell out of here, because we're gonna put a winning industry in. And we're gonna sell that."

I wondered what Green would do to me if I told him I had just finished reading a book about all those people from Montezuma to Jacob Walzer who had come to The Superstitions and died for gold. I never risked it.

On the top steps of Ho Ho Kam Park, looking beyond the scoreboard and outfield to the floor of the desert valley and the crumpled brown hills in the perfect sunlight of early spring, I could think only that Green was so intent on winning that he no longer believed it was connected to losing. Of course, baseball in the spring in America has always been about hope. Some have sold it, some have labored for it as the fulfillment of a dream, some have even died for it. In the spring of one year, Lou Gehrig discovered the first signs of fatal illness in the iron of his body. Gil Hodges fell dead one beautiful spring training morning.

Hope is by its very nature wedded to both victory and defeat.
Emily Dickinson wrote:

> Success is counted sweetest
> By those who ne'er succeed.
> To comprehend a nectar
> Requires sorest need.

I probably share with any Cub fan the secret winter longing
for that triumph to be not so distant. But I also know that there
is more to hope—and even to professional baseball—than in getting the losers the hell out of Dodge City.

"One reason I have always loved baseball," said Thomas
Wolfe, "is that it has not been merely 'the great national game'
but really a part of the whole weather of our lives, of the thing
that is our own, of the whole fabric, the million memories of
America. For example, in the memory of almost every one of us,
is there anything that can evoke spring—the first fine days of
April—better than the sound of the ball smacking into the
pocket of the big mitt, the sound of the bat as it hits the horse-
hide; for me . . . almost everything I know about spring is in it—
the first leaf, the jonquil, the maple tree, the smell of grass upon
your hands and knees, the coming into flower of April."

Baseball manufacturers and T. S. Eliot have probably caused
some peeling at the edges of Thomas Wolfe's prose but it suffices
still in this late-twentieth-century spring—enough to remind me,
in the words of one old baseball man, that spring training is the
game's best time of year.

Spring training. Even the sound of it has attracted me for
more than forty years of my life. But until the spring of 1985 I
had never, save for a bout of Japanese spring (of which, more
later), experienced it. I wanted to experience spring training myself, precisely because what I knew about it existed exclusively
in my imagination—and my imagination, it turned out, was

driven not so much by anything so complex as the problem of putting a multimillion-dollar organization into winning gear as of trying to be faithful to old childhood memories.

It is my childhood, not what I know now, that is in perfect accord with Thomas Wolfe. I did not know then, for example, that baseball was not a game which, following our own mortality, was born in the spring, came to full flower in the summer, glory in the fall—and to death in the network-mandated frosts of pre-winter. No, baseball was conceived, along with Adam and Eve, in the First Seven Days, a game perfect and whole, subject to neither time nor death. During the nineteenth century, baseball was played in the winter—in places like Brooklyn and Greenland. *Dewitt's Baseball Guide* for 1868—the rulebook of the day—has a section called "General Rules for the Game on Skates." The bases, we are told, "except the home base, should be marked out somewhat in the shape of a masonic 'rule and compass'"—this configuration, for the uninitiated, being two interlocking elbow joints, or the Star of David gone haywire. The rules for a pitcher's delivery, baserunning, and all the rest suggest a game that might have had considerably more charm than a night with the Bruins in Boston Garden. Most surprising of all, records of the time show that a few turns at ice baseball were actually undertaken. The baseball historian Irving Leitner noted in *Diamond in the Rough,* "The year 1861—incredible as it may sound today—also saw the start of a series of winter baseball games that were played on ice! The first such game, involving teams of players on skates, was a four-inning affair between the Atlantic and Charter Oaks Clubs of Brooklyn. An estimated eight to ten thousand spectators witnessed the event, which was won by the Athletics, 20 runs to 9." Big place names in New York baseball then, eons before Ebbets Field or the Polo Grounds, were Brooklyn's Washington Skating Pond and Capitoline Skating Lake, along with the Sylvan Lake Skating Pond in Hoboken. This winter game existed for years. Leagues were formed and reached as far out as Greenland, where American whaling men played the game not only on ice but within the few slivers of light left by a midnight sun.

The record books simply do not show, as Genesis does with the Fall, who it was who ate of the tree and understood that baseball, too, had to die. At any rate, my childhood came long afterward, and I naturally mourned for baseball in the winter and dreamed for its return in the spring. Something must have been present in my blood, because in the second or third day of mild weather in mid-February I would wind up slogging around in the mud of the neighborhood park for the sake of a few miserable fly balls.

I waited for baseball—as I waited for spring. I followed winter trades, read my winter books and magazines, and, above all, counted the days till spring training. First there were the sparse newspaper accounts of those initial days when pitchers and catchers reported, then ampler stories when the full teams showed up a week or so later. For me, however, the season really began on the radio. And it is odd, because the strongest memory I carried with me this spring when I headed west and south was of a moment in a spring training game I heard described on the radio almost thirty years ago. I don't know how many people heard the broadcast then, but I am certain I am alone in remembering it now.

"Here comes Mickey. . . . It's just a gorgeous day, I really wish you could see it . . . this is just a spectacular setting for a ballgame. . . . Mickey smooths the dirt out around home plate, now digs in. . . . I wish you could see what we see. There's a huge bay out beyond the outfield fence, and you can see yachts and sailboats out there. . . . Mickey takes, ball one. . . . I tell you, Al Lang Field has just got to be one of the ideal places ever to see a baseball game. . . . Mickey swings and fouls it back. . . . I tell you, I'd like to be on one of those yachts out there, how 'bout that! Lie out on a deck chair with a glass of cold Ballantine listening to baseball and soaking up the sun. . . . Mickey swings and misses, strike two. . . . Maybe two of you out there or you've

7

got friends over and you've got some steaks going and about now you're starting to work up an appetite to go along with your thirst. . . . Mmmm-mm! Baseball and Ballantine—I tell you, there's nothing like it. . . . Mickey swings and bounds one to short, Aparacio in a step, up with it, over to first, and the side is out."

I was an adult before I realized the nonsense song "Mares Eat Oats" was not "Mairzy Doats" (a little girl, sister of Doazy Doats). And it took me until the spring training season of 1985 to understand that the little melody of description from that old radio broadcast actually meant something to me. To be quite frank, I had always assumed that behind this there was nothing more than the fairly uninspired notion that spring training ballgames didn't mean that much. I wasn't prepared for what I was to find.

I spent a good deal of time researching my subject before I set out. Given the fact that this occurred in winter when there was nothing I could do but wait for spring, it was right up my alley. There are far worse places to retreat to than Cooperstown in the snow.

The origin of spring training, like the origin of baseball itself, is somewhat obscure. For years, writers routinely ascribed an 1886 trip to Arkansas by the Chicago White Stockings—ancient ancestors of today's Cubs—as the first spring training. Cap Anson, manager of the White Stockings, collected fourteen players and took them along to Hot Springs; not actually to practice baseball but to boil out a long winter's siege of beer and debauchery. It may or may not be significant in explaining today's Burden of the Curse that among those few who ran the hills and took the baths was Billy Sunday, who left baseball with a lifetime .248 batting average and fire and brimstone—rather than firewater—running in his veins.

More recently, baseball historians have cited an 1870 trip to New Orleans by another group of Chicago White Stockings as the true origin of spring training. These White Stockings, with an eye on the all-powerful Cincinnati Red Stockings, who had won sixty-five consecutive games the previous season, actually went to New Orleans to bone up on baseball. And they succeeded. Twice in 1870 they managed to beat the Red Stockings, thus opening the way for the Red Stockings' demise and the eventual formation of what is today the National League of Baseball Clubs. There are other historians who argue that Boss Tweed packed off the New York Mutuals to New Orleans during the 1860s and there are even a couple of purists around who will argue for an 1840s' beginning, with the New York Knickerbockers dividing up for intrasquad play sometime before the ice melted on Center Pond.

Reluctantly I surrender the great boil-out of 1886 to the vapors of history. Cap Anson was probably baseball's first great showman. He had his players dress in fantastic uniforms. Sometimes they appeared in short, balloon-shaped Dutch pants, other times in form-fitting Nadji uniforms (the name deriving from an extravaganza featuring exotic dancers). Where other teams traveled by bus to the ballpark, Anson's men went by barouche, four to a carriage. What they did, in other words, was usually theater. And other owners of the day, though they did not immediately follow suit, began giving serious attention to the notion of some sort of spring preparation for the baseball season.

The picture of ballplayers in the spring as refugees from the saloons and drunk-tanks of the North seems also, historically, to the point. Until fairly recently, ballplayers were about as socially acceptable as pirates or carnival operators. My mother's best friend's sister once scandalized her family by going out with Fred Lindstrom, the Hall of Fame third baseman for the New York Giants, whose bad luck in the 1924 World Series (a bad-hop grounder over his head won the series for the Senators) changed nothing. Even my mother-in-law, an enlightened and endlessly curious person, drew the line when it came to ballplayers. As a young girl, my wife was under orders never to befriend the son or daughter of a man who played baseball for a living.

Two years after Anson's trip to the baths, the Washington Senators became the first professional baseball team to make a spring training trip to Florida. They went no farther south than Jacksonville, where they were housed in flimsy shacks on the outskirts of town and where nightly mayhem was the order of the day. "By the time we arrived in Jacksonville," remembered Connie Mack, an obscure young catcher on the team, "four of the fourteen players were reasonably sober, the rest were totally drunk. There was a fight every night, and the boys broke a lot of furniture. We played exhibitions during the day and drank most of the night."

What might have convinced reluctant, penny-pinching owners that a trip south prior to the opening of the season might have some baseball value was a trip undertaken by the Baltimore Orioles of 1894. A poor team, the Orioles under a rather crafty manager, Ned Hanlon, spent eight weeks in Macon, Georgia, concentrating on nothing but baseball. They held drills twice a day and concentrated almost exclusively on fundamentals. Hanlon, it has been said, introduced bunting, the hit-and-run play, the idea of hitting to all fields (Wee Willie "Hit 'Em Where They Ain't" Keeler was a member of this team, as was John McGraw). The result of this was an Oriole pennant, the first step of which was a season-opening sweep of the powerful New York Giants team, in which the Orioles pulled off thirteen hit-and-run plays and left Giants manager John Ward complaining that "it's a new game they're playing, it's just not baseball." Baseball it surely was, but the point is that within the decade, spring training became something that professional clubs undertook routinely. The man who later, single-handedly, set the standard for modern spring training camps was, not surprisingly, that old Oriole, John McGraw.

Along with his Baltimore experience, McGraw brought along Cap Anson's sense of showmanship and Attila the Hun's sense of social relationships. "Many modern training camps are little colleges of baseball knowledge," Frankie Frisch, who played for

McGraw in 1920, once noted, "[Each is] equipped with class-rooms, visual aid charts, pitching machines, psychologists and sundry professors. Mr. McGraw delivered no lectures. His language was salty, punchy and profane. He called each Giant by his last name or by a sobriquet, mine being 'Cementhead.' He had little formal education and saw no reason why a man should know more than how to play winning baseball. And to play winning baseball a man had to hit his peak of physical perfection in the spring."

A McGraw training camp was probably equidistant from the lower rungs of the *Inferno* and the back lot of *A Night at the Opera*. The stories of McGraw's rages dwarf Earl Weaver's, while his practical jokes easily reduce Sparky Lyle's to *Reader's Digest* sidebars. McGraw once unloaded a future twenty-game winner because the fellow turned up in camp wearing tennis whites. And he once loaded a picnic chicken with fresh barnyard droppings, which Wilbert Robinson, one of his coaches, unfortunately began to sample in the midst of a pleasant day of fishing.

In 1907 McGraw undertook a cross-country training trip with the Giants, which went as far as Los Angeles and San Francisco. Given the difficulty and the length of time required for travel, it was an astounding feat. And it paved the way for the spring barnstorming tours, which became a regular feature of spring training for the next half a century. Teams like the Indians and the Giants developed spring-training rivalries that took them into the remotest corners of the land. Long before the age of instant communication, these strange traveling caravans of baseball players would arrive in tiny hamlets and way stations to put on exhibitions before people who had never seen a major-league game before and who, in all probability, would never see one again—unless the caravan reappeared the following year.

McGraw was a pioneer in still another important way. He wanted his ballplayers put up in style. They were major-leaguers, not circus riffraff, despite the sometimes unimaginable consequences that followed when the best hotels and dining rooms in Florida began accepting the troops. McGraw might have been an intolerable martinet with his players, but he would brook no challenge to their dignity as representatives of the big leagues. An old friend of McGraw's, Charles Ringling, induced the Giants to move from Texas to Sarasota for the 1924 training season. McGraw had accepted, trusting that his old friend's success with the circus and with Florida real estate would be enough. It wasn't. Ringling had booked the Giants into a squalid cement-block structure on the outskirts of town. McGraw exploded. Too small and too filthy. It had to be changed. The Giants were finally relocated in the Mira Mar, a shiny, new luxury hotel on Tampa Bay. Another time, when the Giants were training in Marlin, Texas, Rube Marquard, who could not get past McGraw's lobby security arrangements to have a good time, began firing a pistol out of his hotel window at a billboard across the way. McGraw's reaction to Marquard has gone unreported, but when the local sheriff insisted on having his pitcher arrested, McGraw, so it is written, thundered at the man, "The Giants put this town on the map, and the Giants can just as quickly wipe it off by leaving." Marquard and the Giants, needless to say, stayed put.

There is a curious and gnawing sense that emerges from going through the Cooperstown files on spring training. To be sure, there is a picture of a changing country, of baseball, in Mark Twain's words, as "the outward and visible expression of the drive and push and rush and struggle of the raging, tearing, booming nineteenth century," becoming something very different in the latter half of this century. But what is most striking is the sense conveyed—directly and indirectly—by many writers over many years that spring training may largely be unnecessary. There are writers such as John Lardner who make no bones about it. In a *Saturday Evening Post* article in 1953, Lardner, citing numerous career-threatening and unnecessary injuries sustained during "meaningless" exhibition games, laid out a picture of spring training as a public relations boondoggle, soliciting what amounted to little more than free advertising space in home markets for nearly two months prior to the opening of the baseball season. ("Winning games down here," says Lou Gorman, vice president and general manager of the Boston Red Sox, "sells tickets back home.") The players didn't like it because they were essentially donating their services (player contracts are paid from the official opening of the season to the official closing) and the training they were getting could be accomplished in half the time or less, while the actual physical threat to their careers was increased.

Lardner's view has been reflected from time to time by management itself. Such sturdy executives of the past as Frank Lane, Lee McPhail, and Bing Devine all went public with their sense that the short season was too long and too costly. Largely as a result of these and other criticisms—coming roughly at the same time—modern spring training, rather than being curtailed, made an adjustment. The long barnstorming tours that preceded the opening of the season—undercut now by the advent of television, which brought baseball to the hinterlands in ways that the Pullman car did not—were eliminated, and in their place were established the so-called Grapefruit and Cactus leagues, the slates of exhibition games at fixed sites in Florida and Arizona. Still, today, there are some players, coaches, and executives who believe that modern conditioning, an all-year round affair undertaken by athlete-businessmen who understand the equation of fitness with high finance, reduces the need for spring training—except for pitchers, whose arms cannot be rushed into shape.

For every outright critic of spring training, there are at least ten ardent defenders of the system—they shall appear in due course—but the Cooperstown files are revealing in yet another way. Much spring training writing tends to downright silliness. There is probably no other single body of prose in the English language in which writers seem quite so hard-pressed to come up with something, anything, than the collected newspaper accounts of spring training over the last half century. Something, anything, more often than not involves the search for yarns, lore, and jokes—rather than baseball. There are hazing stories ad nauseam, the most common involving inspired hijinks like the snipe-hunt or the search, undertaken by rookies too dumb for Ring Lardner, for yards of shoreline. Some stories are retold from generation to generation, with the roles of the main actors somehow getting switched. One well-known spring training pacemaker dates to 1919 and features Bucky Harris and Al Schacht, both in their rookie seasons with the Washington Senators. The older Schacht, so the story goes, convinced the younger Harris that out there in the moonlight, under the swaying palms, a pair of willing ladies of the night waited in perfumed quarters to deliver the joys of Florida unto the travail of youthful Washington. There was some danger to the undertaking, Schacht warned, because the assignation involved married women. The husbands, however, it was assured, were away on business. The inevitable knock on the door—with flowers in hand—was followed by the equally inevitable confrontation with one of the irate husbands, who proceeded to gun down Schacht, so that he fell to the ground with blood all over his clothing, as Harris went fleeing into the night. Needless to say, when a nearly demented Harris turned up at the hotel to tell his teammates what had happened, the man who opened the door to greet him was Schacht.

The point is not the yarn but that in the retelling of it, the roles of Schacht and Harris get reversed. In the retelling, the time becomes 1924, when Harris is a rookie *manager* of the Senators and Schacht, now a coach, is the unwitting rube.

(Come to think of it, there may be something about guns and spring training here. There is a Jim Frey story that has been circulating for some time about an incident with the umpire Ken

Kaiser. When I got to Mesa in 1985 I asked Frey about it. This is what he told me: "Well, what happened was he threw me out of a ballgame one night and the next day I was in the dugout and the clubhouse boy had a starter's pistol, and I asked him if he had a cartridge for it. And he did, and when Kaiser came down the ramp to go out on the field before the game, I walked up to him and I said, 'You're not gonna miss any plays today, big boy!' And I stuck the gun in his padded protector and pulled the trigger. And he jumped back fifteen feet—thought I had shot him in the stomach—and then he came over and knocked the hell out of me. You know, he's six-foot-five and about two-seventy. It felt like some truck ran over me!")

The cumulative impact of reading stories with headlines such as "Preacher Prayed for Rain When Ballclubs Came to Town," "Spring Pranksters Touch Off Laugh Riots," "Camp Comics," and "High Marks in Dining Room League Held by Ruth, Hogan, and Lombardi" is that eight weeks in the swamps left writers with a lot of unoccupied time on their hands. There was only so much space you could devote to ballplayers bending down or playing games that didn't count in the standings. And not all that surprisingly, as spring training became a more settled and businesslike affair, commensurate with the settled affluence of the Sunbelt itself, some writers began to look back nostalgically. "Where are the pranks of yesteryear?" asked *Sporting News* senior editor Lowell Reidenbaugh in March 1980. "The living is plusher now under the southern sun," declared Frank Graham in 1956, "—swimming pools, golf clubs, good food. But there were more laughs in the old days." And beat writer Jack Lang, with the Mets in 1974, remembered this from his early days with the Brooklyn Dodgers in Vero Beach, Florida: "When dinner was over, there were after-dinner drinks. I'll never forget the night that Mike Gaven, dipping the moist end of his cigar in the brandy, inquired why the club didn't purchase a better brand.

15

"'When you buy better cigars, we'll buy better brandy,' was the retort.

"In O'Malley's days—even as now—there were high-stakes poker games in the pressroom every night. But in those early days, the writers also added another bit of entertainment. As soon as the players were asleep, Leon Hamilton [Dodgertown supervisor] and one of the writers would wheel the lobby juke-box into the back room and we'd dance for hours. . . . Perhaps it was because most of us were of the same age group and lived together so closely in Dodgertown that spring training never again was as good as it was in those days of Vero. Of course, we were all young then."

When I finally packed up and left for Arizona in the third week in February, I wasn't suspicious so much as I was curious. I kept wondering what it was so many people had expected of spring training, why so many had seemingly tried so hard to make something out of it that probably wasn't there. Was spring training really important? Obviously it was, to some baseball people, while it was less important to others. Was it six or eight weeks of free hype for the markets back home? Sure. Did players risk injuries they might have avoided had they remained more or less at ease till the bell rang? In a few weeks I happened to see Rickey Henderson make a perfectly unnecessary—and atrocious—slide into third base, seriously injuring his ankle in a game that was probably unimportant even to the Florida Citrus Association. Couldn't teams stay home, work out indoors in armories and gymnasiums, and catch up once the real season began? That actually did happen during World War II, when baseball did its bit to save fuel bills by holding spring training in such exotic places as Bear Mountain, New York, Atlantic City, New Jersey, and French Lick, Indiana. Of course there can be sex without foreplay and nourishing food without the joy of cooking; there was life in Sparta as well as Athens. But even being biased toward the Athenian Way, I knew there was another answer that seemed still more obvious. Spring training was, and is, the coming together of such a variety of characters: veterans with their places already secure, rookies whose places are not; aging players facing the diminishment of their skills; players too young to vote but away from home (and homesick) for the first time in their lives; people on the make to be umpires, coaches, trainers, executives, writers, caterers, groundskeepers, lovers, drinkers, golfers, all of them speaking in the bewildering variety of North America's regional accents, along with Spanish (a lot of that regional, too), dashes of French, Japanese, Korean, and Italian. What you have is a kind of world unto itself. And, like any world, it is a mix of things. As the song says, you can find what you want out on Highway 61.

A first problem for me was not whether or not there was anything to see but how much I could see. Spring baseball occurred in a short season, a giant Azalea Festival gone almost in the moment of its arrival. There was no real way to see it whole—that is, to see it and savor it all. So choices had to be made, and this was no easy matter. Of course I wanted to see something worthwhile and to write in a way that might be representative. But baseball life anywhere—even with the Texas Rangers—can be worthwhile and representative. The drawback, however, was that setting out to find the Texas Rangers did not interest me.

But this matter of the Rangers led me to a home truth: I followed baseball strictly according to the way I felt. As I have gotten older, the locus of my passion has broadened so that I have been able to take in more than a rooting interest in one team. My interest in baseball, as in good wine or music, has grown but still is dominated by the first fires of feeling.

What that meant when I set out for Arizona was that whatever else I did, I planned to enjoy myself. I was going, simply, to see what I wanted. Formally, I decided that I would concentrate my time on the American League East—for me, the most enjoyable, competitive division in baseball. This seemed sensible and in accord with some long-standing predilections. But I knew, from the start, I had no intention of holding rigidly to anything. I would let myself go where I was moved to go, to subject myself—as though I were a farmer or anyone whose work is joined to the peculiar rhythm of a season—to what the weather brought. Ultimately you understood the season best by being in harmony with it. When I turned off the Superstition Highway into the cross-hatching of roadside culture that was Mesa, I was already busily at work improvising. The American League East's Arizona representatives—the Indians and the Brewers—could wait. For the few days that I was to be here before moving on to Florida, I could no more resist the Cubs than I could the desert scenery. Let the Cubs and The Superstitions introduce me to a baseball spring.

When I arrived the next morning at Fitch Park, the Cubs' training facility down the street from Ho Ho Kam, it was uncharacteristically cold. There had been intermittent rain showers during the early morning, and I half-expected to find only a hardy soul or two hanging around. Instead, the parking lot was almost full. The common area between the cluster of practice diamonds was swarming with fans, many of whom were pressed tightly into lines at the players' entrance to the clubhouse. As I approached, players, one after another, came out between the gauntlet of fans, who clapped, cheered, called out. Some of the players stopped, signed autographs, let themselves be photographed; others walked by, seemingly a little dazed that on this very first day for pitchers and catchers, so much fuss was being made over them.

What I did not know was that every Cub regular with the exception of Ron Cey was present, and had been present for nearly two weeks prior to this first day's limited call. This was not the first but the tenth day, and the Cubs apparently had been hard at it all the while. A baseball buff with only limited interest in the Cubs would have recognized immediately what a change this represented from the year before. In 1984, when the Cubs won the National League East, they suffered through one of their worst springs in history, winning only seven of twenty-seven exhibition games and precipitating a team housecleaning that saw the exile of popular first baseman Bill Buckner along with a carload of young talent. In exchange, the Cubs acquired Gary Matthews and Bob Dernier from the Phillies, Rick Sutcliffe from the Indians, and Dennis Eckersley from the Red Sox, the division title following.

I don't know whether it was this unexpected show of *esprit,* the enthusiasm of the fans, the chill of the day, or just because this was the first glimpse of baseball for me after a winter's hibernation, but I was excited, as excited as any of the "snowbirds" who wandered from backstop to backstop, pushing their faces close up to the mesh fences to gaze with rapturous intent upon little more than routine limbering exercises. In these first moments of my trip I was struck by something that stayed with me through the remainder of my time in Arizona and Florida. Players never look better than they do in the spring. Rookies never look more promising, aging players never seem more fit, injured players never seem more restored. Players who are positively miserable as they drag themselves through what amounts to a boring grind never seem more suffused with joy. This is not the result of typical fan softheadedness, either. A couple of days later, when I visited the Brewers' spring camp, Harry Dalton, the Milwaukee GM, as shrewd and hardheaded a baseball executive as has ever gone through the miseries of last place, told me this: "Hope rises each spring like sap in the trees. That's part of baseball, that's one of the greatest things about the game. You have the animal rebirth no matter how disastrous the previous year was." Or how disastrous the coming year will be, he might have added.

"This is spring training," I told myself as I pushed myself

through raindrops and fans toward the fence, hoping to get a closer glimpse of the Cubs doing calisthenics. Actually, perhaps inevitably, I quickly became more interested in the people who were clinging to the mesh. I heard one middle-aged man telling another: "I hope this fan, Frank, shows up this year. He's a real professional heckler. This guy hung his fingers on the fence, and they'd hit a ball past Bowa and he'd yell something insulting at 'im. An' he got to the players, too. You could tell they were starting to get mad at him. And a crowd began to gather. An' he wouldn't let up—play after play. There musta been a hundred people gathered around him when Billy Connors come over and stood right behind 'im—like this. Pretty soon, he tapped him on the shoulder and said, 'Hey, fella, take it easy on the old-timers, will ya. Why don't you pick on the rookies, they're the ones who need it.' Then you know what happened? Billy took off his cap and give it to the old guy. And, later in the day, they came over and took the old guy out to the batting cage an' they pitched to him. You shoulda seen it. I hope he comes back."

On the field, Jim Frey and Dallas Green were standing amid the players, who were in yet another phase of their stretching exercises. Soon the players finished and went to different diamonds, some of them to hit, some to work on fielding. I had introduced myself to a fan and his friends; they were all from small towns in Illinois, and had come to Mesa for the weather and the Cubs. Warren Carlsen, the fan who had been hoping for a glimpse of the heckler, told me about rooting for the Cubs, about the positive ways in which the team had changed, and about how he had, for years, planned his winters around the Cubs, regardless of their fortunes.

"Last year," said Warren, "I went to seventeen games in twenty-one days. You're closer to the game here. I watch a ballplayer here, I can see his face and hear his voice—I feel like I know him. I go to Wrigley Field and I see that number way off there and I don't even know what he looks like. I can talk to the players, get their autographs—the players actually hang around awhile longer; they're willing to stop and visit with you for a little down here."

For Warren Carlsen and his friends, Mesa in the spring was the beginning of a long social event that would end with the last Cub game the following fall. Their talk inevitably turned to the bleachers, which seemed, in this context, to fit perfectly with what they were enjoying in the present moment.

"Last year when we were going hot and heavy with the Mets," Warren said, "I left home at six in the morning just to make sure I'd get a seat in the bleachers. I never had so much fun in my life. That was the day Jody Davis got a grand slam home run. When the ball left the bat I said, 'Holy jeez, *the ball's coming right to me!*' It didn't. It landed a foot or two away. But I was so excited that on the news that night I taped it on the VCR and saved it. But I met a couple from Rockford there, standing on line in the early morning, waiting for tickets, a couple in their mid-sixties somewhere, they came in for the whole weekend. There were four games—Friday, Saturday, doubleheader Sunday—and they come in there spending the night in Chicago, real fancy hotel, but they were staying in the bleachers all four games, they didn't want to be anywhere else."

"I was there one day," Warren's friend Clarence Casey Jones chimed in, "and a guy's standing there with a big fistful of money, standing there, waving it, saying, 'Bet he gets a hit, bet he gets a double, bet he makes an out,' and that carried on for nine innings."

Warren Carlsen returned to the Day the Cubs Did It. "Before the game, in batting practice, a Cub outfielder would pick up a ball and everybody'd yell, 'Throw us the ball! Throw us the ball!' and every once in a while, they'd flip one over their shoulder and the fans would cheer. When the Mets came out, they'd still yell, 'Throw us the ball! Throw us the ball!' But when a Met would actually throw the ball up there, thirty-five hundred people would start chanting, *'Throw it back! Throw it back!'* You had to throw it back. There was a guy there with a little effigy of a Met in uniform, and they were all sticking pins in it."

I was curious. I had no desire to be impertinent, but what, after all, was so special about *baseball?* Could the game have really mattered as much as rubbing shoulders with the players down here and with fellow fans in the bleachers in Chicago? This is what Warren Carlsen said: "Maybe it's special to me because I'm envious of how young they are and how easy they do it. I'm in my fifties and I still try—I used to do it and it's hard to do. Maybe because it's the one sport that all of us, no matter who we are, at one time or another can actually play, or try to. You don't with the other sports."

When I finally drifted into the Cubs' clubhouse, I was feeling both restored and uneasy. Restored because my winter's reading was finally behind me and words, like those yachts in the bay beyond Al Lang Field, were part of what I knew was baseball's natural order. But I was uneasy because Warren Carlsen had inadvertently hit a nerve. Growing older has had a baseball context for me, too. I realized when Warren talked about envying the youth and skill of ballplayers that for years, almost without realizing it, I have made a beeline for those areas of the ballpark where I could get close to pitchers pitching. And being there time and again, without being able fully to admit it to myself, I would play this game with myself in which I would compare the velocity of the pitcher I was watching with my own when I was a high school pitcher. Many times—or so I believed—I came out ahead. Christ, isn't that something, *I threw harder than that,* I convinced myself, and a little backfire of resentment crept up my gut. Without knowing it, I had been angry at being over forty and being consigned by my own body to follow rather than play the game.

I mention this only because I found myself in this distracted quandary, of not being quite sure why I was where I was. I was face to face with the unpleasant awareness that whatever joy

baseball had given me over the years—and it was considerable—it had also turned out to be something I used rather in the
manner of Snow White's stepmother.

I believe that existential crises, even the minor mid-life ones
like no longer being able to throw the high hard one, can be
providential. I am reinforced in the sense that this one surely
was because of what followed. I was about to go home for the
day, when a man in his sixties with thinning red hair passed by
me on his way to the clubhouse door. Someone called after him.
"Hey, Charlie Fox. . . ." I am not sure what followed the name,
but the name was enough. Fox, ex-manager of the Giants and
Cubs, ex-general manager of the Montreal Expos, currently su-
perscout extraordinaire of the Cubs, had once—for the life of
me, I don't know why I know this—confessed, in print, that at
the root of his baseball knowledge was not some old ballplayer or
manager, but the sixteenth-century Japanese warrior Musashi.

Fox, it turned out, was rather easy to talk with. When I introduced myself and told him that I, too, had read Musashi, wondering about its connection to baseball, he removed a copy of
The Book of the Five Rings from his briefcase and showed it to
me. He carried it with him wherever he went, he said. He read it
over and over again and underlined passages in it all the time.
The copy he produced looked like it had kept the colored-marker
industry in business for years.

Later he told me something about scouting: "I'm training some
of our scouts now. I show them what to look for, what not to
look for. . . . I say, when you look, *see*. That comes straight from
Musashi. I'll introduce them to someone and they'll turn around
and say, 'Who was that fella?' Then I'll say, 'Okay, what was he
wearing? How tall was he? What kind of shoes did he have on?' I
practice on guys. I get someone in a car, we're drivin', and he
sees a good-looking girl and he looks back and I say, 'What color
was her dress, kid?' He won't know. I tell him when you're
scouting, you have to see. When you're behind home plate, you
see the catcher and the pitcher. If something moves on the out-

side, if someone tipped something off, you have to look again. *If you look—see!"*

Fox walked right into the middle of my mid-life baseball crisis. When he walked out again, I knew that seeing, really seeing, was more valuable to me than the high hard one—particularly in watching spring training, when, among other things, the game was taken apart and put back together again.

CHAPTER TWO

Old-Timers

And lastly, came cold February, sitting
In an old wagon, for he could not ride;
Drawne of two fishes for the season fitting,
Which through the flood before did softly slyde
And swim away: yet had he by his side
His plow and harnesse fit to till the ground,
And tools to prune the trees, before the pride
Of hasting Prime did make them burgein round.
        —Spenser, *The Faerie Queene*

Charlie Fox learned to look at things early. A year after he experienced his full career as a major-league ballplayer (three games and seven at-bats as a utility catcher for the New York Giants in 1942), he went off to war. "I was in the Atlantic and the Pacific," says Fox. "I went to Russia for a year and a half. Archangel, Odessa, I went the route. I was in special services. There were twenty-seven of us. We had to blow things up. We got into Norway once and got out some scientists. We got in and out by sub—came out by a convoy—went around to Archangel and got frozen in. Had a little old Brownie camera with me all the while. I wasn't supposed to have it. As a result, I took a lot of pictures I wasn't supposed to take."

One of these pictures was snapped in the closing days of the war. Fox was then attached to General Patton's command. "As we were closing in on Berlin," said Fox, "Patton vowed that he was going to piss on Hitler's grave. But when we reached the Rhine, we were told that Hitler had committed suicide and that his body had been burned. You know what Patton did? He said, 'If I can't piss on his grave, then I'll piss in his ocean.'" Charlie Fox has in his collection of old photographs one of General George S. Patton, his britches down around his ankles, a beatific smile on his face, emptying his bladder into the Rhine.

Over a baseball career spanning almost half a century, Fox has refined his understanding and approach to the game. He was one of the first to understand the connection between the game's mental and physical aspects, and from the time he began reading Musashi, even before he began training in the martial arts, he always sought to pass on what he knew to his players, inciting them to train in ways that would enable them to surpass themselves. It did not always work. *Sporting News* correspondent Wells Twombley remembers that Fox went through a period as a minor-league manager when he "considered himself the living voice of the late John McGraw." Recalls Willie McCovey, "As manager of the Giants in 1970, Charlie had his problems at first because he thought all modern players still worship the manager like he was God."

Today, like any guru worth his salt, Fox has learned to lay off, or to lay on far more subtly. "You have to pick individuals," he acknowledged. "You can't get everyone involved in something that just you believe in. I think the greatest thing about Zen or the martial arts is that the person has to come to you with the thought that he's going to better himself or get something out of it. But if you have to entice him to come, he's not going to do anything."

And if he comes?

"Well, one of the stories is of this very learned man who wanted to learn Zen, and he comes to this old Zen master and he says, 'I want to learn Zen.' And the master says, 'Fine, I'll help you.' So naturally before anything, they had tea. And as this person was sitting holding the cup, the Zen master proceeded to pour the tea continually until it overflowed the cup—and continued to do it even after that. The learned man yelled, 'Stop! It's running over onto the floor!' The master then told him, 'You're like that cup, you're too filled up with what you know to get anything from anyone.' You can only get into something as if you're learning it for the first time—even when you may not be. The proper approach is to have a child's mind."

I wondered if anyone was working with Fox at present. When I asked, he looked at me rather tentatively and said, "Yeah. Trout." (Cubs pitcher Steve Trout.)

"Has he read Musashi?"

"I gave him the book."

More than anything, Fox's way of looking at the game itself has changed with the years. As a scout he spends nearly all his time at the major-league level, where the question of physical ability is more or less taken for granted. At the major-league level, the question is really what is inside a player. When the Cubs scouted players like Tim Stoddard, Dennis Eckersley, and Rick Sutcliffe, players other teams had given up on, it was Fox, according to Dallas Green, who was instrumental in convincing the Cubs their services could help the team.

"These days," Fox said, "I'm no longer convinced by seeing a guy work a couple of innings or a couple of games. I don't need a clock or a gun. If it's gonna be a big deal—and I can't name names because some of them are still playing—I may follow them around in the evenings. . . . I'll follow them around, right here in spring training, and see where they go." As though it was still 1943 in Norway, he said, "At times, they never know. I'll buy them a drink, see if they're drinkin' beer or whatever. I'll watch 'em for a while just to see their habits. Sometimes I'll sit around and wait till they come out of the hotel, follow 'em and see what they're doing." He laughed and shook his head slowly. "I've wound up knowing about a lot of players. . . . And during the season, you'll be sitting in the lobby, see a player and say to yourself, I'm not doing anything now, I'll tag along and see what happens. You find out a lot of things. Either you trade for 'em or you don't."

I wondered if it was really possible to see what was inside a player, what might make one trade for him—and eventually shell out big bucks—while others held back. There was probably no better time to pursue such an intriguing but elusive lead as this early February period, when not much was going on, when a day's workout was limited to some light throwing for pitchers and catchers, a fundamental or two, and brief periods of running and calisthenics.

I found Rick Sutcliffe sitting on an exercise bike in the Cubs' clubhouse. With his almost unbelievable 16–1 record the previous season, which most observers say brought the Cubs to the top of the heap and which, as a direct consequence, raised Sutcliffe into baseball's millionaire club, he seemed now to be the picture of ruddy self-confidence. His full red beard and flowing good cheer made him appear positively jolly, in the manner of Van Gogh's Pierre Tanguy. He was totally oblivious to some head-pounding disco music that was blaring nearby. Far too large for the bike he pedaled, he looked, somehow, like an eccentric uncle who had excused himself from a birthday party to seek out the children's furniture in the nursery.

Yes, of course, coming to the Cubs was the best thing that had happened to him professionally. And Cub management, Cub teammates, Cub fans, there just was no way to top them. Cubs, Cubs, Cubs seemed to chug happily out of the rhythm of the exercise bike. "Our season with Cleveland started the first of March and ended the first of June," he said. "When I was with the Dodgers, they expected you to win—not so much in the spring. But the team always expected to win during the year— and they usually did. I hadn't really made it in L.A., and so whenever I got to pitch I was afraid. I was afraid that every pitch I threw, I might be out of the game."

In Cleveland the experience was totally different. Cleveland was the kind of city that Neil Simon thought about when he was stuck for one-liners. "In Cleveland, we didn't win and we didn't draw anybody." Was it pitching totally devoid of fear or was it a well-publicized toothache that had Sutcliffe struggling with a losing record and an earned run average over 5 in June 1984, when the Cubs traded for him? Sutcliffe wasn't too sure. In any case, I had no idea what it was Charlie Fox found in Sutcliffe— other than the black-and-white proof in the record books that he had twice been a seventeen-game winner. Then Sutcliffe began talking about the previous year and the one coming (he would struggle through it). Yes, winning carried pressure with it, and so did having to live up to a big contract. His 16–1 record was pressure, too, because it would obviously be hard to·match, but that was what he loved. He suddenly stopped pedaling his bike. The look of contentment was gone from his face. In its place was a look that probably was the one batters knew quite well. "I love pressure," Sutcliffe said. "Baseball's all about being in the ninth inning in a one-run game. The playoffs were so exciting, you stood there getting goose bumps before the games began. You throw everything out then and say, 'I have to do this now *in here,* not out there.' Oh God, I love it!"

Sutcliffe did not know what he did to get himself "in here" rather than "out there," and it did not seem to matter in the least. "Major-league ballplayers," Fox had told me, "for a long time, never specifically put into words the mental training they put into the game. They call it experience. Their mental approach to the game is a continual, repetitious psalm, as it were. It is knowledge they have, and they go through it before the game so it is mental preparation."

Surely I had just seen the psalm in Rick Sutcliffe's eyes.

More than anything, I was curious to know what a player would be like who systematically, consciously set about psalm-singing for himself. The one player Fox had mentioned was

Steve Trout, and I was drawn to him as filing to a magnet.

"Musashi? It doesn't mean anything to me. I never read it," Trout said. "I don't know anything about it. I don't have the book." He looked at me suspiciously, as though I might have been a narc somehow trying to set him up. For a second, I wondered if Fox had ever had contact of any sort with him. But then Trout suddenly blurted out, "He said he gave me the book but I don't think he ever did."

All through the conversation with Trout, I had a growing sense that it was I who needed to be on guard. This was Steve Trout, all right, but lurking just around the corner or in back of the next locker or standing next to us with the power of invisibility upon him was Charlie Fox. Did Trout sense this, too?

"There's a lot of things you can do to discipline yourself," he said. I could swear he was alert to shadows. "Yoga does it through breathing techniques," he continued, "and through concentration. There's all kinds of martial arts—tai chi, kempo. . . ."

The more Trout spoke, the less comfortable I became. Who could doubt his sincerity? But something beyond words was going on, and for the life of me I couldn't begin to figure out what.

"It's hard to balance the mental and the physical, you see, because what's called for is so physical," he said. "What you want to attempt to do is work on the mental side of it so the physical side will come more naturally, and I do that by my training, by working on my yoga and other things that I feel are really beneficial. My brother Paul is an English professor, and he sent me some books on muscle relaxation. . . ."

"What did he sent you?" I asked, feeling as though I was being drawn to the edge of a whirlpool.

"Techniques on muscle relaxation," Trout said. "And I'm going to start applying them now religiously in my program. It had a wonderful effect last year."

"For sure, last year was your best ever. . . ."

"They're taking me more seriously now—and that's what it's all about."

When I got outside, I saw Fox standing near one of the practice diamonds. He was back in the crowd, where he could watch what was taking place on the field without himself being observed. I could have sworn he saw me, but I wasn't sure. His eye had moved, lizardlike, and was back on the field of play. I pushed my way through the crowd till I was standing at his side. I said nothing. He seemed to be unaware of my presence. His attention remained riveted on the field. I mumbled something innocuous, just to see if he knew I was there. From the way he nodded, it was clear that he did. I felt like I was trapped in a kabuki drama written and staged by Fox. I had no idea how to extricate myself.

"Guess what?" I finally said, feeling about as adroit as a bag of resin.

"What's that?" Fox replied.

"Trout says you never gave him Musashi."

"He did, huh?" If the information was important to him, it barely seemed to register. He remained concentrated on the infield practice beyond the fence. His arms were folded across his chest. I was about to walk away when suddenly Fox began shaking his head from side to side.

"He really said that?" His voice stopped me. But it was as if I weren't there at all. From the look in Charlie's eye, he was in communion with his own demons or angels. I nodded. After a moment, he smiled and said, "I knew it. I knew it all along."

I knew now that Fox had used me, as certainly as if I had been compromised by Mata Hari. Steve Trout had obviously been one of his projects. And, for reasons best known to Fox, it had been important for him to find out if Trout had actually read a volume of Musashi he had obviously given him. He had used me to find out, to get through real or imagined curtains of evasion and half-truths. Charlie had "seen" my curiosity well enough to know he could use me—at least so I thought. Regardless, I am sure he was engaged in actively, if secretly, measuring the mettle of Steve Trout—for whatever personal or organizational ends: to trade or to teach.

Was Charlie an American Zen master or an unrepentant OSS spy? Who knew. The Tao that can be named is not the Tao. But I feel quite at ease in the knowledge that Charlie Fox has given a lifetime to what lies at the heart of the game and to what it is, in seemingly exotic disciplines that might make good ballplayers better and better ballplayers great ones.

Fox had a sense of what a team was and what an individual talent was—or could be—that was revelatory to me. "I have a board in my room," he said, "they always kid me about it—the blackboard—because I always erase and change things, I continually change the structure of the club. I'll wind up saying, 'Well, that looks better, why can't this be done.' I'm always at it. I never quit." A team, for Fox, was an ultimate mystery, just as an individual was. The great teams he had experienced were the ones Willie Mays was on, and the greatest individual embodiment of the mystery was Mays himself.

"Willie Mays had the most unsurpassed instinct or anticipation I've ever seen," said Fox. "You could just concentrate on him on the ballfield—be watching him, and I say, by looking, seeing—you see the ball going to the plate, you actually see a ball hit, and it looked as though simultaneously with the bat touching the ball, Mays was moving. It was phenomenal. I've never seen anyone that quick with that anticipation, as if he had seen it before; he knew where the ball was going and he was there. You see line drives right over second base and you say that's a base hit. He'd catch it. The next hitter would hit a ball clear to the wall, and Mays is *standing there!* And if you didn't observe and watch what he did, you'd say, 'How in the world did he get there?' There wasn't enough time for him even to run out there after the last pitch. But he was there."

Fox was 63 years old, and in the last five months, his wife of forty-three years had died. They had been childhood sweethearts in Brooklyn, where their families had lived on the same block. "She woulda made a great scout," he said. "We had arguments about her way of seeing and mine, but she knew what she was talking about. She knew Musashi and she knew the game." He was alone now, and his job, lonely to begin with, was even lonelier. But it was everything for him. Seeing the inside of the game had become a kind of worship service for him that gave order and meaning to his life.

Because of Charlie Fox, and perhaps because there was so little going on during this week of pitchers and catchers, I became far more conscious of the people who watch and see— rather than play—the game. The camps, save for the Cubs', were largely empty. The workouts were brief and without intensity. The game for these few days was really in the hands of others, those whose job was to tend to it, to see it, but not necessarily to play it. As I never had before, I became conscious of just how important people without the high hard one were to the game. To sow the ground in the spring, you needed tools and a knowledge of both farming and the seasons.

I spent my days going from camp to camp, but my nights were usually far more intriguing. "If you are in Arizona," a friend of mine cautioned me before I left New York, "you can postpone your interest in the American League East—but whatever you do, don't miss the Pink Pony Cafe."

The Pink Pony took up my evenings. It was, in the plainest terms, a baseball joint. There was no other quite like it so far as I knew. It had its birth with the birth of spring training in Arizona, the inspiration, first, of Del Webb's mistress (Webb was a former owner of the Yankees and a Southwest real estate magnate), then of an old pal of Dizzy Dean's, Charlie Briley, who has been its proprietor ever since, a period covering more than thirty years. Briley is 70; he has a face as worn and seamed as an unrepentant regular in a Third Avenue saloon and a manner vaguely reminiscent of Jimmy Stewart. He will tell you how he hornswoggled his friend Pee Wee Reese, whom he refers to affectionately as "a foot-washing Baptist," into buying him out of a losing bet he had already paid for; or how he had once come to bat against Grover Cleveland Alexander—then barnstorming through small towns in Kentucky with the House of David—and heard but did not see three strikes go past him.

The Pink Pony today is comfortable and middle-aged. Its decor seems to look to the past more than to the present or future. On a wall in the dining room is the uniform jersey Ferguson Jenkins wore when he struck out his three thousandth batter. There is a row of caricatures on the bar-side of the house, nearly all of baseball people who won their spurs years ago—Clete Boyer, Bill Rigney, Lou Boudreau. There is a mix of paintings whose subjects are the Old West—*Lawman in the Bradshaws* and others by local artist Wes Chapman. The paintings are sentimental in style, and all of them depict lonely but heroic figures caught against harsh landscapes. There is a photograph of four men, one of them very young, seated at a table. The picture is yellowing with age, and the very young man, who looks like he might have been away from home for the first time, is Eddie Matthews, another of Briley's friends who, at 54, is a garbage worker in San Diego.

Briley's clientele today, overloaded with baseball people, is predominantly middle-aged. Behind the bar is a row of souvenir bats from the last twenty-five World Series, and next to the cash register is *The Baseball Encyclopedia,* the six-inch-thick book that has replaced the six-gun as the arbiter of all disputes. Ceiling fans overhead turn slowly, and the talk, the atmosphere, is as thick with baseball as with the smells of cigar smoke, steak, and booze. On any given night in the spring, the barstool next to yours is likely to be filled by someone whose name is in *The Baseball Encyclopedia* but not the local phone directory. One night, when I was talking with Clete Boyer and Briley, the fellow on the next stool was Billy Martin.

It struck me almost immediately that Martin belonged in this setting, perhaps more than he did in pinstripes. But he was a man without a team in this week of pitchers and catchers in 1985 (though technically Martin was still indentured to George Steinbrenner, thus making him the highest-paid scout in baseball). He seemed, in his Western garb, to be the Man in the Lite Beer Commercial, recognizable to anyone who cared to look. He also could have been another subject of Wes Chapman's—The Old Gunslinger (or ex-Manager) in the Bradshaws.

I no longer remember which one of Martin's divorces from Steinbrenner left me bored and looking elsewhere for my baseball thrills. But frankly, I never imagined I would see him quite as I did that night. I think I came to understand why he carried a marshmallow salesman's scalp in his belt and a Yankee emblem over his heart. Of all of the grizzled characters I ran into or would run into, Billy's instinct for what lay at the core of a ballplayer was unparalleled. There was, however, one major difference. He was his own standard. It was only the light of his own inner fire that enabled him to see what burned in others. He understood the motives of other people as if they were extensions of his own.

"Ralph Houk tried to show me up once," he remembered. "Pitches out with Henderson on first not once, not twice, but three fucking times. Can you believe that? The son of a bitch calls a two and oh pitchout just because he thinks he's gonna stop me from sending Rickey. You know what I did? I stuck it right up his ass. I sent Henderson three and oh, and he took the base by ten feet."

Martin makes no attempt to keep others away when he is in a crowd. He is as accessible as the counter of a bar. If you can get close, you belong. He makes no attempt to hide or put on airs. An owner would never need an ex-FBI agent to discover that Billy's first is a tall, diluted Chivas Regal, but his second is full strength in a rocks glass. It likewise takes no special animus to learn that he currently pays alimony to two former wives, and that the Yankee managing job was just this close from his fingertips midway in the 1984 season, when George was playing cat-and-mouse with Yogi Berra's future, and that a certain American League manager deliberately fouled it up for him with a phone call. It is surprising—perhaps it is part of his fabled inclination to self-destruction—but no one is more vulnerable than Billy Martin in the sense that anyone can get that close to him. Closeness and trouble seem to be synonymous in his life.

"Billy scares you into winning," Clete Boyer says. "That's why he doesn't last long. It's just like a marriage. The arguments finally lead to a divorce." But Boyer believes Martin is a genius. "I've known him so long, been with him, been against him—I've gotten to the point where I can almost sense by instinct what he's gonna do. But there are certain things I'll never figure out no matter how long I'm in this game or how hard I try to study him. There is no one in this game, for example, who understands a pitchout better than he does. You think you understand it, but then he does something you never would have expected. Whatever else he is, Billy Martin is an absolute genius."

Martin is not put uptight by the assertion that he manages by intimidation and fear. In fact, the mention of it allows him almost to poke fun at himself, except for the gnawing sense that he may have no regrets of any kind in approaching managing in this manner.

"You know what happened the first time Henderson, Murphy, and Armas took fly balls with me?" Martin says to everyone within earshot. "I hit a ball to Henderson, and he drops it. I hit one to Armas, he breaks the wrong way, it sails over his head. I hit one to Murphy, he drops it and kicks it. I tell myself, 'What's goin' on here, this is the best outfield in baseball?' So I do it all over again. I hit one to Henderson and he butchers it. I go to Armas, same thing. Hit one to Murphy, he comes in twenty feet and the ball goes twenty feet over his head. I tell myself, 'These guys are trying to fuck with my head.' But you know what it was? They were scared of Billy Martin. That's all. They were nervous and scared 'cause it was the first day they were playin' for me."

Martin even became the main narrator among a group of his ex-coaches, in the recitation of just the sort of incident that makes it hard for any sensible owner to hire him. The episode involved his tenure with the A's, when management had forced upon the team a young first baseman none of the field staff felt was qualified. They were in a game in which the opposing team had loaded the bases, and a decision was made to move the infield in because "we didn't have guys who could turn a double play." On the next play, an easy, one-hop grounder was hit to the young first baseman, who held the ball, waited for the second baseman to back up, and then lobbed the ball to him, too late to get the runner.

"Man, that was it. I was gone," Billy said. "I couldn't fucking stand it no longer."

"He was crazed. He was so crazed he went into the locker room, and no one could work up the courage to go in after him," Boyer said. The laughter was generous and easy.

Martin is closing in on 60 years old. But it is only when you stand next to him that you can see in his face the damages of time that long ago replaced youth with the texture of wax and the drawn lines of a bird of prey. Still his body, devoid of fat, looks deceptively youthful in the disguises of a baseball uniform or of a cowpoke lost in the Bradshaws.

Sometime between the third Chivas Regal and the moment when he disappeared into a swirl of bodies on the floor of a nearby disco, Billy asked, did anyone know how many times he had been named Manager of the Year? "Three times," he answered himself, "and the fourth time I was fucking number two because fucking Ted Williams was in his first fucking year with a fucking third-place team. I finished first and he finished fucking third and they gave it to him."

It struck me when Martin said this that though he had been the center of his own stories for most of the night, this was the single time when anyone could have accused him of pounding his own drum. But in a moment it became clear what had happened. Without anyone realizing it, he had worked himself back in time to something pivotal and essential in his makeup. The only person in history to have won Manager of the Year four times was Casey Stengel.

Martin suddenly began talking about him. "I was with my ex-wife and I went to visit Casey's grave. I wanted to lay some roses on it. They stopped us at the gatehouse when I asked for directions. Was I a relative, they wanted to know. I told 'em I was sort of his son. And when I finally got out there and I was standing in front of his grave, I swear to God I started fucking crying. And I was talking to him, I was yelling at him, I was yelling at him because he was the fucking one who taught me to be the kind of competitor I am. He was the one who taught me."

Like any other unemployed manager, Martin, for those few weeks in the spring of 1985, was waiting for the call that would send him back to work. He didn't know then that Western justice masquerading as George Steinbrenner was about to oblige him once more, but before that great saloon door in the Bronx swung open, the aging gunfighter had a free moment in which he spoke with astonishing innocence: "You know what I really want," he said softly, "I want nothing more than to have people know I can take a bunch of nobodies, players like I was, put 'em all on an expansion team—and win. That's all. Fuck the awards."

Sometime before I left Arizona, I sought out yet another ex-Yankee, Jimmie Reese, the 81-year-old coach on the California Angels, whose fungo bat, over the years, has acquired legendary status at least equal to Wonderboy. (Fungoing, for the uninitiated, is deceptively routine-looking. It is self-generated hitting, usually accomplished with a long, skinny bat. While it has kept generations of odd-lot amateurs happy, whole teams nearly always use fungoing for shagging or for infield practice.)

Spring training normally was Reese's time of year. With his uncanny talent for being able to place a ball on a dime (Gene Mauch, his current manager, calls him "a Russian violinist"),

Reese's usual regimen in the spring was to hit fungoes for as long
as there were players willing to run them down. He stayed in the
field hitting four and five hours at a time, never tiring, never
losing his edge. He got himself into shape during these weeks
even as he went about the business of getting others in shape. At
the end of the 1984 season, as the Angels were concluding a long
road trip, Jimmie suffered a nearly fatal heart attack. When I
got to the Gene Autry complex near Scottsdale that late February morning, I saw him in uniform with his wondrous split bat
in his hands. As I had seen before, he was placing fly balls just at
the fingertips of fielders in full sprint. Later, he said, "From the
time I got sick I didn't come back to the ballpark till today.
Today was the first day I hit."

Though Reese is the oldest man in uniform in the game, he has
never sought advantage based on his years. The game has been
his first love since he was a teenage batboy for Frank Chance in
the old Pacific Coast League—and it will be his last love. He is
childless and has been a widower for many years. His abiding
hope is that he can "remain in uniform until they have to tear it
off me." His work in the spring of 1985, limited by his doctor,
had all of that built into it. Reese is the living repository of nearly
sixty-five years of baseball history, but his gaze is focused stead-
ily on what is happening right in front of him.

On a day when a decent-sized contingent of Angel players
turned up, Jimmie was in their midst on one of the practice
diamonds. He remained long enough to take part in a kind of
orders-of-the-day meeting, hit a few fungoes, and then retire for
a while to the clubhouse. Later, after a rest, he rejoined the day's
practice for simulated game pitching.

"I'm not sure I'd have enough sense to stop," he said. "It's a
new sort of life, you see. I may not travel with the club for a
while. The long travel apparently has an effect."

He saw the problem in the way a person in baseball all his life
would see it. "I have to adjust now more than at any other time.
Got to do it. My God, at my age, some fellas are lucky to put on

a uniform at all! How many fellas have been in the game in uniform sixty-two years? But the main thing now is not to overdo it. Because I could have a snap. Just like that. And I'd be the last one to realize it. Because when you feel good you go all out. You go until you can't go any further. I've hit over two million fungoes in my life." (This is no exaggeration. Bobby Knoop, a friend and fellow Angel coach, said, "He gave me his favorite fungo bat as a present. I have it home. He had used it so much, there were ridges worn in it from his hands. When you pick it up, you can feel where he put his hands on it.") "I could go three, four hours a day," Reese said, "hit thousands of fungoes a day, in hot weather, cold weather, any weather. But the hot weather takes a little more out of you. You know, like in Texas—the intense heat, you know. Kansas City, those places. So you have to adjust."

Reese is surely the only man in the history of the game to have earned his reputation with a fungo bat. To people who have not seen him at work or who have routinely, out of their own experience, adopted the mistaken notion that anyone can hit a decent fungo, Reese is simply a magician. His accuracy extends, apparently, to being able to "pitch" batting practice by fungoing balls as a pitcher would throw to a waiting batter. Knoop says he once played a round of golf with Reese, who used Wonderboy for eighteen holes and "did a hell of a lot better than I did using golf clubs."

Reese's purpose on a baseball field is not merely to whack the ball or even to put it to a certain spot. It is chiefly to enable players to extend themselves in practice, so that their conditioning takes place at full tilt, as though they were actually in a game rather than at practice. "It's completely different when you work with Jimmie," one of the Angel pitchers told me. "When you finish, you know you've been through it. You've accomplished something."

Obviously it requires technical mastery to do this consistently, much as it would to maintain a .350 batting average. And as with any technical skill in sport, the mental part of it is crucial. There are slumps. But, Jimmie says, "not too often. I adjust pretty quickly. The main thing is you have to keep at it." And keep at it he has. That is his secret. Wonderboy and the two million swings did not spring full-blown from the head of Zeus. First, there was failure, the failure of a playing career that did not pan out. In his forties, as a coach with a minor-league team, Jimmie found a split bat that had been discarded, thought he still might make use of it, shaved it, and began experimenting with it to hit fungoes. He discovered that with only one side of the bat rounded, he could hit a ball with topspin or backspin as he chose. It was far easier to hit a ball accurately that way, too. He sacrificed some distance—he had little power to begin with—but distance was never what he strove for. "I saw Babe Ruth hit fungoes one day," he said, "and he hit them eight miles. But with fungoing, it's really not how far but how accurate you are."

Most people who know anything at all about Reese know that he was once Babe Ruth's roommate. This gives him certain advantages *and* disadvantages in the baseball world. The advantages come from his not only being a repository of more than half a century of the game's history but also of having lived shoulder-to-shoulder with the game's greatest player—even if it has meant that the uniqueness of Reese's own career has often been overlooked.

"I don't think there can ever be another one like Babe," Reese will tell you, as much out of affection as admiration; Ruth was a lifelong friend as well as a teammate. "Maybe one man in a century will be like that. There was so much charisma in Babe. He was great and wonderful. The closest anyone comes today is Reggie, but it's not the same. The minute Babe walked out on the field, there was an air. He would *always* rise to great heights. One time when [Tris] Speaker was manager of Cleveland, they were two runs ahead with the bases loaded against them and Babe coming up. They walked him intentionally, cutting the lead to one run. And you know, Babe never made a study of hitting or anything. If he went oh for four, he'd throw an arm around you and say, 'We'll get 'em tomorrow, kid.' When we went north at the end of spring training, we'd make a dozen stops. And [Yankee manager Joe] McCarthy didn't believe in losing. Wherever we'd go, Babe'd walk in and want to know where the 'social activities' were. There are people who say it might have hurt him but maybe that might have relaxed him, who knows? Every town we went to, he'd put on a five-minute exhibition of hitting—and incidentally, wherever we went, there was standing room only, they'd be standing back of the infield. These little towns you couldn't even find on the map and that never saw Babe before. It would be just the batting-practice pitcher and the Babe. He'd hit 'em left field, right field, so far you couldn't believe it."

Living so close to Ruth also allowed Reese to see precisely what it was that made him so much more than a fast fat man who had fun with everything that came his way, including being the number-one player of his time. "I used to go to Babe's house occasionally," Reese remembered. "He had many interesting people there. I just sat back and listened and learned. He had a whole floor and a private elevator. He had a pool table and he hated to lose—at anything. One day, I'm playin' him a dime a ball and I'm up twenty cents and his wife called that it's time for dinner. He says, 'I'm not quitting till I'm even.' He'd go out and spend hundreds of dollars without batting an eye, but he couldn't stand to lose twenty cents in a pool game. That was his attitude and it carried right out onto the ballfield."

Jimmie also saw the Babe in relation to his polar opposite, Lou Gehrig. "Every once in a while, Lou would say, 'Let's go out and raise hell.' But what did he mean? Dinner and a beer and bed by nine o'clock. I used to go to his house for dinner, too. He'd go oh for four, and he'd ask me over for dinner and say, 'Tomorrow, let's go to the park early in the morning.' And I'd throw to him while he used to work on different stances to see what was wrong. After ten minutes once, he stopped and said, 'That's it, I got it!' Just like that. And that afternoon—I remember it—he hit four of the hardest balls I ever saw in my life."

How did Jimmie see the relationship between Ruth and Gehrig?

"Gehrig had a feeling, you could sense it—something like resentment. It was expressed, I think, by Babe doing something, hitting a home run, and Gehrig then having to do it. I think Babe made him a better player. Gehrig competed by having to emulate the great one. God, you should have seen it. When he walked on the field, the whispering started, 'There's the Babe! There's the Babe!' The only answer Lou had was the way he played the game."

To hear Reese tell it, there was no cost to his belonging to such company. His career with the Yankees lasted only two years, and he was out of major-league baseball the following year, after he was traded to the St. Louis Cardinals. "The curve ball got me," he explains. In his first year with the Yankees, he hit .346, dropping to .241 the following year and then hitting .265 in his year with the Cardinals. "The first year, I was hitting second in front of Babe. They didn't want to walk me, so I was always getting fastballs. Then later on, they moved me in the order and I started getting breaking balls." But Reese is an extraordinarily modest man. If he was not Prince Hamlet, he was not quite the attendant lord, either.

"We both joined the Yankees in 1930," teammate Lefty Gomez remembers. "He was part of a great double play combination, Lary and Reese." (The Yankees, at the time, paid a record $125,000 to get them from the Oakland Oaks of the Pacific Coast League. Lyn Lary, the shortstop, remained in the major leagues for twelve years.) "It wasn't the curve ball that got Jimmie. No, no—he had a tough guy to beat out at second—Tony Lazzeri." And when he went to the Cardinals, the second baseman he had to beat out was Frankie Frisch. Reese's fate was the one often reserved for good players forced into utility roles on glamorous teams. His anonymity obscured his talent, but over the years, his talent was transformed by age and who he was. His gift to the game—then and now—is what he brings to it.

Reese was one of the early Jewish ballplayers in the game. The Yankees had purchased his contract partly for the promotional value in the New York area. But being Jewish, while not as universal a problem as hitting a curve ball, was a real enough problem in 1930. "There was probably racism, there always is, but I never had it the way Jackie Robinson did. You're a human being, that's it."

Reese always wanted to be a ballplayer, against his mother's wishes. She wanted him to belong to a respectable profession, law or medicine. "But I never wanted to work in an office or have a business or devote my life simply to making money. All I ever wanted to do was be a ballplayer. And from the earliest time I can remember, what I did was hang around the ballpark. Frank Chance let me be a batboy when I was twelve years old—and I've been with it ever since."

But being a ballplayer—and a coach—has always meant hard work and perseverance. Reese returned to the minor leagues in 1932 and waited forty years to make it back to the majors—too late, because he was then over 55, to qualify for league pension plans; too late to do anything more than give to the game the extraordinary art of the fungo, which he had developed over the years. "Harry Dalton [then Angels' GM] called me thirteen years ago and said Nolan Ryan wants you to come out and hit fungoes for a month. I did and that was that," Reese said, as though there were no more to it than having been in proximity to a telephone. "I never made much money," he continued. "I live in a three-unit apartment, I have Social Security, and my expenses are low."

During the off-seasons, particularly since his wife died, Reese makes picture frames when he isn't working out informally with players. To date, Jimmie believes, he has made over 23,000 frames since 1970, all of them given away at no charge to friends. "I do it for therapy," he says. But then when he talks about the numbers of frames he has done and what it takes to preserve pictures beyond their years, you realize he is still talking about the game.

"I think I've been very fortunate," Jimmie says. "The good Lord's had his arms around me 'cause I only had ordinary ability, but I had ambition and desire, I wanted to make it. I wanted to be a ballplayer. I've always loved my work, and I've always known the inevitable's going to happen. You're going to die. But in baseball, nothing is certain. You never know the best of your life five minutes ahead in this game."

Jimmie sees himself as an artist's helper, a man who enhances the picture, not the one who creates it. Reggie Jackson has another idea: "I'll tell you what I think of Jimmie Reese," he told me. "I think there should be a Jimmie Reese Award for the California Angels. We have an Owner's Trophy. And I've talked to [Angel owner] Mr. Autry about it. . . . There should be a Jimmie Reese Award before he passes on. I don't know what it should be . . . for the guy who plays hardest or loves the game the most . . . something signifying how much he means to the California Angels and the world of baseball. I'll tell you what: if Jimmie Reese likes you, you're one step closer to heaven."

PART TWO

FULL
SQUADS

CHAPTER THREE

Conditioning

... sturdy March with brows full sternly bent,
And armed strongly, rode upon a Ram,
The same which over Hellespontus swam:
Yet in his hand a spade he also hent,
And in a bag all sorts of seeds ysame,
Which on the earth he strowed as he went,
And fild her womb with fruitful hope of nourishment.
                           —Spenser, *The Faerie Queene*

Jimmie Reese is listed in the California Angels' media guide as a conditioning coach. Despite his years and single-minded devotion to a game he learned before most of us were born, he is one of a new breed of conditioning specialists in professional baseball. Baseball teams, of course, have carried trainers on their rosters for as long as anyone can remember. But until fairly recently, a trainer was little more than a water boy who also passed out the liniment and aspirin.

Starting about fifteen years ago, and in earnest with the advent of free agency and the rise of ballplayers whose bodies were suddenly worth more to Lloyd's than some small countries, the man in the training room, along with his equipment, became critically important to success or failure on the field. Rather than prowess at the barstool or friendship with the owner—the previous prerequisites for the job—a college education, with a degree in a field directly or indirectly related to sports medicine, became the calling card of the new breed of trainer, a professional with limited but real expertise—a kind of anatomical investment counselor. Paralleling this, of course, was the emergence of the still robust national craze for fitness. The two phenomena taken together have produced, in the baseball world, a revolution in the way teams condition themselves for the championship season.

"Ballplayers today are bigger, stronger, faster—they're just better athletes than they were in my time," says Whitey Ford, referring to the era of Chubby Checker not Wee Willie Keeler. Surrounding Ford in the Yankees' Fort Lauderdale clubhouse was a group of athletes—from Dave Winfield to the newly acquired six-foot seven-inch pitcher from the Cubs, Rich Bordi— who seemed to prove the point. Even somewhat smaller players like Don Mattingly or Rickey Henderson appeared to have been honed and shaped far beyond their original limitations by the wonders of Nautilus, Inc. In the old days (American slang for two decades or less), players came to camp to get into shape. Today, more often than not, they show up in shape. "When we get to camp," Yankee trainer Gene Monahan pointed out, "our club is expected to be in pretty good physical condition so that the five or six weeks we have in Florida, the guys can devote to baseball skills rather than conditioning."

The Yankees are one of a handful of clubs that have ardently embraced the Revolution. They have invested enormous sums of money in the Revolution's technology—Nautilus, Cybex, AMF—have established ongoing programs complete with body-fat tests, clubhouse diets, and printed pamphlets; and have, with only a few other teams, employed a "strength and flexibility" coach.

The Yankee strength and flexibility coach is Jeff Mangold, a mild-mannered and somewhat tentative fellow who is only a few years out of college. His background, like that of his employer, seems to have been in football. He works in tandem with Gene

Monahan who, in turn, works with Dr. John Bonamo, an orthopedic specialist in New York's prestigious University Hospital. All of these sports medicine revolutionaries serve at the pleasure of The Principal Owner who, in the spring of 1985, became so angry at a couple of routine injuries that he began, in the manner of Robespierre, to conjure images of disloyalty and the tribunal.

On an ordinary weekday morning, Mangold's work is in harmony with the sultry surroundings of Fort Lauderdale itself. There are daily wet T-shirt contests at the local bistros, the annual invasion of eager young college bodies is just blocks away, and there is talk of putting down a tarmac in the Everglades to accommodate a new generation of widebodies. Without distinction, all things are bright, beautiful, and new in Fort Lauderdale.

One of the mornings after I arrived there from Arizona, the Yankees made their appearance on the field in their home whites and went through a series of stretching exercises that seemed slightly more strenuous than the kind on display in most other camps. There were a few more positions to whet the imagination of pretzel enthusiasts, but nothing that seemed too far out of the ordinary. What was exceptional was the absence on the field of certain older players in this phase of the morning's work, players who, in private, confess to the belief that baseball skills—not football calisthenics—are what keep a baseball body in shape. In a conversation I had months before with Bill White, the Yankee broadcaster and former Cardinal first baseman wondered whether the newfangled muscle machinery lining almost every big-league clubhouse didn't wind up adding additional bodies to the disabled lists. "I'm from the old school," he said. "I believe the more games a first baseman plays, the more he gets the muscles he actually needs into shape. How many games does a player today actually play before he's in the majors? A few hundred? A player should have thousands of plays to handle, so he becomes used to the moves he has to make on the field. That's his protection—and the team's."

White's view is shared by others, usually players and coaches whose maturation occurred before the Revolution. "All I need to do is get my fingers into shape," Phil Niekro, the ageless knuckleballer, confessed. "I don't do anything over the winter." "I was never impressed with the fitness craze," said Lou Piniella, remembering his days as a player. "I believe that spring training gives you time for your body to come back. What is really important—particularly in baseball, which requires finesse—is to learn your particular skills. You're getting paid to hit, to learn your mechanics, to know what you're doing up at home plate, and so you should work on those particular skills and don't worry so much about getting in shape, because if you can't hit the damned thing it doesn't make any difference anyway."

There have been, of course, a few scary stories about baseball and pumping iron, the most notable of which are Jason Thompson's bulking up only to lose his home run stroke, and Fred Lynn's Nautilus experience, which upped his home run production but cost him his knees. These and other examples from actual experience have greatly tempered baseball's all-out enthusiasm for pronounced weight programs. Most clubs now, including the Yankees, are skeptical about bulk building and the overuse of systems such as Nautilus. But this skepticism is really fine-tuning the Revolution. The dividing line is still between believers and nonbelievers, and there are enough of both around to make things lively and anecdote-filled.

When you talk to Mangold or Monahan, you are immediately impressed by their attachment to the science, rather than the mystery, of conditioning. Science is what separates them from those who might, on occasion, still use terms like "getting in shape" for "conditioning" or "calisthenics" for "nonballistic stretching." What the unknowing fan watching a Yankee workout—which for all the world still looks like calisthenics—is really seeing, says Mangold, "is fifteen minutes of static exercises to prepare the body for more explosive movements. This increases your flexibility a little bit day by day. And when you do that, you increase your range of motion."

It's all part of a program, year-round and team-wide. "We have our winter program," explained Monahan, "where we monitor the players' weight, their muscle strength. Dr. Bonamo has people in. We monitor their weight so that if they don't send in their cards every two weeks, I'll get on the phone. We do muscle-testing on all the players before they go home—we do it all through the season but we get a last set of numbers on 'em before they go home—and we'll take bodyweight, muscle strength, and body fat, all before they start work here in the spring."

I wondered innocently—and ignorantly—about body fat. How was it possible to measure that beyond pinching the inch? "We do it with Skindex skin calipers," Monahan explained. "We'll choose three sites; it automatically computes body fat, accurately to about a point and a half percent."

Actually, I had had something else in mind. I was more curious to know what they would do with an obviously overweight player, whose girth to the naked eye might be an affront to any program, scientific or otherwise.

"I don't know," Monahan said. "If we had a guy who was overweight, we'd put him on a program of exercise and diet. We'd bring him in every month during the winter and reevaluate him. And if he's not gettin' it done, we'll go after him hard."

Another scientific term that came up and that baffled me was "pliometrics." And this, it turned out, was at the heart of the strength and flexibility program. More than Skindex or Cybex or Nautilus, pliometrics was the future. It was the November rather than the October Revolution of sports conditioning.

"Pliometrics is a series of bounding drills," Mangold told me. "The Russians originated it over in the Eastern bloc, the Russians and the East Germans. People say that speed can't be improved. But that's a fallacy. It can be."

As this seemed to involve some mad scientific tampering with the natural limitations of the body (speed was one of those things that, before the Revolution, supposedly could not be improved), I pressed the point. For example, could pliometrics actually enable me to get over being turtle-like.

"I've seen the biomechanics of running broken down—stride length, stride frequency, arm action, forward body lean, relaxation, along with strengthening the muscles involved with running—the hamstrings, the quadriceps, your gluts, your power area." Mangold was patient, mild, and, like any specialist in the sciences, generously willing to suffer a layman's ignorance. "We're talking about bounding," he said. "One-leg hops, two leg hops. But let's go on in terms of the forty-yard dash. We'll talk about a six-month period. A guy will come in and run 4.8. Then he'll put on thirty pounds of body weight and reduce his 4.8 to 4.65. Just by increasing his strength and working on the actual form of running, stride length and stride frequency.

"You have new ideas you'd like to see accomplished," Mangold continued, "but it takes time. A maintenance program during the season. Work hard, build strength. Then pliometrics. Baseball is a power game. Explosive."

The Yankees seemed to believe more than other clubs in strength.

"It's a game of power. Speed and strength combined. That's the main thing. A lot of people say, 'That's a strong kid.' But it's speed and strength combined. That's the big difference. And we now know how to improve both where years ago we couldn't have even dreamed of doing it."

Mangold is not a mad scientist. A trip to your local library's collection of athletic training publications will be sufficient proof that he is perfectly representative of the new breed of athletic trainers around today. He has time on his side, company in his beliefs, and enough supporting proof to make his work very much in the mainstream. With an adequate building of strength, which comes through controlled and progressive use of specific weights, increased flexibility becomes possible. With increased flexibility and strength, the explosive movements of baseball can be accomplished at peak levels of performance. A batter will be able to hit a ball farther, a pitcher throw a ball faster, a fielder and baserunner move with more speed and fluidity. Mangold is actually helping consolidate things. The *ancien régime* was overthrown long ago, perhaps as far back as the day when the bully on the beach kicked sand in the face of a certain 97-pound weakling.

And yet the doubts linger. The number and severity of injuries in baseball has actually increased over the years. Although such figures need to be examined with caution, the disabled lists of major-league teams on a league-wide basis have shown a percentage increase for every year in the past decade. Fifteen years ago, as one trainer told me, "We didn't even know that rotator cuff injuries existed. If you had asked me about the rotator cuff, I would have thought you were talking about French shirts."

Even more telling, however, is the actual performance level of players over this period of time. Last year, two pitchers in the American League and one pitcher in the National League pitched more than 250 innings. In 1975 (two years after the DH was established) eighteen American League pitchers and nine National Leaguers were able to do it. In 1975, four pitchers threw more than 300 innings. The last time a major league pitcher threw 300 innings plus was 1980 (Steve Carlton did it). Of pitchers currently in the game only Carlton, Phil Niekro, and Nolan Ryan have ever pitched more than 300 innings in a season, and their achievement may reasonably be associated with history rather than with present training methods. More contemporary "workhorses," such as Jack Morris, Ron Guidry, Fernando Valenzuela, Mario Soto, and even Tom Seaver, have never done it.

It is reasonable to suspect that what may be at the root of all this is neither muscle tone nor even the art of the middle reliever so much as money. "With the amount of money players make today," Bill White said, "no one wants to pitch that much. They can't afford to risk it. The other day, I heard a young starting pitcher on a local talk show, and he was saying that he geared all his efforts to going six or seven innings! That was what he was aiming for! It was like he couldn't even conceive of pitching a complete game."

There may even be more. Charlie Fox suggested that awareness of injury has created its own dynamic, and that it is therefore quite likely that pitchers, knowing much more about the nature of injuries than they did in the past, unconsciously nurse themselves into the very damages they fear most.

Whatever the case, the one area the new science of conditioning seems to have ignored almost completely is the mental side of training. "Ninety percent of this game is half mental," Jim Wohlford, former K.C. Royal, is once supposed to have said. "In the big leagues today," Clete Boyer actually said, "the kids have all the ability they'll ever need. At this level, the game is mental. One hundred percent mental." Boyer is one of the few people around in the major leagues who actually experienced a baseball-conditioning program that involved mental training. It occurred in Japan, when Boyer went over there to play out the last years of his career for the Taiyo Whales.

The Japanese, of course, as much as we do, regard baseball as a national pastime. And their approach to the game—and to training—is as distinctly Japanese as ours is American. If we look to the farm or the loneliness of the prairie for our mythic baseball heroes, the Japanese find theirs in a world of self-sacrifice, in the centuries-old sagas of samurai warriors whose training is simultaneously physical and mental. The Japanese spring training regimen, which I saw two years earlier and which players like Boyer experienced, is, compared to our own, punishingly hard, a combination of Marine boot camp and Zen discipline.

"When I went over there," Boyer explained, "I was a fat slob. The way I looked at it, I was goin' over there to make a little money, but when I got there and saw what they did and how much they expected from me, I said, 'I gotta bust my ass to play with these guys.' You gotta get in shape. You gotta work. I couldn't quit, because I couldn't come home and have people say, 'How'd you do in Japan?' when I'd have to say, 'Well, I couldn't handle it mentally. That was a big thing with me. I said, 'I'm gonna get into these people, I'm gonna show 'em I can play infield. . . . I'm gonna do everything they do. I'll train as hard as they train, I'll live where they live, eat where they eat, use the language they use.' I wasn't gonna take any favors just because I was a foreigner. So you know what happened? First time out they do this thing called mental training. You know what that was? They strapped a lotta weight to your back and you ran up and down stadium steps and the sides of mountains. I thought I'd never make it that first day, thought I was gonna have a heart attack. Same thing on the second day. Then you know what happened? Sometime in the middle of this on the third day, I told myself, 'I'm not gonna have a heart attack. I can do this. I can do this as good as anyone else.' Then I understood why they called it mental training. I got two years back at the top of my form. I made plays I had given up believing I could ever make again."

The most striking difference between an American and Japanese spring training camp is in the amount of work put in. Spring training, whether in Arizona or Florida, is accomplished well within banker's hours. In fact, there is usually time enough for nine holes and a trip to the bank. A camp day typically begins at nine-thirty and is over by noon or twelve-thirty. This is not to say that work isn't accomplished. Ken Carson, trainer for the Toronto Blue Jays, described his camp's approach: "Work hard, short days." There's more than a motto in this. "A lot of teams," he continued, "old-style teams, used to work all day at half speed. You do more harm than good that way. If you put in a good hard stint of work and then go and play golf or have a barbecue, that's relaxing and that's good."

The Japanese believe in duration. Where American ballplay

ers typically believe that too much practice actually makes it more difficult to endure a long season, the Japanese, as though from their samurai past, have retained as an article of faith the notion that elevation of both skill and fighting spirit are the direct result of almost endless practice. Jim Lefebvre, currently manager of the San Francisco Giants Triple A affiliate in Phoenix, once played for the Lotte Orions in Japan. This is his description of a typical spring training day:

"We'd start with a wakeup call at seven a.m., then we would go on our morning walk at eight o'clock. And we'd always walk in formation. We ran in formation, we did our exercises in formation . . . and that walk wasn't a stroll through the park. It was a very intense speed walk. Then we'd stop and do a series of ballistic exercises and then we'd finish right around eight-thirty or a quarter to nine. Then breakfast—together—then back to our rooms and then down to go over the program we were going to do for that particular day. And they were very detailed and organized about that. Then when we would hit the field, we would run for one hour—every day—in formation, just like you see in the Army: down the lines, around the outfield, around home plate. Some days we'd stop after forty minutes and finish with wind-sprints, other days do a hundred meters—it was one hour. . . . We'd have two hours of batting practice every day, fifteen minutes for lunch—together—then we'd have two hours of defense. Then we'd do our baserunning, which was very extensive. After that was over, they kept guys out for extra BP and fielding practice, then, after that, we'd go back to the hotel. You're looking at five o'clock now. We'd take a bath and have dinner between six-thirty and seven—and we ate like kings. We had what they call sumo-style training tables. We had four to a table, and they would bring out these big platters of beef and chicken and noodles and fish—it was like a feast every night. They felt that you earned that. It was like a celebration for making it through the day. Then we had a meeting every night! We went over bunt defense and relays. It would usually last about half an hour. After that, we broke up into groups. The hitters would go into one area, the pitchers would go to another. We'd work on form. The hitters would hit into nets or work before mirrors, and there were all kinds of drills for pitchers. Then after that, everyone had to get a massage. When you finally hit the sack, believe me, it was lights out. You had been through war and you had won it, and you knew it."

There is far more than a difference over quantity of hours between the Japanese and American approaches to conditioning. Both are geared to preparing players for professional competition and are, therefore, necessarily, mental and physical at the same time. But where American programs—with one notable exception—make very little attempt to link mental and physical work directly, leaving it to the psalm of "experience," the Japanese believe you can train the mind as well as the body. Spirit leads technique. The goal of training is to engage the spirit so that it can provide great bodily strength and almost unbelievable powers of concentration. Concentration, rather than, say, pliometrics, is the key.

On a recent trip to the United States, Sadaharu Oh, the legendary home run hitter, was once again seeking to explain the way he used the Japanese long sword in his training. The mechanics of the swing were surely important, but the real secret of his success lay in an unusual form of concentration derived from his martial arts training, which enabled him to approach the task of hitting the ball as though far more than sport was at stake. "When a warrior killed himself," he said, riding in a limousine through rush hour along New York's Fifth Avenue, "he needed an assistant who would finish the job by cutting his head off. The task was always left to a trusted and highly skilled swordsman, because this had to be done with one clean, perfect stroke. If the stroke was not perfect, the result would be a horrible mess. I approached the task of hitting a baseball in the same manner."

One of the newer Yankees in the spring of 1985 was the pitcher Marty Bystrom. Bystrom had been traded to the Yankees the year before for Shane Rawley and was a refugee from the one conditioning program in American professional baseball similar to the martial-arts-inspired programs of the Japanese. This was the regimen initiated and run by Gus Hoefling for Steve Carlton and other members of the Philadelphia Phillies. Bystrom, without Hoefling, has tried on his own to keep up. "I have my boots and my weights and I do the stretching and the kicks and the punching," says Bystrom, "but there's no rice and no poles or anything like that." The Yankee program, though it derives some of the stretching exercises from Hoefling, is just not the same.

"Jeff's approach," Bystrom said, "is really more from football, more tuned into weights. Gus was one of a kind. He was a kung fu guru back when he was younger, when he was in China, so his background gives him a lot."

Hoefling's regimen combines brutally difficult physical work with mental training. As was the case with Clete Boyer in Japan, the two cannot be separated.

In Hoefling's "back room" at Veterans in Philadelphia, there is a little booth that looks vaguely like an execution chamber. It is a mood room. The soundproofed walls are covered with thick blue carpeting, and there is a single painting bathed in soft light. It is a seascape featuring two circling seagulls, waves crashing against a rocky shore, and a mysterious light shimmering across a stretch of ocean. In the center of the room, facing the picture, is a Barcalounger, one whose onboard motors permit it to vibrate while the occupant of the chair faces the picture and listens to specially designed relaxation tapes. It is surely an odd accouterment to find among professional athletes. But psychologists and their techniques for quieting the mind and inciting it to winning ways have been an infrequent but regular part of the baseball scene ever since Branch Rickey and Bill Veeck. Several teams, including the A's, Mariners, Orioles, and White Sox currently employ psychologists or their equivalent. The "mood room" will probably survive the retirement of its chief occupant, Steve Carlton, and of its designer, Gus Hoefling.

"Hell, I go in there with my Conway Twitty tapes. It's just a nice black place," said Phillies' coach Dave Bristol.

But the room really says no more about the nature of Hoefling's program than the usual line of expensive conditioning machines that are also present. Hoefling's program is Gus Hoefling. Eccentric, down-to-earth, assertive, contradictory—obvious and puzzling at the same time—he is exactly, as Bystrom described, "one of a kind." As part of the winter preparation for my spring travels, I visited Hoefling's pre-spring class at the Vet and had a chance to see what is surely one of the most talked-about and least understood conditioning programs in the game today.

On the day I turned up, Greg Gross, along with a handful of younger players, was there. None of Hoefling's more celebrated students—including Carlton—were present nor would they be until camp began in Clearwater. I had hoped, before I went, for more, but I was warned in advance, with an appropriate sense of mystery added, that getting to see an advanced class was not all that easy.

Hoefling, as much as Mangold or any other strength and flexibility coach, believes that increased strength and flexibility augment performance. An athlete could be trained to run faster, throw harder, hit with more power. But there the similarities ended—at the water's edge of a painting in the mood room, of approaches centuries apart. "Strength and flexibility," Hoefling says, "are not only physical, they're also mental." The source of his teaching, he will tell you, is not the AMA or the National Association of Athletic Trainers, but Kwang Tung, a Chinese Buddhist monk who died in A.D. 520. Kwang Tung's gift to Gus is ongaku, or northern-style kung fu.

"Who am I?" Gus says. "A fifty-year-old kung fu guy. But I've studied something that's stood the test of time. How long has

Nautilus been around, fifty years? Marcus of Catonia was the first man in history to record a weight-training program, what we call progressive resistance exercises. He did this by lifting a baby bull, and he observed that as the bull got heavier he had to exert more strength. When the bull was little he could lift it over his head ten times. Three weeks later he could only do it seven times. But he was getting stronger and bigger. Marcus observed that, too. Okay, now Kwang Tung and many others understood all this long before Marcus and long before the Southern California Trojans and their Nautilus conditioning program. It was around long before the American Medical Association. Shit, we only started washing our hands two hundred years ago, and the AMA sets itself up as God."

Initially, nothing seemed out of the ordinary in Gus's class. It might easily have passed for a typical high school gym session save for its atypical setting in the bowels of Veterans Stadium and the weights strapped to the ankles and wrists of some of the students. Gus, too, *looked* typical enough. In his sweat pants, cutaway shirt, weight-lifting belt, and boxing shoes, he bore a certain resemblance to a high school coach I once had who was fond of telling Marine stories, slapping people too hard on the back, and continually wondering aloud about his students' sex lives.

The exercises in Gus's class began with simple neck rotations, reverses, and then stretching movements with the extended arms. Gradually, the full torso became involved and, aside from the obvious exertion that was involved, seemed no more unique than any other set of stretching exercises. It was only when the students, on orders, held their palms in pushing position before them and began a series of forty-nine palm pushes—one for each year of Kwang Tung's life—that you realized more than calisthenics might be going on. Gradually, over the next forty-five minutes, the exercises became more intricate and more punishing. Simple stretching gave way to variations of situps, twists, pushups that would have made a wimp of Rocky Balboa. All the while, Gus walked through the rows of students, calling out to them, teasing them, prodding them—an amalgam of affection, exhortation, challenge.

"Come on, be a great athlete . . . this is for baseball, there'll be no wars, no Boxer Rebellions in America. . . . Bend your knees, the Lord said, on Sunday! . . . Twist! Twist! Twist! Hands on your waist! . . . Don't be bashful, don't change. . . . We love Jerome. Don't be happy, Jerome! Don't you smile! C'mon, Crimson Tide, good athlete!"

When a student arrived late, Hoefling walked up to him and aimed a devastating kick toward his groin, stopping short a millimeter from target. With another student, who was apparently doing an exercise incorrectly, Gus came close to knocking his feet out from under him. Toward the end of what turned out to be only a preliminary series of routines, a few of the students began doing brutally difficult variations—fingertip pushups, side scissor kicks with weights attached to the legs, pushups done spread-eagled over four buckets. All of the students were soaked in their own sweat. Then the sweeps began.

In squatting positions, the students moved forward, slowly sweeping one leg straight out, planting it, then moving the other. To do this at all, a tremendous sense of balance was required. And this balance was possible only after the building of much strength in the lower and middle torso. The players moving across the floor looked like they were doing a variation of the Russian *kazatzka* in slow motion.

The players, only two of them now, Greg Gross and a young pitcher named Tony Ghelfi, went into a pattern of slow, intricate moves—the Northern Salutation, Gus called it. Done from a standing position, the hands and arms were in constant circular motion. Coming forward step by step, the legs, too, were raised and lowered in patterned, dancelike movements.

"Flow—mind and moon!" Gus called out. "Look out, see the moon across the water. Your mind should be like that—without ripples!"

These *kunes* (sequenced movements), which were in fact forms of tai chi (the centuries-old Chinese physical exercises), were at one with, not apart from, the skills of a baseball player. "Motion never ends, even when you're still. But we don't understand that. We flow from one movement to another. And in tai chi, that is exactly what we experience. Your body shifts when you pick up the ball. Between one movement and the next, no matter how much time between, a shift is taking place. In reality there is only one unbroken movement.

"Why do you have to move so slow?" Gus asked. And then, answering himself, said, "He who moves fast is hiding something. From himself, from his body—and from his teacher! Doing it slow shows where it is in the body; it also shows fatigue. Speed hides a multitude of mistakes."

When the players finished this part of the workout, Gus brought Gross to a table. Hoefling stood on one side, holding a short, exotically colored stick—"I paid eleven cents for it. It is the ultimate weapon." He held it below the edge of the table. Gross leaned across the table and with one hand gripping the opposing wrist for support, tried, against the full weight of Gus's downward pressure, to raise the stick to the level of the tabletop. It required almost superhuman strength.

"Pop it, kid! Pop it!" Gus exhorted. "Try harder, Gregger, fight for it, try harder! Come on, Gregger. Fight for it! Great athlete!" Millimeter by millimeter, Gross slowly raised the stick. The cords in his neck stood out; his breath escaped between his teeth in explosive bursts. When he got the stick to the level of the table, he turned his wrist the other way, palm down, and tried, against similar resistance, to force the stick down.

When Gross had finished his work for the day, I wondered what he felt he got out of subjecting his body to such punishment.

"When I'm playing now, I feel a little more flexible, a little quicker. There's so much standing around in this game and you can get stiff so easily. The other part is mental. Just learning basic balance. With baseball, throwing and hitting requires so much balance—everything starts from the waist down, power starts from your legs. A good swing does. Fighting or anything like that really doesn't enter my mind, but over the last five years, I have a little better feel when I come into a game. . . . You can't use the excuse 'if only I had been ready' when you come off the bench—and I've come off the bench a lot. I'm also an older player. And players are basically lazy, until they start seeing the end coming and they don't want it. You should be able to extend your career if you're willing to work for it. I happened to start this when I was younger. It's become a habit for me."

In another part of the room, a very young player, John Russell, was standing in a nine-by-three-foot bin of rice. Of the many devices Hoefling has employed in training, "the rice" is the most well known. If you ask anyone in or around baseball about Hoefling, the odds are the answer will be about either Steve Carlton or rice. The most familiar story involves both: It is that Steve Carlton has acquired his fabulous strength by learning to work a baseball down through a pail or a barrel of rice until he gets it to the bottom (this is a progressive resistance exercise; ordinary mortals usually can go no deeper than the length of their own fingers). While the bucket and the barrel are standard equipment in the "back room," it is this long, two-foot-deep pit of rice that commands the most attention. The sight of it is enough to make you aware that trials of an extraordinary sort may be involved.

Russell is 24 years old. The previous season he played for the Phillies' Triple A affiliate in Portland, joining the parent club at the end of the season, in time to hit .283 in 99 at-bats as a catcher. But the winter brought knee surgery and doubts about his future. A bona fide "prospect," Russell had undergone an intensive rehabilitation program using Nautilus and Cybex. It did not work. After a period of weeks, the tendons at the side of the knee had been strengthened, but the ones directly over the knee itself had not been affected. The knee remained swollen and Russell's future was clouded. It was then that he began working with Hoefling. In three weeks' time, he said, he made more progress than he had in all the time he had put in previously on the machines.

Russell stood in the pit of rice and, under Hoefling's direction, did a series of tai chi movements. The slow, dancelike pattern in the rice was as much the result of the extraordinary effort required to move the layers of grain as of any intention on Russell's part to be deliberate. As he moved, he ground himself ever more deeply into the rice. The muscles of his legs quivered and jumped from the intensity of the effort. The color of his face slowly turned dark, almost black. If he had been enacting the scene in the *Chanson de Roland* where Roland's head explodes from the effort of blowing a horn, he could not have exerted himself more. It was frightening and spectacular and, because the movements in themselves were so dancelike, it was eerily beautiful.

"The rice," Gus said to me, under his breath, "is a humbling experience. J.R. has done things in rice I have never seen another human being do."

I wondered, how could he move at all, and then, at what risk?

"I don't feel the rice," Russell said. "I block the rice out, just move right through it."

"It doesn't exist," Gus added. Simple.

"When I first started doing it, I was fighting the rice," Russell continued. "I was only thinking about what I had to do to move it. I couldn't do it until I stopped thinking about it. I had to do that in order to move through it."

But, I wondered, wasn't he mindful of the extraordinary, seemingly life-threatening effort that was involved?

"When I was on the bottom," he said, "I didn't worry about the effort. It wasn't even there. There were only the movements."

J.R. knew nothing about Eastern disciplines, Gus said. The

only reason he had entered the program was to rehabilitate his knee when all other methods had failed—and it had worked. The swelling in the knee was finally gone and, Russell said, he was feeling stronger than at any time since the operation. He was hopeful he would win a place on the 1985 Phillies.

"How does a joint work?" Hoefling said after Russell went in to take his shower. "You see, we're always looking for machines to give us answers in this country. Okay—if you sit on a machine, not once do we walk on our ankle, do we? The weight is suspended off the ankle. I change the so-called momentary arm or change the angle of the weight. The momentary arm is defined just that way—where the limb is *at the moment*. Say you have a 140–73 range of motion in this knee joint. That's average. Some will have more, some less. But not one of these machines works you in a normal manner. A leg bent in motion does not normally have the weight suspended from it in that way. Second, when you walk or run or dance or play baseball, the knee is *rotary* in motion—not linear—see it! None of these machines give you that. The only way you can correctly work any joint in the human body is through *natural motion*. Notice I said *correctly* work it. There are many ways to work it, but there are also many ways that are wrong."

The rice, like Hoefling's eleven-cent stick or the wooden horse or the long stave he will use in some exercises, creates resistance—just as the exercise machines do—but calls forth from the body only those motions that are absolutely necessary and natural. Rice resists and yields exactly in accordance to what you do, unlike an exercise machine, which will keep to its calibration no matter what. In the class I had just seen, the tai chi movements had even been incorporated—by the use of partners locking their arms as though they were dueling swords and then doing the patterned movements from the shoulder out—so that strengthening the area of rotator cuff could be done naturally and without the use of weights.

"Tai chi," Gus said, "is the ultimate in exercise, but it takes so many years to understand how it works. It takes years, maybe centuries—the foot and the toe are working the mind! . . . I've had writers come and say that all this is useless exercise—no range of motion, no cardiovascular. Can you believe that? What do you think John's heart rate was in the rice? In America we have hundreds and hundreds of black belts and all kinds of experts. Lao Tse said, 'Beware of the teacher who teaches flowery moods.' We get taught nonsense. All these guys are doing is putting on their belts or wearing their degrees. It starts with the ground you stand on—if the ground we stand on is bad, we're bad . . . if this is bad down here, then this is bad up here."

As if Hoefling had anticipated the question I was going to ask him about the demand his work placed upon the body, he continued. "The recuperative power of the body depends on how well conditioned you are. More conditioning means better recuperative power. . . . People who don't work like this are ready to keel over but not the ones who are conditioned. There are so many misconceptions brought on by God knows what—a drunken coach or trainer back in the twenties or thirties. You'll hear them say, 'Don't do this, it'll hurt you.' But there's nothing to found this on. It's like saying, 'Don't drink that iced tea, it'll hurt you.' Well, why in hell will it hurt me? Hard work never hurt anyone. They don't begin to understand why we work in this manner. If you mention mental training to them, right away they assume you mean the hypnotist, the psychologist, the masters of meditation. And I have nothing against them, except when they have you believing that you can train the mind without the body. Look, every move a person makes can be martial, every object, even a toothbrush, can be a weapon. It depends on your intention, on what's inside you. These hands can belong to an angel of mercy or an angel of death. I can take the fly off your shoulder or I can take your shoulder off. It all depends on what's going on in here."

I wanted to know how, specifically, Hoefling saw martial arts training in relation to baseball. And his answer, not surprisingly, had to do with concentration. He expressed this in a way that was surprisingly familiar.

"In this training, you're talking about concentration before you're talking about confrontation. Confrontation is an energy drain. If you're in a sword fight and a guy hacks your arm off, you can bitch and scream about it, but you'd better get a tourniquet and protect your other arm so you can go on and try to win.

"But this is 1985 and the age of hand-to-hand combat is past. Nuclear war is possible, and you better believe that won't be hand-to-hand. I can no longer train men to fight and go into battle. I would love to have lived in a time when I could have. But I do know this: when a guy goes out to the mound to pitch, he's ready."

I wondered, of course, with every other baseball fan in the country, about Steve Carlton and his study of kung fu with Hoefling. Contrary to some published accounts, Hoefling did not come packaged with Carlton from St. Louis. The two did not know each other until Carlton had taken up labors for the Phils. Hoefling had emigrated to Philadelphia from Los Angeles, where he had been a martial arts teacher and where one of his few students was Roman Gabriel, the Rams quarterback who was subsequently traded to the Philadelphia Eagles. It was Hoefling's association with Gabriel that got him into the conditioning of professional athletes. It was his association with Carlton and baseball that made him famous, and mysterious.

Carlton's workouts, Hoefling assured me, were as brutal as anyone had suggested. Perhaps more so. He worked a minimum of four hours a day—his lightest day being the day he pitched—and his capacity for work was almost unimaginable. But there was more. Carlton had what Gus called a "photographic mind" (this was the first time I had heard the term used in such a context), where he would be able on the first try to reproduce exactly whatever moves he was being shown. "A man like this—a Carlton, a Gabriel, a Seaver—is really a kind of genetic freak," Gus explained. "When you or I tell our fingers to do this or that, the message gets out there and back at about five hundred miles an hour. But with a man like Carlton, the message gets out there at about fifteen hundred miles an hour. Carlton is so far ahead of anyone at the moment that he's just in a different category. I haven't seen human beings move like that since I was in Hong Kong ages and ages ago. He's six foot four, he weighs two hundred twenty pounds, and that man is as good in my special world—maybe better—than he is in the baseball world."

Kung fu, as Hoefling defined it, meant "skilled labor." There were, or could be, kung fu bartenders, kung fu shoemakers, and so forth. With this skill, the weakest man in the world could disarm and disable the strongest if he knew what he was doing. But Carlton was altogether different. He was, as far as Hoefling knew, the "last practitioner of Sil-Lum kung fu left on earth.

"There was no sport back there," Hoefling said, the tone of his voice changing as he spoke. It was almost as if he were talking to himself or, perhaps, to Carlton. "There was only hit. It's that deep. We talk of Mind of Moon and Elephant techniques—like 'Elephant Walks on Lily Pads.' Clichés, eh? Well, conceivably an elephant could walk on lily pads, couldn't he, if he was deft and quick enough. We both know he can't, but it's conceivable—what the mind conceives, the body tries to achieve. Even if you know it can't exist. But that's how he trains. He trains that hard."

There are twenty-four professional seasons and more than 4,700 innings to go with Steve Carlton's 41 years of life. He is, by baseball standards, nearing the end of his career. Some pitchers in the modern period have gone longer but it is conceivable that by the time he finishes playing, only Cy Young, Pud Galvin, and Walter Johnson will have thrown more innings. It is even possible, in Hoefling's mind, that Carlton himself might be the one to shatter all the records. "Carlton," Gus said, as though injury and age were inconceivable to contemplate, "is gonna go nine more years, and that will take him over fifty." More, so much more than baseball is involved, and to understand what this man of baseball did, how he actually played the game, you had to see him not as someone 41 years old, but as someone whose life went back to A.D. 520 in China.

"All of these games, baseball, football, karate, all of the so-called martial arts—except the northern Sil-Lum kung fu—all of it has changed. Only this practitioner of Sil-Lum hasn't changed. Now listen to me: the caveman ran out of necessity, to catch his prey or not be prey. The game was life and death. Your caveman of the East, Genghis Khan, and all of the feudal warriors of Japan, reached the top: slash, hunt, kill—whatever, right? And he did this because the game, if you call it that, was life and death. Now, all of the heirs, the game players and all the phony martial artists, don't do that anymore, do they? Your samurai or your man of karate trains in the old way, but he doesn't kill anymore, does he? He wants to—oh, God, does he want to kill! All right. There's only one form of training left in the world—northern Sil-Lum—where the practitioner still trains to kill. He takes his training as he learns it. Step by step or station by station. There's an old legend about the origin of this training. It is the origin of the 128-movement exercise you saw in class today. All of these movements in tai chi originated here. There was this temple where these warrior monks trained. The training involved having to pass 128 stations, each one constructed as a deadly, intricate trap. In order to pass these stations you had to learn such movements and strategies as would enable you to survive. The entire course, so the legend went, took thirty years to master. One day, one of these monks escaped from this monastery, after only eleven years of training. He did this in defiance of his discipline; he escaped through a sewer. But because of his powers, he eventually became emperor of China and ruled as a terrible despot until a man named Kwan Tung emerged from his training—after thirty years—and killed him. Kwan then became a champion of the people until he was ordered to commit suicide by a succeeding emperor, who was jealous of him; this Kwan did, at the age of forty-nine, which is why we do forty-nine palm pushes in our exercises, one for each year of his life. In legend, he was equal to Jesus Christ! Think: there was no modern medicine, no psychologists, no doctors, no athletic trainers, nothing like that—and this man perfected a training for the human body, for life, that's still alive today, and men like me would swim to China to learn it. Okay, okay. I'm not the system, I know that, we're just the purveyors of half-truths as far as that goes, and maybe I'm a little insane. It's frustrating to find yourself in Veterans Stadium in 1985. But let's go back to the hall of obstacles.

"Once you were out you had to move a giant urn of boiling water. The only way you could move it was to stand as a perfect horse, grab it, move it either to the left or right. This is the way you had to do it. . . ." Hoefling suddenly demonstrated a massive lurching movement left and right. A cry, seemingly from the center of his body, tore from his lips. "The boiling water, it is said, branded a tiger and a dragon on your forearm—the emblem of this training then and ever since. To verify that you had passed through all one hundred and twenty-eight obstacles. Then the practitioner was free. Freedom. He could go all over China and the people knew because they saw the tiger and the dragon. He was a priest. He knew what it was all about . . . that's Carlton."

Before I left the Vet that late winter day, I tried a move of my own. I asked Gus if I could watch one of Carlton's workouts. To my total amazement, he told me where he held his workouts in Clearwater and to contact him when I wanted to come. This I did and was once more diverted from the highway of the American League East—this time by almost four hundred miles—when Gus, answering a phone call I made to him from Miami, invited me to turn up the following morning shortly after dawn.

I confess to not being as eager to see this workout as I might have been. An all-night drive left my body feeling as though it had, from head to toe, been forcibly pressed through the rice. Also, I had, in a few weeks' time, more or less convinced myself that Gus's portrait of Carlton, like that of Whistler's mother, was probably better than the original. And while I surely did have Carlton's durability on my mind when I watched him work out—because he had pitched injury-free so brilliantly for so long and because Gus in an almost offhand way had said that he thought Carlton would pitch till he was 50—I was not nearly so taken as I might have been when Carlton briefly stopped his workout, held his shoulder, and, in reply to Hoefling's query about what was the matter, answered, "I don't know, can't seem to get it loose."

Actually, I stayed to see two of Carlton's workouts. The first was surprising because after all the Garbo-like shrouds and stories there was so little to see. Carlton appeared to be just one of several people in a class I had already observed—except that he looked older, slower, and about as tired as I was. He had been out drinking the night before, Hoefling told me later. He seemed irritated and slightly embarrassed. Probably, if I had seen no other workout, I would, over the years, have added to it a dash or two of make-believe as well. But at Gus's bidding, I saw a second workout—and it was like seeing two Steve Carltons. One was flesh and blood mixed with Cabernet Sauvignon. The other was the Sil-Lum killer Gus had talked about.

In the early phase of this second workout, performing a series of progressively more difficult stretches, Carlton worked in a far corner of this large armory room, a little apart from the others in the class. He seemed to need the space and privacy because he added little extra movements of his own to the standard ones followed by everyone else. He worked slowly and effortlessly, and with the weight cuffs attached to his wrists and ankles you understood—but could not otherwise tell—that every movement required extraordinary strength as well as coordination. What I noticed first was that some of the other players—John Denny, Jerry Koosman, Pat Zachry—were not nearly as effortless. At one point, Pat Zachry suddenly barked: "Shit! Shit! Fuck!"

"Now what's the matter?" Hoefling said, as though to a life-long *kvetch*.

"It's fuckin' cramped up on me," Zachry said, holding his calf.

"In your next life, tell 'em you want a different fuckin' body," Hoefling said, walking past him.

"You aint' shittin'," Zachry called after him, "I've been telling 'em that for thirty-three years already."

Meanwhile, Carlton continued on his own. Long after the rest of the class had moved on to another exercise, he worked at a series of pushups on his own. Later, when pairs of students worked at a locked situp exercise, Carlton and Greg Gross, like two rims of a rocking chair, continued. At the finish of their routine, Carlton said, "I think everybody else counts by twos."

But when the class moved into the phase of the work that involved more clearly recognizable martial arts movements— the spins and kicks and hand chops—the difference between Carlton and everyone else became obvious. Carlton worked at all these movements as though he had performed them not for years but centuries. Each movement seemed exquisite and per-fect, the epitome of dance as much as of combat. Where others seemed like they were shadow-boxing, Carlton seemed to be moving like a shadow—or was it mind and moon?—through that fifth-century Hall of Trials, effortless and perfect, within himself totally and yet totally alert to everything around him. One student after another went to the front of the room, led the rest in these patterned movements, and Carlton, following, was always apart. Sometimes, particularly as the movements became more intricate, Gus called out, "Remember these movements will kill a man! What you are doing is killing, not playing!"

Gross, the only student whose fluidity even remotely resem-bled Carlton's, suddenly stopped in the middle of one of these exercises. He was obviously upset. He gathered his belongings and started to leave.

"What's the matter"

No reply.

"You're in an in-between stage, Gregger," Hoefling called after him—to no avail. Gross left the class. The work continued, the patterns ever more intricate, always demanding more effort and coordination. Gus eased over to me and whispered, "He's advanced to the point where he understands what has to happen. He can't accept it yet." He moved back out to the middle of the floor, to the others.

"There's no set pattern to killing," Hoefling said, "it might come from a touch, a pull, a strike." He pantomimed a series of rapid motions, free-style, vigorous, breath bursting from his lips as he struck or kicked the air. "No black belts! No brown belts! You can't buy them here. Open the left heel! One, two, *step-through!* My teacher would absolutely roll over in his fucking grave if he saw what you guys were doing!" That is, except for Carlton, who continued his inexorable progress through the centuries to the caldron that would eventually scald a tiger on one forearm and a dragon on the other. Only the sweat pouring off his body, soaking his shirt, indicated that his perfect center of gravity had been maintained throughout at the cost of an almost superhuman expenditure of effort.

"Today we worked with five systems," Hoefling told me afterward, after Carlton had gone silently on his way. "The Le-Mon system, Tiger and Crane, northern Hung-Gao style, Long-Hu. I start out with baseball, as it goes on, I drift back to the smoke and dust or whatever and I try to get them to do the same. You can't play with it, it's not a sport. When you look at them," he said, "you can tell instantly which one's best, can't you? If we cross the street and cars are whizzing by us, you just have enough time and space to make it to the other side. But if you slip you don't just lose, you lose your life. We will die, not just get injured, we will die."

Carlton got injured. In the season that followed, the twinge he reported in his workout became a career-threatening injury to his rotator cuff. Had I not seen Carlton's workouts, I am certain that, with all fans, I would simply have hoped that he would get back to pitching soon, skeptical that anyone at his age who depended on power for his performance would very easily be able to do it. But because of what I had seen, I was left with something else.

Carlton refused standard medical treatment for his injury. He saw a chiropractor—not a surgeon—and he put all his hopes on the program to bring him back—the only change, I was told later, being the stripping away of the wrist and ankle weights he used during his workouts. What I had been witness to—and what was strangely illumined by the phenomenon of injury— was Carlton's total commitment to what he did. He may or may not have been the last Sil-Lum killer on earth but he risked everything in his work—as though life and death hung on the outcome. There is no more advanced form of training than that.

CHAPTER FOUR

Fundamentals

I placed a jar in Tennessee
And round it was, upon a hill.
It made the slovenly wilderness
Surround that hill.

The wilderness rose up to it,
And sprawled around, no longer wild.
———Wallace Stevens,
"Anecdote of the Jar"

A spring baseball camp in full swing is a carnival sideshow, a boot camp, a country fair, a street festival, a meditation on things slow, easy, and tranquil. There is a certain look and feel to a southern Florida sky that overarches the steaming concrete mazes of Overtown, Liberty City, and Little Havana; the faded opulence of Collins Avenue and the newer, far more stylish affluence of Key Biscayne. The passageways between the southern, the central, and the northern areas of the state do little to lead you away from this special sense of climate that once lured Ponce de León and subsequently such diverse types as Al Capone and Al Lang. Florida has long since been turned from a dense and luxurious wilderness into an overdeveloped chaos. There is no visible coherence anywhere under the palms—unless, perhaps, it is to be found in money: its presence in huge, spectacular strips of development, its absence in equally visible stretches of neglect. Gunrunning, cocaine trafficking, gorgeous seascapes, international intrigue and terror, children seeking Mickey and Donald in the company of grandparents seeking the perfect condo and retirement community are all of a piece in the heavy air, sometimes laden with the scent of orange groves, sometimes with the heavier aromas of automobile and jet exhaust.

But chaos, like plenitude, produces its own rewards and punishments. In the special, interconnected world of Florida's baseball camps, this can mean, on any given day, the chance to rub shoulders with the game's greatest players or to be caught in the game's nastiest traffic jams. Nothing is more pleasant than to be so close to the game that you can hear the actual conversation of the players. On the other hand, there are few indignities like trying to escape the dirt parking field at Kissimmee when the drivers of two thousand cars are trying to do the same thing.

On any given day, you might bump into an old legend or two. At Vero Beach, the chances are excellent that somewhere along one of the many walks lining Dodgertown, the person passing you by or walking along with you will be Sandy Koufax or Maury Wills or Vin Scully. You might come face to face with Al Kaline in Tigertown or with Ted Williams or Carl Yastrzemski in Winter Haven's Chain O'Lakes Park. If you come from a small town in America, one that has happened to give a player or two to the national game, you will, for a moment, share a sense of old home week with someone who, only weeks later, would not be likely to look at you or sign your autograph book.

Most of all, the game the teams play is on display in these different camps. And the game is different, depending on where you are. Teams, like people, have a character. If you go to a Yankee workout at Fort Lauderdale Stadium, the chances are you will be struck by the confluence of two powerful currents that define Yankee baseball: security and show biz. Unlike in other camps, it is hard to have any real contact here with the players or the several Hall of Famers who regularly migrate to the team's spring camp. The field entrance and exit to the club-house is along a fenced-in corridor well removed from spectators, whose only chance of contact with the players is at the edge of the grandstand or outside, when the players leave to retrieve their cars. Were it not for the show biz side in all this, a day's visit with the Yankees would be about as pleasurable as getting a clearance check at the Pentagon. But whether because of their Principal Owner, whose background includes several stabs at Broadway producing, or because the Yankees themselves are and always have been celebrities, a day's workout inevitably is a happening. Where other clubs in that phase of training before the exhibition schedule would draw only a handful of people, the Yankees draw thousands. For the most part, the people get to see only calisthenics and batting practice. One to two additional fields, beyond the left-field fence, where the day's fundamentals are practiced, is off-limits to both fans and media. But even that is part of the happening. You can see enough bodies in white moving out there to become half-convinced that Yankee fundamentals, unlike those of other teams, are imbued with the kind of secret stuff from which the downfall of nations flows.

It is hard to believe that the fans—and the media—who come out in such numbers are really there to see baseball. It is more like the old Schwab's Drugstore round of seeing and being seen. On Rickey Henderson's first morning in camp, media people lined up like customers in a bakery shop to get numbers to interview him. Fans sat packed into the small, single-decked grandstand to watch—and applaud—every batting practice home run. And, on a morning I was there, the loudest applause of the day was reserved for the appearance on the field of the Principal Owner himself. From the moment he appeared out of the runway until the moment, over an hour later, when he went back in, it was clear that the Yankees might have had Winfield, Mattingly, Henderson, et al., but that the cleanup hitter—no doubt about it—was the man from American shipbuilding who had somehow managed to be born on the Fourth of July.

I know nothing about shipbuilding, but I have spent enough time around the theater to recognize one of our own when I see one. I ascribe this to no particular list of known hits George has produced (like most struggling theater people, he has somewhat inflated his résumé), but to the manner of the man. If he didn't exist, someone—perhaps Gene Wilder or Zero Mostel—might have created him. He is a rather typical sort of producer, who knows—or believes—that money and superlatives can overcome anything, even the burdens of taste and bad reviews.

For a while, George made his way along the retaining wall of the grandstand, signing autographs, shaking hands, even stopping to kiss people. Applause, excitement, and cameras followed him every step of the way. I saw Don Baylor hit a batting practice home run over the left-field wall, but in the special circumstances of Steinbrenner's visit, little attention was paid in the stands. Soon George moved out to the area near first base, engulfed by reporters and photographers. Was he playing Caruso getting off the boat in New York, or was he walking into Sardi's after a Nederlander revival of *Guys and Dolls?*

"Boys," he said, with that special expansive twang common to assembly-line movies of the thirties and forties, "go easy on me. I've just gotten back from Pompano this morning working out horses, and I tell you my arms and shoulders are really tired." I'm sure it was my own jaundiced eye and not really the objective problem of poundage once cited by Graig Nettles, but it struck me that the Principal Owner's chest was bulging just a little too much in his powder-blue shirt.

Someone asked him how spring training was going. He responded, "Spring training is like opening night in the theater. There is nothing like it, nothing!" Then came a question about the American League East. "It's the greatest division that ever existed in any professional sport—and that includes football, basketball—I've been in them both. This will be the greatest division." Rickey Henderson was a man, a real man. Of Ed Whitson, the questionable million-dollar acquisition: "I only know Ed Whitson as a person. I've never met a finer person. He's an outstanding young man with an outstanding young wife. He's developed a new pitch, the palmball. He knows how to use it. I'll be very happy with whatever he does because I know whatever he does he's going to give one hundred percent."

Inevitably, the question of Yogi Berra's tenure as manager came up. In light of what followed during the season, the well-reported reply that followed has been cited as proof positive of the Principal Owner's recidivous hypocrisy, psychopathology, or worse. What I knew was that when Mike Todd couldn't fill up a theater, the first thing he did was put out an SRO sign at the box office. Then again, the deadliest words spoken in the theater are "I love you, darling." The Yankee media guide for 1985 refers to Yogi Berra as "one of America's most beloved" celebrities, and on that beautiful spring day, weeks before he was, in orthodox show business fashion, canned out of town, the Principal Owner tossed his bouquet, adding, "I said last year, Yogi's going to be the manager no matter what happens, and I say the same thing this year—even if he comes in last place." It is simply wrong to think George was lying. People don't lie when they talk to *Variety*.

There is a well-known Broadway producer who keeps a little plaque on his desk that reads "I love the theater, it's actors I hate." This should not be judged too harshly. It is the product of neither excessive paranoia nor eccentricity. Generations of actors, directors, and other "creative" people in the theater have, through the very force of their temperament and imagination, made life tough for the people who have had to pay the bills. Actors are just not to be trusted. One did in Lincoln; another got his revenge by becoming President. Years ago I knew a producer who consciously and deliberately set out to create in people's minds that he was the reincarnation of Napoleon. He carried this even to the point of keeping his hand placed inside his jacket. It was his way of dealing with what is now loosely called in the theater world "the talent."

The analogy is really not so farfetched. When George talks about his players, there is a combination of resentment, paternalism, and envy. The people who are out there on the field for him are a special breed—better and worse at the same time than ordinary people like himself—who wish they could have it so well but who do not qualify because they are not "talent," and so have to work for a living. Says the Producer:

"Let me tell you something about being the boss. I'm a disciplinarian, but baseball players, they don't do too much. They have to get up, get on the bus, what time's hitting, what time's infield, what time's the game, what time's the bus leave to go back to the hotel? They don't do too much. That's a pretty good life. But what I want my young men to be ready for is the real world, when they're finished playing baseball. So if I'm extra tough on them, if I'm extra hard on the discipline, it's only because when they're done here as Yankees, I want them to have careers and amount to something and not be in a home in Arizona for old ballplayers. They may not appreciate it now, but I think if you go talk to Bucky Dent [manager of the Class A Fort Lauderdale Yankee farm team]—I think he made some statements about how great it was to be in Texas, how great it was to be away from Steinbrenner—Bucky's back with us. Maybe he would say that he understands what I'm talking about . . . he's part of the family now. He'll be a great manager someday."

Probably the greatest testament there is to Yogi Berra is that he never seemed to feel threatened by Steinbrenner, although he was every day that he sat in the dugout. Other people close to the Principal Owner have been Napoleonized to the point where they have even wound up sounding like him when talking about baseball and the Yankees. I was, for example, mainly interested in finding out how the Yankees came together as a team, how they prepared on the field.

Clyde King, the Yankees' vice president and general manager, one of the game's knowledgeable men and also chief among George's "baseball people," advised me thus: "This is one of the most thorough camps I've ever been in. Yogi is a stickler for organization—and Gene Michael and Jeff Torborg. Every day after workout, they get together on what we're gonna do tomorrow—it's printed up and the sheets are distributed to the proper people and they've got the guys running back and forth between the drills this year. They've got the cutoffs and the relays and the rundowns all booked at special times, because by a certain date they feel they need to have been through that at least once. And then later down the road, they need to have been through it twice. The pitcher's drills—we add things every day to compensate for their increased ability to throw—we use the two other fields. All the pitchers participate. Phil Niekro leads the group. Forty-six years old, like it's the final game of the World Series. And when these young kids see that, they say, 'Oh my, how can I not give my best or do my best?'"

In all fairness, while I had surely not meant to ambush King, I already had some idea of how the Yankees and some other clubs prepared. Jeff Torborg, for example, also explained that the Yankee program was based on people constantly moving around. "But," he added, "there are only so many things you can do in baseball." The Yankees divided their pitchers into four groups, their hitters into six, and then kept rotating them from field to field. The work they did, though, was fairly circumscribed: twenty minutes of stretching ("stride stretches" was the term used by Mangold), a brief period of easy throwing, then mainly hitting on the different fields—with a round of infield practice in one place and catchers catching pop-ups in another. The Yankee camp, Torborg said, paid attention to fundamentals, but because the club was mainly a veteran one, it was assumed that players handled fundamentals well enough so that "you don't have to harp on certain things like cutoffs and relays." Two hours of concentrated work each day (what the schedule called for) was enough and, in reality, aside from the job of getting pitchers' arms ready—something that could not be rushed—two weeks' training was about enough. (All of this left me, months later, with the uneasy sense that Billy Martin had probably gotten the same spiel from Clyde King when he publicly—and gracelessly—attacked the team he inherited from Yogi Berra for poor spring preparation in fundamentals.)

The reality in the Yankee camp was that individual players, as was the case on other teams, had their own regimens. With the Yankees, however, you had the feeling that this also was the result of a general climate in which a celebrity star was a small duchy or fiefdom. Dave Winfield, who has regularly drawn taunts from the Principal Owner for failing to be the team leader Reggie was, takes his two million, plays at full throttle at all times, and largely tries to sidestep the noise and hype of Yankee Productions. He does his own thing. "I don't have to be one hundred percent sharp when spring comes around," he said shortly before a freak injury sidelined him for a few weeks. "I have to be ready to start the season, that's all. I do a couple of things to stay in shape over the winter. Run periodically, do free weights periodically, shoot some baskets periodically, get a little rubdown once in a while." Winfield's major preoccupation at that moment seemed to be the marketing of a new line of athletic training machines, on principles of Sagerkinetics. "It has to do with isokinetic exercises with resistance," he explained, sounding more scientific than Mangold. "It duplicates the movement of specific sports. Nautilus is variable resistance. This is completely different. You duplicate the movement of the sport with resistance and at high speeds." As for spring training, Winfield prepared for the season as he has all along—largely on his own. He was a student of the game, he said, and this gave him whatever additional advantage his natural abilities had not given him to begin with. "The players who are up here have good to great ability, but the ones who can mentally apply themselves to the task at hand are the ones who are special. There is a certain group of players who don't know the fundamentals. They don't know the techniques, so they never become as good as they might be. I am a student of the game. I have studied the fundamentals, I know them, and then it is a matter of how you apply them. . . . It's a science. When I started off, I had the ability but not the fundamentals." The "fundamentals" came, Winfield said, not by belonging to any team's program but by "talking to the best players in the game, working my butt off," and by looking at himself over and over again on videotape. This last might really belong to Charlie Fox's psalm-singing. "When you finally put it all together," Winfield explained, "you put it on videotape and you analyze every movement of your body." But this is only when things are going well. "Oh man, I don't look at it when I'm going bad—I don't want to. A couple of times a year, I may ask the batting coach or whoever what I'm doing wrong. It may be one thing, it may be nothing. I may be tired or overmatched or distracted. But I'll take one good swing—not even a sequence— just one at-bat where I have a good swing and I replay it, replay it, replay it, and I'm locked in once again."

Away from the game, Winfield says, he neither thinks about baseball, practices it, nor even talks about it very much. His answer to stardom is individual effort to enhance it and individual separation to escape its unpleasant side effects.

"I'm not into the stardom thing," Don Mattingly says, with no intention of pointing fingers. That is simply his manner, as much as the confidence mistaken for cockiness is Winfield's. The two have been set up as opposites by the New York media, and in the race for the batting crown the previous season, the hype, fanned very largely by the club itself to generate lagging gate receipts, made them seem actually estranged. The truth of the matter is that estrangement and rivalry have little to do with who they are, but both, each in his own way, owing to the peculiar atmosphere of New York baseball, remain largely isolated. It is not on the team or the program so much as on themselves that they must rely.

"I came out of a very modest family," Mattingly said, "and

everything I've ever gotten, I've had to work for. Baseball didn't just happen; I've had to work for years and years." A nineteenthround draft choice in 1979, Mattingly rose through the lower minors without the benefit of great expectations or great public relations. It is almost as if his real training program, his psalm, was the private experience of the minor leagues. "Nothing was ever given to me. I remember those years in the minors, too. But I remember them as great times, as good times. I remember everything. All my apartments, even the rents. What kind of circumstances it was, the bugs, waiting for a paycheck to pay the rent and get some food. . . . Remembering those things makes me appreciate what I have now."

And what Mattingly has now, aside from a following, is one of the sweetest swings in the game. He has worked on it with Yankee coaches, mainly Lou Piniella, but he knows that what is most decisive comes from himself. "I've seen myself on film," he says. "[My stance] changes all the time. You get wider or lower, it depends really on how you feel. Your stance changes all the time. It's not a big, wide change, but it's there just the same."

The spring of 1985 was special for Don Mattingly because in his private preparations for the season, he injured his knee on a weight machine and required arthroscopic surgery and then rehabilitation to repair the damage. But the overriding sense was that in this Yankee camp, he—along with most others—was about the very individual business of triumphing over chaos.

Down the road in Miami, the setting is very different. In a week's time, there was: a riot over a nude bather, which resulted in a five-hour traffic jam on the Rickenbacker Causeway; a carnival in the Orange Bowl featuring mariachi bands and Latin politics; an unbelievably grisly murder, featuring a naked man walking down a Miami street holding the severed head of his victim; and spring training featuring the Baltimore Orioles at Miami Stadium.

Miami Stadium itself is situated in a seedy part of town, at a midpoint between Overtown and Liberty City. Beyond the right-field fence is a large white, windowless building. It is a state hospital for the criminally insane. And if there were windows in the building, the inmates therein would have a view of a ballpark that would do little to ease their stressed nerves. Built in the postwar period as a come-on for major-league teams and as a permanent home for the now-defunct Florida International League Sun Sox, Miami Stadium used to be a crown jewel among minor-league parks. It has subsequently become a study in decrepitude. Its once glittering cantilevered roof is now a covering of rusting tin; the appointments of the original building are long since gone; the passages and entranceways, with peeling paint and mottled railings, are dark and vaguely aromatic in the manner of New York subway stations. If that were not enough, the playing surface, worn down by innumerable rock concerts and political rallies, has all the appeal of a minefield. None of this matters.

In these first weeks of workouts, the Orioles, as in the past, drew only handfuls of spectators. The sprawling reaches of the single-decked grandstand remained largely empty, and the few people who showed up moved down to the low railings by the field at will. Autographs and conversation were as available as the sun.

"Hey, mister! Hey, mister!" a couple of kids called out. Cal Ripken, Jr., looked their way and smiled. "Who are you?" they cried to him. Ripken shook his head in disbelief and then showed them the lettering on the back of his uniform jersey. The kids consulted for a moment, then nodded in agreement. "You're okay, can we have your autograph?" Ripken rolled his eyes to heaven in mock exasperation and obliged. It was all part of the day's routine.

The Orioles, too, have a highly visible and active owner. He is Edward Bennett Williams. But EBW, as his employees refer to him, comes and goes without fanfare. His appearance during a workout is hardly noticed. He can wander up and down the deserted aisles of the stadium, onto the field, back into the grandstand again with little or no comment from anyone. His clothing is a little rumpled, his hair is not quite groomed, he looks deceptively avuncular. What he wants from his team is as simple as a verdict in a court of law: "A pennant," he says. The chances, he believes, after a winter of free-agent signings, are stated just as simply: "They are excellent."

It takes a while to see what others have said about him: that he, like the Producer, interferes with the running of his team. But he is as far from show biz as anyone who is truly on intimate terms with the uses of power. There is neither bluster nor bravado in the words he chooses to express what might ensue if his "baseball people" ignored his suggestions. "I wouldn't think it would be prudent," he says. The words are softly, almost thoughtfully spoken. But there is no mistaking the steel and menace behind them. "I don't tell them what to do," he continues, "but I do make suggestions. And I wouldn't think it would be prudent to ignore them." This is a man no one in his right mind would put on an enemies list.

Williams is also a man who has been through several cancer operations, the most recent one having come that winter. It is not other men but nature itself that appears to have dealt him his harshest challenge. But he is no Lear raging against the elements. Danger and mortality seem to have worked on him in different ways. He has surrendered none of his power, but has acquired along the way a kind of second sense, gentle and subtle and deeply appreciative of the life he has. It is inextricably bound up with his ownership of a baseball team. Over these past years, he said, he had quite specifically become a baseball rather than a football person. He had his explanations.

"I prefer baseball, I think, because it's a game of strict accountability," he said, keeping an eye on the practice routines on the field. "You know, it's much more like the American system than football. If somebody screws up, you know who it is, you don't have to look at the films. You know who is doing well and who isn't without needing some expert to tell you. You can look and see. You can see errors and strikeouts and you can see home runs. You don't need to run a play twelve times on film as I did in football. I also find that I think the country—subliminally, perhaps—is attracted more by nonviolence in sports than by violence. What could be more peaceful than sitting here in March, in the sun, looking at spring training. There can't be anything more tranquil or pleasing. In a sense, it's true of watching baseball. You have a chance to sit and talk without missing important things—it's a great and beautiful experience."

One of the great and beautiful experiences Williams has had is that not only the game but his own team has somehow been larger than any one person's will, including his own. The Orioles came into being as the transmogrification of the St. Louis Browns, baseball's own Duchy of Fenwick. Between 1954 and the early eighties they built themselves into the kind of flagship organization the Branch Rickey Cardinals and Dodgers once were. When they won eighty-five games in 1984, it was the seventeenth consecutive time the Orioles had a winning season. In major-league baseball history, only the Yankees of 1927–1961 have had a longer streak. Since 1956 the Orioles have won more games than any team in either league. But, perhaps most telling of all, since the inception of the team, the Orioles have had only four managers. Going into 1985, thirty-two years of Oriole pitching had been under the tutelage of only three pitching coaches. Their third base coach, Cal Ripken, Sr., managed in the Orioles system for fourteen years before he joined the parent club in 1976. He has missed one game—for his daughter's high school graduation—in a decade. The Oriole signature has always been stability and continuity—and regardless of what followed in the regular season, this was amply on display in Miami. The Orioles were long ago converted to the notion that spring is for taking the game apart and putting it back together again.

In late 1983 the Orioles were driving for a pennant. Half a

game out of first place, the Toronto Blue Jays came to Baltimore for a crucial three-game series. The Jays assaulted the O's in the first game of the set, 9–3, and were ahead 3–1 in the 9th inning of the second game. In one of their familiar late-inning rallies, the Birds tied and sent the game into extra innings. Having shuffled and played a full deck of role players, the Orioles sent what looked like the remnants of Falstaff's army into the field for the 10th. John Lowenstein lined up at second base, Gary Roenicke was at third, and for the first time since he did it in Little League, Lenn Sakata looked out on the world as a catcher. Cliff Johnson opened the Blue Jay 10th with a home run and Barry Bonnell followed with a single, bringing reliever Tippy Martinez into the game. Martinez promptly picked Bonnell off. Jesse Barfield then walked. Martinez picked him off. Willie Upshaw lined a single to right, and as he stood at first base, staring wide-eyed at the skewed Oriole defense, Martinez picked him off as well. Three pickoffs in a single inning! Of course, the Orioles won the game in the bottom half of the inning on a three-run homer by Sakata, but to everyone on the bench—and to some aficionados who knew how the Orioles spent their time in the spring—there was an explanation to it all. It was called Little Field.

Little Field is the name the Orioles have given the area in Miami Stadium off to the side of the left-field foul line where the grandstand ends. The Orioles have packed into this space—just barely—one infield diamond. They have also packed into it a primer on baseball fundamentals that is a standard for the game. The pickoff play, which all teams practice to some extent during spring training, has been elevated to an art at the Little Field. The Orioles have led the majors in this relatively obscure department for years, and last year, when they finished in fifth place, they led the league with twenty-seven pickoffs, "a whole game of outs," in the words of Ray Miller, then pitching coach of the O's. But the pickoff play is only part of a comprehensive overall approach to defense, one that has been in place and systematically practiced almost from the time the club came into being.

"The first year I was in the Oriole minor-league camp was 1962," said former major-league manager Billy Hunter, who had been in the Oriole organization for many years. "Earl, I think, was in Elmira. I was going to be rookie manager in Blue-field, West Virginia. Harry Dalton [then Oriole GM] felt that we needed a manual on player development. It seemed like all our clubs were doing things their own way. So the need was for us to develop a program throughout the whole system, that would apply to everyone."

Hunter and Weaver, who was also a minor-league manager at the time, worked on assembling "the book." Hunter had come out of the Dodger organization, and Weaver's background was in the Cardinal system. Branch Rickey, a pioneer in devising programs in fundamentals, was the common denominator. "Even though it was a kind of mixture of both organizations," Hunter emphasized, "it's really Rickey. And we just decided we would set down some things, even to the point of using the same signs throughout the system (which we didn't do). The catcher's signs to the pitcher and the switchoff, those were adopted. Our cutoff plays and our bunt defenses, those were established as organizational things. And everybody would be executing those things the same way. It caught on. We found that in the progress of various players through the system, they felt comfortable moving up the ladder because the things that were being taught were being used as they had been before."

Most clubs have organization books on fundamentals. The Milwaukee Brewers, for example, have a variation on the Oriole book—thanks to Harry Dalton (he had been with the Orioles before he went to Milwaukee)—that was published several years ago. The Yankees have something called "The Yankee Way," which goes back to the Mantle era. But the key for the Orioles is that their book, because of the extraordinary continuity of the organization, has been operational all the while. "The Yankee Way," with Steinbrenner changing managers, GMs, and farm directors faster than the Borgias switched wine tasters, has been in mothballs for years. The Orioles, like the Dodgers in the National League, approach fundamentals as though they were the guardians of an ancient, honorable, and still living religion. Even as its forms are constantly to be renewed, its traditions are to be preserved at all costs.

There is no single routine or fundamental exercise that dramatically catches the eye in the Orioles' spring. But then again, almost everything that is done has in it that peculiar thoroughness and intensity that separates practitioners of the faith from those who merely pay lip service. When I watched the Brewers, for example, working on having their pitchers cover first base, it was clear that each pitcher ran from his position in line toward the first base bag according to his own mood. One pitcher would be into it, another would not. One would hit the bag, looking down at it as he went by, while another would simply amble directly across the bag and on into foul territory. No one—when I was watching—told any of the pitchers to make sure the ball was in his mitt before he looked down, or that *crossing* the bag was an invitation to the next world.

The Orioles' pitchers by their years of training within the organization and by the degree to which responsibility is delegated to them by the pitching coach—Miller said that when a starter went to the mound, the remaining starters were actually four additional pitching coaches on the bench with him—approach even the most routine drill with the faith that really getting it right means several ballgames in the standings or, in a tight pennant race, the difference between first or second place.

The pickoff play, practiced by everyone, has only a certain number of moves. The leg-kick of the pitcher can be modified so the baserunner can be held a little closer; the pitcher's throw to the bag can, like his delivery to the plate, be done with enough deceptive variation to upset timing. Usually, a club will practice pickoff plays once or at the most twice during the spring and leave it at that. The Orioles practice it daily in the first days of camp, let it alone for a while, then come back to it with ever increased attention as the season draws near. When you watch the Oriole pitchers go through their moves, you realize that they are doing more than getting the details down. They are also learning something crucial about timing—something that involves other players and, rather oddly, something about their own bodies. When they whirl and throw, it is not enough simply to deliver the ball; they must do it so that they, the fielder, and the ball are really part of one complex single motion. If any of it is out of synch, it will not work. The regular team infielders take part in the drills, and all the pitchers are asked to cover infield positions themselves so they will better understand what is demanded of everyone to make the play work. In the overall Oriole approach to infield defense, plays are not sent in from the bench; they are put on by any of the players at any time—and that, of course, includes the pickoff.

By far the oddest-looking part of these drills is when Miller has the pitchers work in slow motion. The pickoff move, the delivery of the ball to the plate—the pitchers' standard mechanics—somehow manage to look like underwater ballet or tai chi. Not Gus Hoefling, but baseball surely.

"You'll wind up doing it at game speed when the time comes," Miller explains, "but you want that automatic thing, that habit, to be right. You stress the mechanical part of it. I've seen Frank [Robinson] do that with the outfielders. They roll the ball sometimes. Get 'em down and roll the ball. I do it with pitchers. I have 'em throw slow, slow, slow, always tell 'em slow your body, slow your body, slow your body—all other organizations say drop your back leg and push hard, drive, drive, drive. And I think that's the least thing you have to teach a young pitcher. It's the one thing he can do naturally. And more often than not, that's the one thing he does wrong. I gradually back off and back off till I don't say it anymore. I force guys to find keys and habits. Every day's a different day and over time you can do that."

"You have to overexaggerate," pitcher Mike Boddiker explained. "It gets to the point where you're barely moving." For Boddiker, these drills are essential. Over the years, Boddiker says he has been plagued by rushing. From his years in the Oriole minor-league system, he learned that doing "the little things" correctly kept you in a lot of games. His pickoff move is not what it should be. "It's great," he says, "except for throwing the ball into right field all the time." He has a tendency to rush to the plate because he gets "this energy buildup inside me." So the slowdown is a way of working on *both* mechanical and mental balance. "I work at slowing myself down, I work at it, I work at it every day. The drills are vital because if you can't get your balance, everything else will go from there. . . . All of this is easy to say and hard to do for someone like myself."

The Oriole pickoff play is part of a comprehensive understanding of pitching and beyond it of the importance of defense itself. Every phase of defensive play, every scrupulous detail, is gone over with the sense of how it contributes to winning. "The thing about the pickoff play," Miller says, "is not just the twenty-six or twenty-seven guys you get a year—and I don't want to minimize that—but it just kills a ballclub. It happens to us every once in a while, and you can just feel the whole club go flat. Jesus, we worked so hard, got men on base, had such a good chance—and then it's gone. And the other thing is it's just impossible to calculate how many runs it saves. You look at the corners and their coaches are yelling, 'Be alive to the pickoff,' and everybody's shortening up, because they know we use the play. They're shortenin' up and shortenin' up. And how many base hits does a guy get held a third because his lead was too short at second, or how many times does a guy miss taking an extra base he might have had if he wasn't staying close for fear of the pickoff? Eddie Murray's the greatest you've ever seen with runners on first and second in bluffing the runner back to first. He's puttin' on so many plays, and there's so much bluffing, that there's a lot of times when there's almost a base hit in the hole at short and Ripken can't make any play at first, but because the runner had been held that close, he can make the one play for the forceout at second."

Whatever the Orioles are doing—whether it is a cutoff and relay, particular formations for bunt defense, rundown plays—there is always this scrupulous attention to detail, repetition, and that book. If you have ever watched Ripken handle a relay, for example, you probably have marveled at his seeming effortlessness. The ball comes to him and is on its way again as though it had merely passed through him without pause. It is one of the perfections of our game, as Joe DiMaggio's taking a fly ball once was. Ripken's natural talents, in this case, blend with what it was he had learned growing up as an Oriole, and what is still practiced today. The important thing in an Oriole relay drill is correct positioning, not in running down balls to distant parts of the outfield. The infielder presents a full target with his body for the outfielder. But then, says Billy Hunter, "your feet aren't nailed to the ground. So many catch the ball on the wrong side and make a kind of half-turn or full turn in order to throw the ball when all they had to do was move over a foot and catch it on their glove side and have their throwing arm in position to throw. A lot of our—I say 'our'—a lot of the Oriole outfielders end up with a number of assists they might not have had. It isn't that they threw someone out at the plate or third base. It's Ripken on the relay!"

The Orioles have run these plays so long and with such success that they have put their own style on them. With a runner on second and a base hit to right or right center, for example, the Oriole second baseman will neither go out for a relay nor act as a trailer. He will, instead, go toward the outfield, then double around to first base as the first baseman handles the relay or not on the throw home. The first base bag, normally left unoccupied in this kind of situation, is suddenly covered. And the hitter who takes his normal turn around the bag winds up as an ex-base-runner.

When you listen to Oriole players talk about the way they play the game, you become aware of just how deeply this devotion to fundamentals has affected them. Very few of them feel comfortable talking about themselves apart from their role on the team. Fred Lynn, a glamorous newcomer in the spring of 1985, was struck immediately by this dual sense of attachment to fundamentals and to the team. "Everything around here is pretty much team-oriented. There's no special favors for anybody. That is not often the case with other clubs," he said, adding that it made him feel very much at home. Eddie Murray, the team's mainstay, put it another way: "Playing just for yourself is not the game I play."

This sense of cohesiveness—which very much comes out of how the Orioles play—also allows them to do things on the field other teams would be reluctant to do. Not only do players call their own defensive plays in the field (other teams do that), but, says Ray Miller, "There's been times when the guys put three different plays on at the same time. They've worked long enough and together enough to know that when the pitcher has the ball in his hand, he'll know where he's going, and so everything will work out. It does more than that. For example, you might have a time play on with runners on first and second where the short-stop isn't gonna break right away but later on; at the same time, Eddie at first base has a quick play on that the shortstop doesn't know about [a "quick play" involves the first baseman breaking to the bag from a set position away from the base]. Well, Eddie thinks the quick play is on, and yet the pitcher and shortstop have the time play on, so this is what can happen. The pitcher comes set, Eddie breaks, and their first and third base coaches start yelling 'back' to the runner at first, who goes back to the bag. Nothin' happens but then, boom, guy's picked off at second by the shortstop because everybody's concentrating on what Eddie's just done. We go over and over everything with them, and we say to them, there's nothing wrong with having two plays on at the same time, because the guy who has the ball knows where he's going. A lot of times the seeming confusion makes things work better."

This intricate sense of timing, which can only come from trusting the performance of your teammates, has enabled the Orioles over the years literally to steal a few games from the opposition. Seven or eight times during the past decade the Orioles have worked a double steal of home that would try the sanity of both friends and foes. The play works with runners on first and third and a left-hander pitching. When the pitcher comes to his set and just as soon as he has turned his glance away from third, the runner there breaks for home. At the same moment, the runner on first makes a move—usually clumsy—to draw a throw to first. If the throw—or a balk—is made, the run scores easily. If not . . .

"I remember one time," Miller said, "Flanagan went twelve innings. He was pitchin' great, and Earl said in the seventh, 'Give me one more inning.' So he struck out twelve and went to about 160 pitches and in the twelfth inning he had the bases loaded and one out and I remember Earl saying, 'If you get in trouble, I'll go out and get you.' So there was Flanny lookin' in the dugout. Later, he said, 'Jesus, I wonder what trouble is.' So he got a double play and got out of the inning. He went and sat in a corner of the dugout and our half winds up with Belanger up and two out, Eddie Murray at third, DeCinces at first. And then Earl started yellin', *'Put the play on with two strikes! Put the play on!'* Well, Flanagan came walkin' over to me and he says, 'For chrissakes, twelve innings of work for a lousy trick play,' and he no more went down in the hole when DeCinces fell down and grabbed his leg, the pitcher threw over there, and Eddie, who had broken from third at the same time, stole home with the winning run!"

The overriding sense one gets from watching the Orioles at work in the spring, however, is just how conservative they are. The heirs of the St. Louis Browns have purged themselves of all traces of the sort of gimcrackery that was needed to keep a losing franchise going. They have been baseball-respectable for years now, without anyone really calling them conservative. Their dress code was in place long before Sparky Anderson's advent in Cincinnati. Years before others the Orioles have had mandatory drug screening throughout their minor-league system. In addition, the team has had a working arrangement with the Sheppard-Pratt Clinic in Baltimore for cases involving alcohol and drug abuse. The director of the drug and alcohol program, Dr. James McGee, a psychiatrist, is on the Orioles' staff. McGee has also been operating an organization-wide counseling program for players and their families. Dennis Martinez credits Dr. McGee and the Sheppard-Pratt program with saving his career—and his life. The Orioles even have a semiofficial in-house agent for the players—lawyer Ron Shapiro—who has the confidence of both players and management and who is, when the time comes, a perfectly keen advocate for the players in bargaining. There is no other arrangement like it in baseball.

Yet what defines this conservatism, perhaps more than anything else, is the team's approach to what takes place on the field. In striking contrast to most other teams, the Orioles possess what can only be described as a philosophically coherent sense of the game. Though it is nowhere so directly stated, this sense is that success in baseball, first and last, depends on a proper appreciation of the vulnerability of things. The Oriole approach to pitching, which emphasizes changing speeds and total defense over power, rests on two explicit assumptions: first, that the human arm is not strong enough to throw a ball past major-league batters consistently over a long period of time; and, second, that it is only the strength of nine that can offset the weakness of one. By changing speeds, a pitcher turns not only to wile, he allows hitters to hit the ball, and thereby throws fewer pitches than a strikeout pitcher, who has yet to learn that the human arm, as designed by the Creator, was probably not meant to throw baseballs at ninety miles an hour. "The most perfect game I ever saw," Ray Miller said, "was a twenty-six-hit 3–2 game we won in Anaheim with Scotty McGregor pitching against Tommy John. The game was over in less than two hours, and Scotty threw less than one hundred pitches." Miller—and every Oriole starting pitcher—can tell you exactly how many sub-one-hundred-pitch games the staff has thrown during a season.

In the spring of 1985 the Orioles went into camp having finished fifth in the American League East the year before. Atypically, the Orioles reached outside their organization in a big way—to free agency—to fill needs for the coming year. "Sometimes, you have to veer off course to get back on course," the soon-to-be-released manager Joe Altobelli said. But getting back on course wasn't simply a matter of filling needs. In 1984 when the team fell out of contention they began playing sloppily. That year saw the loss of three key players—Jim Palmer, Ken Singleton, and Al Bumbry—as well as Benny Ayala and Tom Underwood. Age, and the shield afforded them by fundamental baseball, had seemingly folded in upon them. "We have to get back to playing baseball the Oriole way," Eddie Murray said. "That means getting back to fundamentals. We made an awful lot of mistakes last year. Out there on the field, on the bases. We have to have people turn their years around." But Murray, like many Orioles, could not think of the team without thinking simultaneously of the organization. It was as if the team itself were a vulnerable entity without the strength of the entire organization intact. Years before, Cal Ripken, Sr., had given up running the minor-league camp. Murray wondered about what was happening there now. "When we were down there, he even taught the game. I mean not everybody really knew how to play the game of baseball. The game was taught by him. The Oriole way. We had booklets on cutoffs, everything. Where to be on certain plays, men on this base, men on that base. . . . That's where the fundamental Orioles came from."

"The Book," in other words, was no better or worse than the

rest of the organization. You simply could not predict from Oriole tradition that the Orioles' future was secure. An organization was too complex for that. But still, to watch the Orioles slowly remind themselves in their daily work that winning depended ultimately on this collective recognition of individual fallibility and of the need, therefore, to do all those "little things" required to offset it, was to be curiously renewed in an irony that went beyond baseball but yet lay at the very heart of it: that the small, detailed labor of individuals, bound by rules and conventions and always slow to change, still had in it the astonishing capacity to transform the surrounding and illimitable force of chaos into patterns of beauty and order.

CHAPTER FIVE

Hitting School

The light has sunk into the earth
The image of Darkening of the light.
Thus does the superior man live with the great mass:
He veils his light, yet still shines.

—I Ching

History has not been kind to the Boston Red Sox. Three times since the end of World War II they have come within outs of a world championship, which has eluded them since 1918. They were close enough on each of those occasions to taste it, and on each one, as though some lowering zealot emanation from the Puritan past had it in for them, they were denied. Twice in the same period they were in a first-place tie at season's end, and twice the grim judges of the canon bound their hope of joy to flames of memorably unbearable defeats. It is not really surprising to find people among the Red Sox who still have visions of Bucky Dent's pop fly skittering over the Monster and Yaz's closing pop fly settling, as though from the fall of some cosmic guillotine, into the basket of Graig Nettles' glove. (These same keepers of the vigil remind you of the eerie coincidence that the final out in the '67 and '75 Series, along with the '78 playoff game, was, in each instance, delivered up by The Captain.) What is surprising is that Enos Slaughter chasing home with

That Run in '46 still pricks at the flesh of memory. Ted Williams, a perennial fixture at the Sox spring camp in Winter Haven, remembers, as does Johnny Pesky, who, one morning in the commissary adjoining the clubhouse at Chain O'Lakes Park, told a group of reporters that the fault for the poor relay was really not his but reserve outfielder Leon Culbertson's. From the manner of Pesky's telling it, it was as though it all took place during the World Series of the previous fall.

None of this would matter, of course, except for the feeling of settled gloom that one finds in and around today's Red Sox. Why this is so is arguable, but the evidence of one's senses is not. I have been a lifelong Red Sox fan (that is, ever since the Dodgers left Brooklyn), with all the credentials in suffering one needs. I know unhappiness when I see it. The Red Sox are an unhappy family. But a special one. As we all know, every unhappy family is unhappy in its own way.

"I'll get out of here one of these days and restore myself with the Celtics," said a *Globe* writer. He was just one of many Boston beat writers who let you know that covering the Red Sox and the Celtics was to travel between worlds 180 degrees apart. Winter Haven in the spring was little more than doing time. In this sleepy central Florida town, the day's attractions began and ended with the Red Sox, and it had been years since the old Earth Opera song "But the Red Sox Are Winning" had any real staying power against the indignities of a world gone mad. My landlord advised me that a swim in the pretty lake behind my rented trailer was inadvisable because I might find an alligator or two for company. Even sleeping was risky: I awoke at five-thirty one morning to find a possum sitting on my chest. The Red Sox just do not provide a winning environment.

Perhaps it was the incongruity of finding New England's team in the setting of an Erskine Caldwell novel. Pickup trucks rambled down the main street of town; the shopping malls were full of men in plaid shirts and feedcaps. The women wore neat plain cotton dresses or candy-colored pants suits. When a dispute broke out between the Red Sox and the local Elks Club over a "whites only" invitation to the team, you knew you were in a time warp depositing you somewhere back in the fifties. The invitations to the team, accepted each year until the present, were torn up by the team's new general manager, Lou Gorman. One of the writers said that if the same thing had happened to the Celtics, Larry Bird would have simply torn up the Elks Club. The local press said people from Boston had nothing to say to anyone, coming, as they did, from Boston. The Red Sox couldn't win for losing.

And yet, this sense of gloominess that seemed to envelop the clubhouse, the press room, and the team offices like a low coastal fog, seemed puzzling in light of the team's chances. The Red Sox probably had the best hitting team in baseball. The year before saw the emergence of a trio of young pitchers who promised, for the first time in memory, to provide real wings for the powerful flying body. Also for the first time, the ownership had put aside its don't-spend-as-you-go philosophy nearly to give away the store in signing Jim Rice and Bob Stanley. There were some expert opinions in print that even had the 1985 Red Sox winning everything. Yet, the overriding feeling was unmistakable: the Red Sox were a team out of touch with themselves and out of touch with their own fans, who, in recent years, had begun to return the favor in the cruelest way of all—with indifference. In 1984 Red Sox attendance was 1,661,000, down by almost a million in less than a decade. In Maine, the left chamber of the heart of Red Sox country, the most popular team on the summer airwaves was the minor-league affiliate of the Cleveland Indians, the Maine Guides.

As a Red Sox fan, I have had strong opinions over the years for the lamentable slide suffered by the team since its near championship year of 1975. Heading the list of explanations has been the new ownership and the inability of local fans and media (Yankee fans should sympathize) to throw the rascals out. For years, the sickening squabble between partners at the top—

culminating in attempted takeovers and court battles, the kind of sleazy shenanigans that were the staple of the old Perry Mason show—led me to almost long for someone like the Producer to step in and set things straight. I knew all along this proceeded from a certain heat-maddened way of thinking. The Red Sox of today were not the Red Sox of '75 or '78. Anger was no explanation.

Peter Gammons' recent book, *Beyond the Sixth Game,* blames the decline of the Red Sox on the inability of the new ownership to cope with the economic revolution brought about by the abolition of the reserve system at the end of the 1975 season. I am not so sure. Red Sox co-owner and chief operating officer Haywood Sullivan acknowledges that economics had a great deal to do with the fortunes of the team in those years, as they did with baseball in general. The unloading of popular stars such as Fred Lynn, Carlton Fisk, and Rick Burleson (which probably soured things in New England as much as John Adams' defending the murderers of Crispus Attucks), Sullivan says, was done "on principle, for baseball as much as for the Red Sox. Unfortunately, it was never really explained, the context of it. Those contracts were negotiated whereby we had that first option—which we had paid a certain amount of money for—and so they formed a test case and we tried to win it for baseball in general," says Sullivan. His view is that he, along with other owners, is caught between a rock and a hard place, with salaries escalating wildly on one side and the need to pay the talent in order to keep them on the other. "This game," he said, in his slow Alabaman drawl, "was never predicated on havin' General Foods puttin' the money in to run things. That's where the fear is right now. If the costs keep escalating the way they are right now the game will not be able to sustain itself. That's not a threat, it's just common sense. Every five or seven years, you're getting a five hundred percent increase in costs. You just can't pass that on to the public."

All of this would make sense if Sullivan's leadership had

shown consistency or strong direction over the years. It has not. The very first decision made during his tenure was to enter the free-agent sweepstakes in 1977 for Mike Torrez—to the tune of a then whopping two and a half million dollars for seven years. Subsequent to that, perhaps because of the unfortunate results, the freeze set in. But the loss of free agents Luis Tiant and then Bob Watson wedged opened the purses a bit for Skip Lockwood and Tony Perez. Ultimately, threatened by falling attendance and rising hostility, Sullivan renegotiated a contract for Dwight Evans, who had asked to be traded and then moved his team from sixteenth to fourth in the salary lists with two strokes of a pen and an arbitrator's wink. Unable to trade Jim Rice, he made him (for that moment) the highest-paid player in the game. Bob Stanley simultaneously joined Millionaire's Row, as did third-year man Wade Boggs. Neither a borrower nor a lender nor—obviously—an owner lacking resources (a standard explanation), Sullivan has approached the exercise of ownership rather like the person who chooses to get into a poker game and then constantly worries about how much he has to bet. This is not necessarily the way of a piker but it inevitably is that of a loser. It is not villainy so much as lack of character and direction that marks his reign. Extravagance and penury exist side by side, achieving a mean that is neither one nor the other.

Nowhere is this smoothed-over clash of tendencies more apparent than in the way the Red Sox prepare for a season. The Red Sox are one of many teams that do not live or die by their devotion to fundamentals during spring training. They go through them but the manner of their going is ordinary. I watched a pitchers' fielding drill one day. The pitchers lined up at the mound, threw to the plate, at the same time a coach fungoed a ground ball wide of first base and the pitcher went over to cover the bag. I had been here before. The Red Sox pitchers, not known in history for throwing low-run ballgames, did their variation of the Brewer Trot. Each man seemed to be doing his own thing, ranging from the hustle to the hospital collision. I watched another pitcher's routine. This one involved the players lining up in two different rows. Out in front of them, at intervals of about thirty yards, were a series of baseball caps full of baseballs. Each pitcher would run out to the furthest cap, bend over, pick up a ball, and bring it back to the line, then go out to the next farthest cap, bend over, get a ball, and bring it back. "We're squirrels storing nuts," one of the pitchers explained, while the supervising coach urged his charges on in the manner of a drill sergeant.

I asked another pitcher what the purpose of the drill was. I might have been asking why certain naval captains rolled steel balls around in their fingers. "Beats me," I was told. "I guess we're doing wind-sprints," another pitcher explained. On another occasion, I watched a more orthodox drill in relays and cutoffs. The supervising coach, with each swing of the bat, put the ball in the gaps or down the lines, never directly at the fielders, where most throws from the outfield develop.

"Successful teams, nearly all of them, really work on fundamentals," Billy Hunter had told me. "Then there are teams that go down to spring training to get their pitchers' arms ready and to get enough batting practice." At the time I spoke to him—shortly before spring training began—I asked him if he had any sense of which teams were like that. At first he would not answer the question directly. Instead he told me a story about his taking over the Texas Rangers one year in midseason. The team, he said, was so deficient in executing the most routine plays that he decided to hold a mini-training camp at four o'clock each day in the Texas heat; this created an incentive to get the work done correctly as quickly as possible. Then Hunter said, "I've never been to a Boston Red Sox spring training camp, but their team reminds me of a team that goes to camp to pitch and hit. I may be way off base. I don't think Houk would run a camp like that, I don't think McNamara would; but just watching their team perform—I'm just talking about the results—it looks like that's what they do."

What Hunter was absolutely on target about was hitting. The Red Sox hit. And hit and hit. This is a team that has had only three regular left fielders in forty-five years—Ted Williams, Carl Yastrzemski, and now Jim Rice. The Red Sox approach hitting the way medieval pilgrims approach Rome—with reverence and effort. Rice gets into the hitting area near the clubhouse, has the pitching machine turned up, then moves up to a distance half-way between the machine and the plate, swinging at each ball as it whistles past, backing with each swing farther toward home plate, till he's settled in at sixty feet six inches. Dwight Evans, as Yastrzemski did before him, shows up early, too early for the media, to work with Walt Hriniak, acknowledged by many to be the game's best hitting instructor. Hours after the day's work-outs are concluded, Wade Boggs, Rich Gedman, Mike Easler, or Bill Buckner labor on, working with Hriniak. To watch the Red Sox have at it is to turn up yet another coherent answer to yet another of those perennial questions: "How do they manage to keep turning out those hitters?" But even this lifeline out of the depths of Red Sox history is at present curiously divided. There are two very different approaches to hitting on display in the Sox spring camp. One is Hriniak's and the other belongs to Williams—the game's greatest hitter in the last half-century and the living embodiment of Red Sox tradition. That there should be different approaches to hitting a baseball, called by Williams "the single most difficult act" in sport, is not surprising. As rookie coach Tony Torchia put it: "Hitters are like snowflakes, no two of 'em are alike." What does raise an eyebrow, however, is Williams' gladly given opinion that Hriniak's approach is an unmitigated disaster. The "Lau" method taught by Hriniak—head down, going back to go forward, good weight shift, and follow through with the bat winding up in a high position—actually rouses the ire of Williams, who, at 67, is still a towering presence and a relaxed and easy spokesman for a science of hitting he feels has been undermined. Williams, during the spring, dresses, goes down to the fields behind Chain O'Lakes Park, and

oversees the work of the young hitters in the organization, ranging from those in the low minors to those on the forty-man roster
of the big team.

"I get a lot of fun trying to appraise the talent, troubleshoot,
talk to these young kids," Williams says. "In fact, it means ten
times more to me than with the older players, who are more set
in their ways." The danger out there in baseball land for the
younger players is the harmful virus of the Lau-Hriniak approach to hitting.

"I'm talking about theories of swinging down, I'm talking
about theories of shifting the weight, I'm talking about theories
of keeping your head back and looking at the ball over the
plate—hell, you don't even do that! You're looking at the ball
out front and deciding where you're going to swing when it's
fifteen to twenty feet out and you're gonna hit it in here. But
you're *still looking out there as you hit it!* You don't come back
into the plate and look at it—impossible! You'd be surprised
how many ballplayers—because this stuff is supposedly up-to-
date—think it's gospel. I really in my heart feel that some of this
junk has retarded hitting ten to fifteen years. That's what I
think."

But there is more. When Williams looks out at the mound
from his perch behind the batting cage, the force and charm of
the man seem to make the years drop away, and once again,
with the barest of imagination, the man standing there is The
Splinter, Teddy Ballgame, the one who had five seasons taken
from him by wars and another four by bases on balls (2,019 in
his career) and who still managed to hit 521 home runs with a
lifetime batting average of .344. Williams has put on weight over
the years, enough so that with his rawboned, sharp-eyed face
and gravelly voice, he seems downright John Wayne-ish in manner. Except when he shows you something about hitting. When
he assumes the familiar stance and in slow motion brings his
imaginary bat into the ball, his eyes suddenly become hard diamonds of light, his face an almost frightening mask of concentra-

tion. Just a few years ago he played a game of tennis with Yastrzemski that is still talked about in Winter Haven. The match lasted for hours and Williams, who was then 62, battled his junior successor to the Hall for hours before succumbing. When he pantomimes or talks about any part of hitting, you realize that it is John Wayne who resembled Ted Williams.

"I just disagree with a lot of the Charley Lau school, that's all. The poor guy's gone now but I still don't adhere to much of what he said. 'Keep your eye on the ball.' Christ, you gotta keep your eye on the ball! 'And don't pull too much and hit it back through the pitcher.' Okay, those are things everybody said. But when you talk about the real mechanics of a swing, and what you gotta do to get that bat on the ball and hit it with authority—it's a quick, strong game! You've got to have length of stroke. You've got to do that length of stroke as quick as possible. You can't do it, you can't do it, buddy, *you-can-not-do-it,* without utilizing hip actions to the fullest."

I made peace thirty years ago with a lifetime high school batting average of .221, so challenge was the very last thing I had in mind when I asked Williams to explain how what he was saying was at odds with the basic Lau-Hriniak premise that you had to go back to go forward.

"All right! All right!" Wiliams thundered. "As you go forward, you're movin' toward the pitcher, aren't you? And you want that sixty feet six inches to hit the ball, don't you? Well, why cheat yourself six inches or a foot or ten inches or whatever it might be—that's what I say! Don't cheat yourself. *Wait for the ball!* Don't go back to go out after it! *You wait for it!*"

There is not a trace of insecurity in Williams' anger. It is large and bold and good-spirited, as he himself is toward the end of his seventh decade of life. He is a passionate, outgoing man, as he once was passionate and ingoing. He is generous to the point of being able to make others who are all too easily in awe of him feel at ease. A father and teenage son stopped by to gawk at Williams. The father, with faltering voice, asked Williams if he could take a picture of him with his son. Williams gladly consented. The teenage boy stood alongside his family's hero, so awestruck that the blood seemed to drain from his face. Williams put a steadying, friendly arm around his shoulder and the picture was taken. Above all, this greatest of living baseball legends seems to be a man reconciled to the career he has put behind him and to his role as an elder statesman. To a local reporter's question about whether he felt he might have been born too soon, he responded, "Naw. Naw. Shit, if I can live another eight or ten years, I'll be happy and see ya later."

There is just this little matter of hitting. I had over a period of time come to realize that Russian violinists never die so much as change with age, and that the beauty of their tone transforms the music they play. I had grown up believing Williams actually saw the seams on a ball when it was pitched. He says now he never did. "Oh, they wrote so much shit," he said. "Jesus Christ! I didn't see the ball hit the bat and I didn't see a lot of things. The ball looked as small to me as it looked to a lot of guys. Once in a while the ball looked big as a balloon because the guy didn't have anything on it. Bill Dickey one time—I was hittin' real good—I had Bill Dickey say—I had taken a couple of real close pitches outside—I knew they were balls—Dickey said, 'Ted, tell me the truth, just how big does that ball look to you?' Shit, it didn't look bigger to me than to anyone else."

Second on the all-time career list for walks, Williams hated this invitation to someone else's dance. "Oh, how I hated it. But there was nothing I could do about it. Shit. They didn't want to pitch to me. They had a fine on the Yankees when Stengel was there, automatic fine if Williams beats you in the seventh, eighth, or ninth inning. Automatic fine." But when Williams talks about the contemporary players he most admires, he mentions Eddie Murray, a hitter who also detests, but accepts, bases on balls. "Whaddaya gonna do if they walk ya? Shit, I'll tell ya this—Eddie Murray's the one guy today I wouldn't let beat me. He'd be number one. You know, we got guys here like Rice who can lead in home runs, RBIs—big, strong guy in a great ball-park—an' he walks forty-four times a year! He's got to hit a whole lot of bad balls to do that."

Invariably Williams steers all conversations that begin in the past into the present. Present Red Sox players—Evans: "He's got as much ability as anyone in baseball but . . . [in following Lau-Hriniak] he's dumb about it." Gedman and Easler: "Twenty points better because they're playing in Fenway. You damn well better believe Fenway is a left-hand hitter's park." Boggs: "In practice he pulls the ball, but he won't do it enough in a game. We talked about it earlier. I said you should pull the ball. So we went from here over to [the main field] to play an intrasquad game. And the count got to be two and oh, and I hollered to Boggs, 'Now's the time! Now's the time!' and he hit a line drive against the right-field scoreboard. See, he's capable of hitting twenty, twenty-five home runs and still hitting .320. Brett is capable of hitting twenty-eight home runs a year. My criticism is there because they're not as good as they ought to be."

As good as they ought to be. This signature of Williams' own drive as a player is so much with him in the present that it comes as no surprise to see him at work only in the limited space of these spring training weeks and then no more—it is almost as if the organization that has hired him is too small really to make use of him. It bothers him that young hitters can go up to the parent club and fail because they have been "changed" by what is taught there; it bothers him that conditioning techniques emphasize size and speed, which cover a multitude of mistakes. And it always gets back to hitting. Hitting, at 67, remains, for Williams, the great, unfathomable mystery the gods ordered him to devote his whole life to. You have the feeling that his devotion as a teacher carries to the edge of still wanting to swing the bat himself. It is an absurd notion. The urge, he swears pungently, has long since left him. Except that as he describes its leaving, you are not quite convinced. The moment he acknowledges did not come really with that famous final Fenway home run in his last official major league at-bat. But it did come, once and for all, many years later:

"It was a funny little incident. About five years ago, I was in spring training here. The pitchin' machines were just throwing lollipops, and the kids were really teeing off on them. I said, 'Put some speed on that machine, get it pepped up.' Well, they pepped it up to, jeez, where the kids were havin' a hell of a time gettin' it out of the cage. And I'm watchin' the ball, watchin' the ball, watchin' the ball—and I said, 'I *know* I can hit that stuff. Well, I went in there and I couldn't get it out of the cage either. That's when I realized that things were all done for me." What was left was teaching. And the feeling in this Red Sox camp was that his teaching—because it was so forceful and opinionated—represented, as Williams did himself, something of a puzzle.

If Central Casting were given the job of finding Williams' opposite, they might look no further than Hriniak. Hriniak in appearance is everything Williams is not. A physically unimposing man, he is of slight build and his hair, hanging stringily down from his baseball cap, is almost orange; his face has been scarred in an automobile accident that nearly took his life. As Williams is booming and outgoing, Hriniak is soft-spoken and intense. There is about him the look of a person from another century. Dickens or Hogarth might have found him in the crooked back lanes of teeming London.

Hriniak has been with the Red Sox for nine years. For eight of them he was officially listed as a bullpen coach. Only in the last year has the club bothered to acknowledge what he has been all along—the team's hitting coach. His major-league career as a player consisted of two seasons as a catcher for the Padres and Braves. He had ninety-nine at-bats and a lifetime batting average of .253. But for Hriniak this brief time was as important as a career studded with records and glory. He got to the majors, he feels, largely because in 1968, playing for Shreveport in the Texas League, his manager was Charley Lau. Everything he learned, Hriniak says, he owes to Lau. Lau made him realize that a .220 hitter might become a .250 hitter and that a .250 hitter might, with a proper sense of what he was doing, become a .300 hitter. He has never forgotten.

"I was never a talented athlete," he says, "but I like to think I went about my job in a workmanlike manner. And I just believe if you practice right you're gonna play right. I've learned over the years that a lot of hitters didn't practice right, didn't get enough quality time out of practice, and I believe if guys' work habits were better they could learn to do it—that is, practice right."

Hriniak's work habits are impressive, even to those who disagree with his theories. Though spring workouts do not officially begin till ten, he is there at seven-thirty in the morning, setting up, getting buckets of baseballs ready, moving the mesh screen he built for his flip drill into place under the large open shed opposite the clubhouse. "I got guys comin' in early," he explains, "guys who wanna work on things." He might also have said the same thing about his staying late. He is the last staff member to leave, because there are also those who remain behind in the afternoon "to work on things."

During the official workouts, Hriniak—as he has for the past nine years—throws batting practice. He estimates that he has thrown the equivalent of about six hundred innings each season. His pitches are sharp, accurate, and odd-looking. He throws with a minimum of motion, most likely to conserve his arm, which years ago was operated on, unsuccessfully, to repair a torn rotator cuff. Most often, he pitches in pain. He does not care. He does it, he says, sounding suspiciously like those kindred eighteenth-century New Englanders who wrote discourses on Unlimited Submission, because he enjoys it through the pain. In fact, Hriniak has given his body to his work. Five years earlier Joe Rudi, then a member of the Red Sox, shattered Hriniak's elbow with a line drive during a flip drill.

Early morning. This is his time. Before the press turns up or fans or even most players. The ones who come, like Dwight Evans and, until he retired, Yastrzemski, seem almost like large rare birds briefly out of their inaccessible morning sanctuaries. One morning, though he was retired, Yaz showed up again. His early-morning work habits, probably established on the potato farm of his boyhood, match Hriniak's perfectly. Yaz came at the beginning of his own workday as minor-league instructor to go over a cable television interview he was to do later with Hriniak. Together, they reviewed what they had practiced for eight years as hitter and coach—as friends. There was a kind of stiffness and formality in their exchange, which you knew came from their trying to put into an unnatural form what had been living practice between them.

"If you don't have a move back," Hriniak said—as Yaz practiced being not a hitter but an interviewer—"if you don't have that move back, you won't be fifty-fifty when you land."

"But, Walter, I don't want to be charging out," Yaz said, in that hard East Island accent that sounded so akin to Hriniak's genuine Boston.

"That's not what I call chargin' out, Carl. To have a movement back means you have more weight on your back side, you pick your foot up, put it down, you get back, you're perfectly balanced—*now* you shift your weight. *The last thing you do in a baseball swing is swing.* . . . So what you used to tell yourself was you had to come out nice and soft. Many times I heard you say, 'Walter, I got to get out soft, I got to get out soft,' or 'I got to step on an egg, I'm comin' out too hard, I'm comin' out too hard.'"

To anyone who knew anything about the endless abuse Carl Yastrzemski subjected himself to in his twenty-three year quest to overcome the limitations of a talent he truly felt he did not possess, it will come as no surprise to hear that in this seemingly simple matter of stepping forward softly rather than jerkily, there was no sense that the task had ever really been accomplished. "I spent my entire career trying to do it," Yaz said, "I was trying on my last day." Sometime later I would hear Dwight

Evans, himself an inordinate exponent of the work ethic, remember that Yaz was a model neither he nor anyone could match. But in Yaz, Hriniak saw a *raison d'être* that went far beyond the game itself: "The eight years I spent with Carl were a lot of fun—a lot of work but the one thing was he was willing to do anything to make himself a better hitter or to prolong his career. Numerous times at eight o'clock in the morning, in the rain, in the mud, till his hands bled, he was constantly looking for a way to be better. He would never give up on that. To the last day of his career. One of the biggest talents he had was his ability to concentrate and the burning desire he had to excel. It was tremendous. He was not a talented athlete—he wasn't a Willie Mays. There's very few people in this world who get the most out of themselves no matter what they are, but Carl Yastrzemski's one of them."

Though Hriniak is reluctant to admit that he has deviated from the teaching of his friend and mentor Charley Lau, the fact is he has. Technically, he says, the differences are slight—but they are real. "One of the differences is that I teach more of a downward swing than a level or an upward swing—to some hitters. There's a few guys I think have a better chance of hittin' if their bat starts down and then finishes up."

But it is a search through the esoterica of hitting to find what it is that separates the teaching of mechanics by each of the two men. Experience—working intimately with individual players over long periods of time—has made Hriniak his own man, a hitting instructor unlike any other. He is, it turns out, not quite so wedded to theory as all that. "When I started here, I didn't know as much about hitting as I do now . . . I don't know it all and never will . . . but what I have learned over the years, the biggest thing, is that you can't teach people to hit the same way. You just can't. There's different offshoots of it, different ways to get the same thing done. You have to find out about other people, how they're thinkin', and be honest with them. And you want them to be honest with you. All you can ever do is help them help themselves. You can't push anything down some-body's throat."

This is far from idle talk. Hriniak does work differently with different hitters. There are certain Lau-Hriniak hitters—Carlton Fisk, Dwight Evans, George Brett—who are home plate clones. But there are others who are not—who, in fact, deviate considerably from Lau's old "Absolutes of Good Hitting." One of these hitters is Mike Easler, who maintains that he hits off his back foot rather than off a rigid front foot (violation of Lau "Absolute Number Seven"). "With me," Easler said, "Walter's approach has not been to get me to hit off the front foot. He's been working with me to keep my head down on the ball, and it's made a difference. He talks to me about the psychological part of hitting—one thing at a time, not worrying about a multitude of different things. He won't even talk to me about back foot, front foot. If he's talkin' to another hitter, he'll turn to me and say, 'Don't even listen to this, it doesn't apply.' . . . He doesn't sell me, he helps me."

As Hriniak sees it, there is no war with Williams because he does not recognize that he stands in any way as an adversary. "I don't know if what we do is that different. He explains his way and I explain mine. I don't teach the upswing, the downswing [anathema to Williams], or the level swing—I teach them all. Every hitter is different."

What distinguishes Hriniak most is this acute sensitivity to what Easler called "the psychological part" of hitting. What exactly this consists of is perhaps easier to describe than where it comes from. One is tempted to see in Hriniak yet another incarnation of an Eastern master, but in doing so there is a danger of overlooking this special quality of showing up before anyone else at the crack of dawn and leaving after everyone else has gone home. His labor is as much a glory to traditional Yankee stick-to-itiveness as to whispers of the East. In either case, the labor is defined by his relationships. And out of these relationships, carried on through the medium of "quality" hard work, there has emerged this sense that is Hriniak's own, of sharing with a hitter that most elusive and private mystery: hitting a baseball well.

Wade Boggs, who Hriniak unreservedly says is the best hitter in the game, probably arrived in the majors with as clear an idea of what he was doing at the plate as anyone. Hitting has been a religion since his father began coaching him as a boy. For biblical inspiration, there are two Great Books: Ted Williams' *The Science of Hitting* and Charley Lau's *The Art of Hitting .300.* Boggs believes the rival approaches have more in common than not. Hriniak is the coach who understands best what he is doing as a hitter. "Walter has never changed anything," he says, "he watches, puts me under a microscope, and knows when I'm doing something wrong. That isn't always easy to pinpoint because a lot of times it can be something subconscious. But Walter will pick it up."

Hriniak works with a hitter in stages, progressively rather than all at once. He goes only as far as his students take him. This is either appropriately Himalayan or Massachusetts modest. It is his students who seek him out, not the other way around. Dwight Evans, in the midst of an agonizing slump in 1980, having changed stances so often that people had begun to laughingly refer to him as "the man with a thousand stances," came to Hriniak for the help he says turned his career around. Rich Gedman, the young catcher, said that he turned to Hriniak when he first came up because he was helpless against inside pitching. "So I went to Walt and we got together and worked. The first thing I remember his telling me was to keep my head down. And as time went on, he'd take piece by piece and add in other things like getting back to go forward and following through with your swing and the path of your swing. It took a while for all that to come about."

Hriniak always goes back to what he calls "the one thing," which began the process of work with a hitter. This is a psychological as much as a mechanical adjustment, having the peculiar quality of an amulet or a magic circle. "It's impossible to go through a season with your mind that sharp," Walter says, "and your mind is everything. When I played, I wasn't a very good player but I remember at certain times I'd be hitting the ball real good and in those times I realized I wasn't thinking anything. My mind was almost a blank. Now when you're goin' bad, your mind is full of a hundred different things. And there's always a fear of failure there because hittin' itself is about failure. A good hitter fails seven out of ten times. So what I try to do is find out what a guy is thinking, what he can believe in. Take the way I used to work with Jerry Remy. I'd go to him and say, 'Jerry, what are you gonna think about tonight?' He'd say, 'Well, I'm gonna think about my hands, my feet,' whatever. I'd tell him. 'No, it's too hard that way. It's too difficult to think of three or four things—let's get one thing we can think about that will take care of all the rest.' With him it became keepin' his shoulder down. That was a mechanical thing, but it cleared a hundred thoughts and the fear of failure from his mind. It made him concentrate." For Gedman, the "one thing" is keeping his head down, for other players, the "one thing" may be something else. In each case, it is personal, precise, the result of shared labor. Above all, it is gospel only to the point that it is believed by the individual player.

The Red Sox camp is a very quiet place. And because of that, it is possible anywhere within range of the clubhouse to hear Hriniak at work. The sound is peculiarly compelling in the near fog of soundlessness surrounding the team. It is the slow, flat staccato of batted balls, amplified by the corrugated drum of a roof over the practice area. The sight of Walter on his knees behind his little screen; of his students, stripped down to their undershirts, lashing at the underhand tosses over and over again out of their practiced, disciplined stances—all of this leaves the unmistakable impression that it is in this place where hitters work, this place alone, where an organized sense of purpose is alive and clear-cut, the surviving remnant of something older and bolder than the new ownership. The Red Sox, long before

Sullivan and his principal partner, Buddy Leroux—and even before the advent of Hriniak—have always worked on hitting as a seven-day devotion, another old New England worship service designed to deliver those who are flawed from the hands of an angry God.

The more I saw Hriniak work, the more I wondered why he hadn't answered any of the calls that had come to him from other teams. He could have left the Red Sox and their dreariness for more lucrative employment many times over. It was, he said, because he wanted to remain near his daughter and near his lifetime home in Natick, Massachusetts. There were relationships, too, built up over the years with these few Red Sox players which he could not walk away from. Hitting was inseparable from something close, personal, and caring. The previous winter Walter opened to girls a hitting school he ran in Massachusetts. It was his hope that his daughter might become interested. "You don't have to be strong to play baseball," he explained. "Baseball is the last pure sport, because you don't need physical strength to excel. Girls can be good hitters. They're good now. Good hitters are not born; they develop techniques, and girls are as capable of learning those techniques as boys. If you know what you're doing, if you go up to the plate with an organized idea, with a plan, and you've worked hard enough at the mechanics, you will succeed, no matter who you are." Was he tough on his daughter? "No," he said with a shrug, "easy." She did not come to the school. If he was disappointed, his strong New England upbringing prevented him from showing it, any more than it did in revealing his feelings about the drift and decay that had come upon his team in the years of the new ownership.

By early afternoon on a typical spring training day, most of the team had dressed and left the grounds—except for Hriniak and his few students. The new Red Sox manager, John McNamara, a glum and quiet man whose principal attractiveness to management seemed to be his long-standing friendship with

Haywood Sullivan, held forth in the commissary with a few beat writers.

"Springtime is the time to go to work," Hriniak was saying, as he set forth for the shed. On his way, he remembered that Ted Williams had always loved to hit and had always worked inhumanely hard at it, and that Yaz, in more recent times, had done the same. "It wasn't what I call bullshit hittin'," he explained. "You know, some guys just stand out there and hit for an hour as though it's a drivin' range. It's foolin' around. Our guys don't do that. We're workin' on things. We really work on things."

The work carried on hour after hour in the humid stillness of the Florida afternoon. The shed and its few occupants against the deserted grounds of Chain O'Lakes Park seemed like a ship adrift in a quiet sea. With the engines gone and no one sure of the direction, was there anything better under the sun than to turn the torpor of these hours into honest New England labor?

CHAPTER SIX

Champs and Challengers

All who joy would win
Must share it—happiness was born a twin.
—Byron, *Don Juan*

Tigertown is twenty-five miles from Winter Haven, in neighboring Lakeland. It might as well be twenty-five light-years away. The canopy of sky covering both baseball camps is the same, but the atmosphere in each belongs to different planets. As you turn into Al Kaline Boulevard on an early weekday morning, the crowds are already four and five deep, waiting to get into Joker Marchant Stadium, spring home of the 1984 world champions. Tigertown used to be a wartime airbase. Three large converted hangars and the old tarmac, now used for parking, are still part of the scene. The Tigers have trained here since 1934 and continuously since 1946, a record matched only by the Reds in Tampa and the Cardinals in St. Petersburg. If war had once been the inspiring spirit for this place, the more recent ruling deity has been joy. It is apparent in the faces of the fans and players; it seems attached to the physical entity of the stadium, named after a Lakeland Parks commissioner who apparently had a reputation as a *bon vivant* and practical joker; the mood seems even to have affected the groundskeepers. Diane Yost, the only woman on the crew, had the unseemly assignment of cleaning up the swamp of tobacco juice left behind by the players. The overpowering stench of the stuff should have been enough to sicken anyone. Not so with her. "I come from an Italian family," she said. "This is the same smell of the *grotto,* where good wines are stored." These Tigers spit, she maintained, answering one of baseball's oldest conundrums, "because a lotta the guys are really shy and they gotta do something to quiet their nerves."

As was the case with the Yankees, the Tigers, at least in the spring of 1985, drew thousands rather than hundreds to their morning workouts. But where the Yankees seemed to attract stargazers, the Tiger crowd seemed all part of one giant family.

"I've worked in Tiger Stadium for thirty-two years," said a woman who identified herself as Gertrude Moore, "so I'm down here to check up on 'em, make sure they're all okay."

"We gotta get 'em in shape for the year," another fan said.

"Haven't you heard about Detroit Tiger fans?" still another added. "We do the wave beautifully."

When the Tigers finally appeared on the field, they did so as a unit. The full squad gathered in right field and, in formation, began running slowly around the warning track of the stadium. As they circled the perimeter of the outfield, turning in toward the diamond and the single-decked grandstand, the fans rose to their feet, applauding. There was no shouting, no vocal sound at all—only this building, joyous tribute of applause, as for a star at a curtain call. But it was for an ensemble, an entire company. The team, in fact, *was* the star. And as the Tigers, in their sparkling home whites with the Old English "D" on their jersey fronts, rounded the area back of home plate, running parallel to the first base stands, they seemed actually to be a single-segmented creature, one of those fabulous Chinese dragons borne aloft by a hundred souls on a festival day.

Ernie Harwell, the Tiger broadcaster, was sitting out under the overhang by the clubhouse along the right-field foul line. There was no reason for him to be in camp—the first exhibition game was still days away—but as he lived in Palm Harvest, he just wanted to be there, for the pure enjoyment of it, "to let people know I'm on the scene." He explained that to come here as a fan and sit in the sun was a little like being able to watch the rehearsal process of a good play. "Plus, everyone sits so close they can almost reach out and touch the guys." For fans, he said, this actually changed the way you saw the game. "That's why the old ballparks were so conducive to fan interest, far more so than the new parks, I think. We've got a park," he added, watching his team, "Tiger Stadium, where people are right down close to things and you're really far more part of the game than at Shea or Yankee Stadium."

The Tigers, like the Cubs, drew unusual media attention in the spring of 1985. As with any people who do their work in a glare of publicity and public attention, this was not an unmixed blessing. "This is all kinda crazy," said Al Kaline, who first began coming to Tiger camps when he was 19. "You get over a thousand watching these drills and then five hundred of them stay around for autographs afterward. Sometimes you just have to walk away. You don't like to, but you have no choice." None of this appears to make any difference. The Tigers won by being the embodiment of a team in 1984, to the point where more than one observer believed it might have all been luck.

But you can't be around the Tigers for any length of time without realizing that luck explained little or nothing. Of course the Tigers had luck with them en route to their wire-to-wire championship. All winning teams do. But the Tigers won because through one season, at any rate, they achieved this remarkable sense of balance, a single dancing Tiger balanced on twenty-five pairs of simultaneously celebrating legs. In classic fashion, they were strong up the middle, produced runs more abundantly than any other team, and had powerful pitching from a simply unbelievable bullpen, which, among other achievements, *did not lose a single game all year* in which a lead was held going into the ninth inning. How did such a team come to be? What immortal hand or eye framed its gorgeous symmetry?

"A lot of it," explained Jim Campbell, Tiger president, "is minor-league instructors, managers, Ralph [Houk] and Sparky and the coaches, and everybody. An organization like ours isn't a one-man show. It's a lot of people. It's Bill Lajoie and Hoot Evers [the GM and director of scouting, respectively], or I'll tell you a story about John Fetzer [longtime former Tiger owner who sold his interest in the team at the end of 1983]. We had a chance to move the team to Pontiac—the way was wide open, the deal was unbeatable. I sat in on the meeting when it was proposd, and Mr. Fetzer said, 'Gentlemen, I'm going to turn you down right at the start. . . . I thank you, but I consider myself merely the caretaker of this franchise, and it belongs to the city of Detroit and to the workingman who has helped build whatever success we have had here.' No one person, no instructor, no player, no manager or executive is solely responsible. It's been a long and sustained team effort at every level, and I'm not saying that because it sounds good but because I really mean it."

At the center of the Tigers' '84 ascent to the top was Sparky Anderson, the only manager in the history of the game to win world championships in both leagues. At 51, taking his ease, pipe in hand, in the far shade of the right-field corner, Sparky is a picture of such contentment that you might mistake him for a fantasy camp version of Huck Finn at a bass hole. What he has reeled in seems not nearly so important as the simple freedom to lie there enjoying himself, dreaming, concocting yarns, occasionally dropping his bait into the water.

"I don't get involved in none of it anymore," he said, pulling happily on his curved pipe. "That's what the coaches are gettin' paid for. I told 'em, if you see any sweat on me, come up and slap me alongside the head. I don't get involved in anything. Put on my uniform in the mornin' and take it off when I leave."

There is a widely told joke among baseball writers that when Anderson and Tommy Lasorda get together, there is a surefire way to tell when they start to pile it higher and deeper. The telltale sign is either of them moving his lips. At various times, Sparky has told reporters that his reserve first baseman, Dave Bergman, is the greatest he has ever seen at that position, that the one team he fears in the American League is Boston, and that his widely publicized five-year plan to bring a pennant to Detroit was just a ploy he planted with the press to keep management from firing him for at least that length of time. "You see, what I love about the game," he said, straight-faced but with eyes twinkling, "is that it gives you a license to speak. Because you don't ever work. I've been in this business for thirty-two years and I haven't worked for thirty-two years."

There is always the danger that one will get hooked on one of Sparky's stories and fail to see the real man and what impact he has had on those who labor for him. It probably doeesn't matter because he is such good company either way, but as with Huck the younger, Sparky is, in Jim Campbell's words, "a beauty." Sparky telling tall tales is like Charlie Fox's Zen master pouring tea over the rim of a cup. You can afford to take it in the lap.

Sparky, in his careers with Cincinnati and Detroit, has been perceived variously. With the Big Red Machine, he was "Captain Hook," the autocrat who demanded high knickers and pitchers placing the ball in his palm "as though it were an egg" if ever he came to the mound to remove them from a game. With the Tigers he has become the Man Who Delegates. He was seen as less the autocrat and more the man who needed pitching coach Roger Craig to win. What is to be believed? The key, as far as I was concerned, lay exactly with this curved-pipe, feet-up approach in spring training, 1985. Only a fool would mistake it for a man dozing.

"I don't do nothin' in the spring," Sparky explained. "For me, the players become the coaches' responsibility. So the more time they spend with them, the tighter they get. That's the way it's supposed to be. This is supposed to be a game of players and coaches. I learned. What good would it do for me to be out there?"

Somewhere along the line, Sparky also learned that star players and coaches could be replaced. "Joe DiMaggio left, Mickey Mantle left, Casey Stengel left, Walter Alston left. Baseball's not run that way." Delegating for Sparky is founded on an unshakable belief in the existence of absolute leaders in the midst of democracies where equality reigns. "There's nobody in our business who's smarter than the next person," he says. And then: "I don't know why, I never felt anyone was bigger than me—not the President of the United States, not nobody. To me, the President of the United States has to put on his pants in the morning—I hope—and has to eat breakfast and brush his teeth and do everything else. The both of us are just human beings."

Sparky allows his coaches—he always has—to work intimately with his players because it is essential to the success of his team, because it allows the coaches, who are underpaid and often neglected, to feel more involved, and because it costs nothing. "I'm gonna get the credit anyway," Sparky says. "I'll never ask a coach to do my dirty work; only the stuff that can keep friendship with the players. But I know every minute where the credit's gonna go."

Sparky may not have had a five-year plan, but he has always known how people fit together on a team. He apparently knew as a child. "Ever since I was a kid," he explained, "my mother says I ran everything. At school, the teacher called up and said, 'You've got to talk to George, he just won't let certain kids play.' Right. They couldn't fit in, they couldn't play. Go play by yourself against a wall."

It is this seemingly uncanny ability to know which players

were meant for each other that separates him from other managers. Here is his latest explanation of the five-year plan:

"All I did was take a look at where our strengths were. Our strength was in young Parrish, young Whitaker, and Trammell. When I got here, they were the only three strengths, so, okay, there's three guys that can play winnin' baseball, that could play on a championship team. The rest of 'em can't. So now the thing is how you go about acquiring some people that can. Well, our first shot is we got Herndon—and we gave up two young left-handed pitchers who I did not think were going to pitch in the big leagues [Dan Schatzeder and Mike Chris]. Next step was we traded Kemp for Lemon. We needed a center fielder. That was just a heckuva deal for us. We were able to trade a left fielder for a center fielder, and we already had a left fielder in Herndon, so we were able to block off two spots, And then Gibson. It all depended on how long it was going to take for Gibson to come. And we had to wait awhile. He had to come around if we were going to be a championship team. We could have always been a second- or third-place team, but no higher. And then being able to come up with that Hernandez deal was just unbelievable. So we did some fantastic trading. If you look at it—Herndon, Lemon, Bergman, Hernandez—our key things have all come from the outside. Our foundation was Trammell, Whitaker, Parrish, and then Gibson, and then we went from there and were able to do some good things."

The "foundation," as Sparky calls it—particularly the double play combination of Lou Whitaker and Alan Trammell—has been part of the scene for years. Though the pair is still young (Trammell is 27, Whitaker 28), they have been expert together so long you get the feeling they must have been yoked together in a former life. Actually, Whitaker was a fifth-round draft choice in 1975 and began life in the minors as a third baseman. (Sparky toyed with and wisely abandoned the idea of restoring Whitaker to third to make room for a rookie, Chris Pittaro, at second during this spring camp.) Trammell signed on a year later, a second-round choice, and the following winter, during instructional league, the two were finally matched as a double-play combination. They spent a year together at the Tigers' Double A farm team in Montgomery, Alabama, before being promoted to the majors together at the end of 1977. In their year at Montgomery, the pair roomed together, took extra practice together, dreamed together of one day playing for a championship team. Having watched and marveled at their play for years, I was half inclined to believe that they did not play separate positions—they were two people who actually played a single position called something like middle infielder.

"I think it would be a mistake to see the two of us as one position," Whitaker said. "That's like the pitcher-catcher kind of thing. The best way is just to leave it alone and remember the way it was designed for baseball."

"The combination is more than us," Trammell added. "Include the catcher and center fielder. We're very strong up the middle. I know that's a cliché—to be strong up the middle—but that is true for us and not only defensively but offensively as well. Lou and I try to set the stage for the big guys, that's all. We each have our jobs to do."

What is most interesting about this baseball version of Castor and Pollux is how they have handled being themselves rather than each other's counterpart over the years. In the beginning, their teamwork was born of necessity—precisely because Whitaker was not a natural second baseman.

"I think it was a little tougher for Lou," Trammell explained, "because I was a shortstop all my life and he was converted. He had to learn to pivot, get his footwork, and as far as that goes we didn't do it by talking about it but by going out there and saying, 'I'd like the ball right here, or here, so now I can almost see when I'm catching the ball where he is at the bag and I just instinctively throw it to that exact spot. There's no God-given talent in all this—we went out there and worked on it. I don't think there's any secret to it other than work."

To this day, Trammell and Whitaker dress side by side. They are still a team and will—like Tinker and Evers—always be. But time and success have made clearer just how individual they are.

"When we first came up," Trammell remembered, "everything was Trammell and Whitaker, Whitaker and Trammell, and I liked that because it wasn't just one guy and because we were middle infielders and our numbers were one and three and we were always together. But we're both married now and have families and so we go our separate ways. But when we're on the field, we're a team."

"It was always the both of us," Whitaker said, "it just became a habit to us. We worked our first three or four years together, so it's not like we have to go out there and work at it the same every year now. We don't. We're into the game, both of us, we're not waiting for the game to come to us. We're approaching the game right from the first pitch."

Success, like family life, has brought out different things in them. Once they could count on sharing obscurity, as they did the middle of the infield. Long before the championship year, but forever after that, this part of their lives vanished. There are probably more people who know about them today than who ever knew about Castor and Pollux. They have handled celebrity—both of them—as if it were yet another double play ball, but each with the grace of a very individual style.

Of the two, Trammell is easier with words and more at ease with a limelight he has never sought or believed was essential to his game. "I try to be a team player and help out any way I can," he said. "If any of that leads to success and media attention, fine. But I don't ever want to get away from the way I play the game. I know I can pop the ball out of the ballpark now, but I don't try to. I'd be a fool to go up there and go for a home run because I'd lose my stroke. You can't let anything take you away from knowing your limitations and staying within them." As for the media crush around him? "You answer the same questions every day, and that gets tiring. There are certain days you just don't feel like doing it. But I try to be as accommodating as I can."

Whitaker, on the other hand, remains more withdrawn. He is a bright and cheerful man but is ill at ease reading or hearing about himself. "You draw a lot of attention to yourself when you look to be in the limelight," he said, "and it requires a lot of time and effort, so much so that it can sometimes get you away from your real purpose, which is to play baseball, to try to be out there with the rest of the guys and not be doing something off on your own."

Whitaker maintains that so long as his name appears in the box score, that is all the confirmation or praise he needs from newspapers. There is no sense of defiance or hostility in this. It is simply part of his nature, as a person and as a ballplayer.

"I always played well," he said, "even when I was thirteen and fourteen. I was approached by scouts and radio announcers who wanted me to go on the air. I never heard of anything like that before. You know that sorta stuff is usually reserved for major-leaguers or other professionals. Well, that first time—I'm sort of shy, I didn't want to do it then because I knew the sorts of questions that would be asked—there would be a lot of emphasis on 'Lou, you did this,' and 'Lou, you did that.' I didn't want it then and don't want it now."

Whitaker actually seems protected by his own nature against the urge to talk too much. "I even don't like myself on tape," he said, "because it just doesn't sound like me. I've heard myself on tape and somehow it's just not me—I mean, I know it's me only because it's saying the same things I just got finished saying. I've always felt this way."

Because he is so self-effacing, it is possible to mistake him for a kind of wheel within a wheel. But this overlooks how much he has improved over the years. For the first six years in the big leagues, he was not a .300 hitter. In 1983 he hit .320, tailing off to .286 in 1984 (and .279 in '85). But, more remarkably, beginning with the 1982 season, Whitaker began to hit for power. Through his entire minor- and major-league career prior to the 1982 season, he had hit 17 home runs. Then in '82 alone he hit 15, followed by 12 and 13 in '83 and '84. (In the '85 season, he hit 21 homers, a record for Tiger second basemen.) Typically, he places the credit for this beyond himself:

"Gates Brown [former Tiger hitting coach, decidedly non-Lau, credited by many on the current team with improvement in their hitting] helped me the last three years. It was his approach and his way of showing me the fundamentals of being a hitter. He taught me to go up and take nothing—he said I had power and that I could learn to use it. He saw me when I was eighteen and nineteen, saw me hit a ball 400 feet. He said, 'You hit a ball that far to left center field—400 feet. It's only 325 feet to right.' . . . I never thought about hitting home runs. I always thought about hitting the ball through the infield, I never thought about hitting the ball up in the air."

In mechanical terms, Brown taught Whitaker to "turn on a ball" more quickly, something, Whitaker says, "a power hitter goes up doing." In addition, Whitaker began working on his bat speed and to begin thinking of hitting as something that took place from the waist down, not going back to go forward so much as "staying back, going straight forward and just turning—there wasn't a whole lot of movement to it." But the more Whitaker seemed to describe what he had done in mechanical terms the more he seemed actually to be talking about some vital change that had taken place within himself, in the way he saw himself as a hitter.

"I do what I can with the pitch," he explained. "If it's not the pitch I'm looking for, get a better pitch—you know, don't swing at every pitch that's a strike. Set the pitcher up. Get the pitch that you want, and then, don't miss it. Because a pitcher will always give you one good pitch to hit—so don't foul it off or miss it. I used to go up there and say I'm gonna take a walk, I'll take a pitch, see what he's got. So Gates told me, 'Man, go in there and take nothin'; before you even step in the box, you be ready to hit.' That's where I started to get these first pitch home runs from. First pitch. Hit 'em before they're even ready. For me, the goal isn't to hit one out—just to hit. If it's a strike. But, see, now they know. They know. With a lot of good pitchers, I could count on seeing their fastball. Now it's gonna be a change. I never saw a changeup in my life because I had a real slow bat, but now it's all changeups—I get more changeups and curves than I've ever seen in my life. But, they're always out of the strike zone on that first one. I'm still gonna get my pitch, and I'm gonna hit it."

Though he is young, even by baseball standards, it is harder now for Whitaker to get his body ready for 162 games. The spring season, which used to be an easy time for him, seems now to be too short. "When I was twenty-one or twenty-two, it was one thing but now I need the whole spring. Even if I'm going good, I need that one more week. Oh, yes! I never say I'm ready and then walk right into a big slump." Conditioning for Whitaker does not involve weights or unusual stretching, it is all baseball—to get his hands and legs and eye ready. The previous season, Whitaker rarely took batting practice. He didn't, he said, because lacking the pressure of a game, it could too easily lull him into bad habits. He was never criticized because his play never seemed to suffer. But what his manager and teammates did not know was that all the while, he went off to a small room in Tiger Stadium and got himself ready by swinging over and over again until he felt his body was loose enough for the game. He told no one about it because, typically, he could not put up with the notion that he might be calling special attention to himself. "All my thinking goes into what I have to do on the field," he says. "Baseball has never been easy. It wasn't easy to learn when I was young and it isn't easy now. Do my job, get my check, give the credit to the others. That'll do. I don't need more than that."

Another one of Sparky's building blocks is the six-foot-three-inch, 215-pound former All-American football flanker from Michigan State University, Kirk Gibson. In fact, if appearances alone determined things, Gibson is not at all a block. He is a cement wall. He came into the league heralded as another Mickey Mantle. Paul Bunyan–sized, stronger than the mountain giants of *Nibelungenlied,* faster than Clark Kent changing in a phone booth, he developed more in the manner of Myrtle the Turtle. When he came on in 1984 to ransack the American League, he left no doubt that he had finally arrived. He became the first Tiger ever to hit at least twenty home runs and steal at least twenty bases in the same season. He had 7 game-tying, 23 go-ahead, and 17 game-winning RBIs (the latter another team record). The sight of him streaking across the outfield or thundering around the bases, his hair flying, ferocity and ecstasy contorting his unshaven face, gave him all the appeal of a twelfth-century Christian at the gates of Jerusalem. It is an image Gibson would gladly accept. "I enjoy myself, there's no doubt about it," he says. "I enjoy beatin' the fuck out of other people. I enjoy whalin' at 'em. I enjoy taking extra bases, I enjoy breaking up double plays, okay. I enjoy throwing people out at the plate. I enjoy running balls down in the alley that everybody thought was a hit . . . see, I love to watch guys pitch seven, eight, strong innings—like Charlie Hough did against us last year. He pitched eight and two-thirds strong innings, ended up losing 5–4 when I hit a three-run homer off him in the top of the ninth. Charlie, too bad you lost. I don't care. I come out here to win and play hard. . . . I don't cheat, I'm not putting cork in my bat. I don't have to. You can say I cork my mind."

This last is a clue to how Gibson went about adapting his avenging angel attitude toward the competition. It did not come with his birth certificate or upon spoken demand from Odin or

Thor. Rather, it came from a most modern and civilized West Coast mecca for self-realization, the Pacific Institute.

For two winters prior to his big season, Gibson, at the behest of his agent, went to this enclave of yuppiedom and was taught, in essence, that you are what you picture in your mind. If you see wimp, wimp you are. Same formula for Conan the Barbarian. Between such extremes, of course, lies the rich tapestry of life's possibilities. The picture Gibson chose for himself undoubtedly involved the destruction of other baseball teams. "The way it works is, you move toward what you believe, okay. Now it ain't anybody else's business what my exact picture is—they'll find out," he explained menacingly, adding, "That's for me to know." He thought about what he just said for a moment and then, as though he were calling up the images of Hough and other crestfallen American League pitchers, said, "See, it would be destructive motivation if I said I was going to hit fifty home runs by May first. I'd be putting a time limit on myself, so I'd be working against myself. You don't do that. But you're always going for the end result. My end result is to win the world championship this year. So I'll do what it takes to get there—we will, too."

Gibson is a hulking, volcanic temperament packed into a baseball uniform. He has that sort of chaotic febrility about him that seems more suited to the war zones of football than to the comparatively peaceful pastures of baseball. In fact, it is almost impossible to imagine him standing still (in percentage terms, standing still has about the same relation to the game of baseball as water covering does to the surface of the globe). Gibson, no matter what image he carries in his head, has the sort of super-charged inner wiring that makes him seem like he wants to jump out of his own skin. Under duress, it is hard to imagine him ever being able to get past the rampaging demands of his own nervous system. That is what makes his evolution into stardom so remarkable. This journey involved more than making up a positive mental image because it took him out of himself, carried himself past his own nervous system. It was about the way he related to others. It involved discovering his own innate modesty, a force at least as powerful as his hurricane center of energy and one that, in the end, allowed him to belong comfortably to a team that eschewed superstar egos.

When Gibson came to spring training in 1984, he was coming off his worst year in the majors, a year in which he hit .227 and drove in only fifty-one runs. Sparky told him the time of waiting was over. He would have to win a job in right field if he wanted to remain in the starting lineup. For Gibson, the challenge was even more imposing because he did not feel right field was his best position. But nothing else was open. "Basically," Gibson said, "I didn't know how to play the outfield. I had said previously that I hated right field, that I'd rather catch than play right field. And it came down to right field being the only place I fit into the lineup. I had to reassess things for myself. Maybe I had been babied a little. I realized I was going to have to learn how to play right field."

Tiger management was not quite as Darwinistic as all that. The hopes they still harbored for their Mantle-who-never-was were too great. The stick they held to Gibson had a carrot dangling from it. If he chose, Gibson could, during that spring training period, work with Al Kaline, the former Tiger Hall of Fame right fielder, who was in camp as an outfield coach.

Temperamentally, Kaline was everything Gibson wasn't. Low-key and evenhanded, Kaline had lived peacefully in his own skin and within his own limitations as a player for twenty-two illustrious seasons. Gibson described his coming together with Kaline this way:

"They [management] told me, 'Lookit, we're going to give you every opportunity for this job. We're gonna have Al Kaline down here for you. If you want to use him, use him, if you don't, it's up to you.' I said to myself, from what I knew of Al already, if you can't let Al Kaline coach you, you're uncoachable. From the previous camps and the few times I had talked to him—and he was my boyhood idol—I knew he was just a fine person. He was a great person. He had twenty years or more experience, he was a Hall of Famer and one of the best right fielders who ever played the game. So if I ever wanted to succeed at my job, that sure was a good place to start. So we started. I said, 'Al, you know better than I do what I should work on, you just come up and tell me."

Day after day, the pair met. They worked and they talked. When Gibson was standing in a group of outfielders shagging flies, Kaline stood next to him and asked him to watch the different ways a ball came off a bat, to note particularly that when a ball was hit to right field it had a tendency to slice and that therefore it had to be played differently than if it was coming straight at you or was hooking to the side. They met privately. They reviewed all of the techniques an outfielder needed— proper footwork, where to go on fly balls, how to circle the ball in order to achieve a proper throwing position, how to charge a ball. They worked on a flaw in Gibson's throwing technique. Gibson had had a tendency simply to take a ball in his paw and fling it. Kaline taught him to grip the ball firmly enough so that when he threw it it would be on target. But most of all, what happened was this interplay of opposites—the coming together of a baseball odd couple that resulted in the making of one bona fide baseball superstar.

Kaline's evenness of temperament and modesty was legendary. When he retired from the game in 1974, he was one home run shy of being the first player in the history of the American League to reach career totals of three thousand hits and four hundred home runs. He retired not because he was indifferent to the record. "Had I known it," he says, "I definitely would have played another year—at least played till June 15 to have become the first to have done it." But he didn't know. The truth of the matter was he didn't pursue records and he didn't think that much about them. In retrospect, there is no bitterness or real regret. In his mind, it is almost as if that record rightfully belonged to players he judged greater than himself. "You know, Hank Aaron, who did it, actually played in the American League, so I really wouldn't have been the first. And he passed it long before. I knew that Aaron and Mays, great players like that, all had accomplished four hundred home runs and three thousand hits; I just didn't think that I was ever so close to it."

In the years following, Kaline made the transition to the relative obscurity of private life as smoothly as he had made difficult plays look easy in American League outfields. Confronted wih the peculiar existential dilemma of every professional athlete— that the high point of life arrives and passes just when other people's lives are taking off—Kaline tried his hand at sales promotion for automobile companies, only to find the business world generally unsuitable and unsatisfying. "I'd been playing baseball ever since I was nineteen years old when I came out of high school, and nobody knows exactly how reaching the end is going to affect them. And many of us only hope and pray that when our playing days are over, there will be something still available in the game of baseball." For Kaline, there was. The job of doing color work for Tiger telecasts came along, and so did the opportunity to put on the uniform once every year in the spring as a special outfield coach. Because he was so clear in his love for the game, he fit back into it as easily as he had left it, and nowhere more devotedly than on the field in Tigertown. Working with Gibson was a pleasure, not a chore. And, characteristically, Kaline downplayed the assistance he was able to give.

"It's been blown out of proportion," he said. "You can only work with someone who's willing to work and willing to learn." But looking as lean and sharp as he did in his playing days, acknowledging in his middle age that what he misses most about the game is a competitiveness that cannot be carried on, Kaline gave a reading of Gibson that was a tribute to them both, and to what it was they were able to share. "Gibby came to camp that year with a great attitude, willing to work harder than anybody

I've ever seen," Kaline explained. "He had some weaknesses and he knew it. The only thing I see in the game of baseball—probably every sport—is that all the players like to do the things they can do well. And they don't like to work on their weaknesses. And Gibby came to spring training knowing he had some weaknesses, and he wanted to work on them. . . . He always had a lot of confidence in his abilities. There are going to be times when he looks bad, because that's just the kind of player he is. But he has a great attitude. He wants to be the guy up at the plate in tight situations. He just has a great, positive feeling about what he has to do and he gets extremely upset with himself if he doesn't do well. . . . The difference in our temperaments is a mistaken way of looking at the two of us. It's true he does have a temper— but only where it affects himself. Strangely enough, he doesn't get mad at other people. I don't think he takes an oh-for-four home so long as the team wins. So long as the team wins, I don't think anything else matters to him."

Though Gibson's free agency was only a cloud on the horizon in the spring of 1985, I wondered about its possible effect on the team—and, for that matter, whether Kaline saw the team now as he had a year ago.

"I think we have the best team in baseball," he said without hesitation. "You can't predict about free agency and injuries but this team is so professional and so good they can reach back and win. I really enjoy seeing professional players go out and play hard every day. It's a joy to be around a team like this."

If you travel due west from Tigertown on Interstate 4, you will, within an hour, come upon Tampa, the oldest continuing spring-training site in major-league baseball. But if you branch north across the Courtney Campbell Causeway, you will pass through Clearwater on your way to Dunedin, winter home of baseball's youngest team, the Toronto Blue Jays.

Because the Blue Jays have come on so strongly so quickly, it has suddenly become possible to forget that they are a team without a tradition. Seeing their play in the last two years, however, has been a little like coming upon the sight of a great mountain through a suddenly opened rent in a covering fog. Their stature, you are sure, has somehow always been there. It has not. The Blue Jays did not exist when Jimmy Carter was elected to the White House. They were an infant of three when 69-year-old Ronald Reagan headed down Pennsylvania Avenue for the first time. But they have, in their short life, made up for all the tradition they do not have. They are the model of what an expansion team should be, the hope of youth-just-starting-out everywhere. None of it, however, is an accident.

Pat Gillick, the 48-year-old executive vice president for baseball in Toronto, was once an obscure player in the Baltimore Orioles minor-league system. For three of his five seasons, in Fox Cities (1960) and Elmira (1962–1963), he played under Earl Weaver. He credits much of his own achievement with the Blue Jays to what he picked up from his Oriole experience. His narration of the Blue Jays' rise is a short course in how to build a baseball organization.

"In 1976, we set out a game plan that we followed," he said, sitting in the shade at Grant Field. "That plan was that over the first five years of our operation, we were going to try to collect, regardless of position, as much talent as possible. We realized that as an expansion team, we would have a honeymoon with the fans for a couple of years—so consequently we had time to play with. We drafted as young as possible. We have three players [Jim Clancy, Ernie Whitt, and Garth Iorg] who are from the original expansion draft in 1976. . . . We went about it in four different ways. We went through the amateur draft—that is, of high school and free-agent players. We tried to do it—not very successfully—through the reentry draft. The only players we acquired that way—until last winter—were Luis Gomez, Rico Carty, and Dennis Lamp. We sought to do it through the December professional draft, which is the draft of players who have had three years of professional experience, and through that draft we acquired George Bell, Willie Upshaw, and Jim Gott. We got two kids who are here now, Manny Lee and Lou Thornton, and we got Kelley Gruber. The other avenue we planned for was trading. So we consciously established four avenues to follow and we tried to give emphasis to all without favoring one. And then, of course, we have a very heavy Latin American operation—we have been very deep in that."

It is this last which is the most visible hallmark of the patience, caring, and skill that have gone into the building of the team. The Blue Jays, nearer to the Northwest Territories than to the tropics, seem new-flown from the rain forests and barrancas of Hispanic America, the most unlikely collection of birds in Canada. More than any team in the majors, the Blue Jays reflect not so much a Latin influence as a Latin community. "It's like you come to the baseball park and you don't feel alone," said the 28-year-old second baseman, Damaso Garcia. "If I was by myself, it would be one thing, but we really are like a family. With the team, yes, it's good, but with the other Latin players here it's like my brothers and a little bit like my hometown."

Garcia's hometown is Moca, in the north-central part of the Dominican Republic. The Dominican Republic has long been to the baseball world what the United Arab Emirates has been to the world economy. One small town in Dominica, San Pedro de Macoris, home of three current Jays—George Bell, Tony Fernandez, and Manny Lee—along with eleven players from other teams, has more per capita representation in the big leagues than any other city, town, or hamlet on earth. The Blue Jays, long ago recognizing this seemingly limitless vein of baseball talent, established a recruiting program in Santo Domingo under Epy Guerrero, the great Latin scout. It has been the envy of the competition.

Guerrero, a solid, pleasant-looking man, has worked for Gillick for twenty-two years, following him from Houston to the Yankees to Toronto. The Jays' organization, he says, "is the best

I have ever worked for." Years of patience and experience have enabled Guerrero and the Jays not merely to sign players to contracts but to discover them, nurture them, move them gradually along so that when they arrive in Toronto it is as though they have been expertly transplanted, carrying a little of the soil of home with them. Guerrero's operation in the Dominican Republic is so thorough, it amounts to a rookie league camp where players are not only evaluated but trained.

"We know where to get the players," Guerrero says. "We know the culture, the language, the people, the customs, the manners. Our people have played together for some time before they ever get to Toronto. It is no accident they feel so much at home there." At the time I met him, there was a story circulating—I thought it was apocryphal—that Guerrero often traveled by mule into the jungle to discover talent. There was nothing apocryphal about it. "Oh yes, I do that," he said. "I go as far as I can by truck, keep the mules in the back. I took someone from the States with me last time, and you know, we may have come up with our best prospect yet. Watch. His name is Sylvestre Campasano. Remember the name."

Another player Guerrero brought into the fold is the 20-year-old shortstop Tony Fernandez. Fernandez, honed and hardened in the sandlots of San Pedro de Macoris, then carefully brought along through the Blue Jays system, hardly seemed like a rookie about to take over a major position on a pennant-contending team. "I'm very young, yes, but I don't feel any pressure here," he says. "It's very comfortable because when you're alone, those guys who speak Spanish make you feel at home. You feel like you're playing in your hometown. There are lots of guys who speak your language, and when something goes wrong, you have them to talk to in Spanish. It's good when you have somebody."

Newcomer Manny Lee speaks no English, but similarly feels as though he belongs. The other Latin players look out for him, but so does his rookie sidekick and roommate, Lou Thornton, from Hope Hull, Alabama. The opportunity to learn English is something the team apparently feels is just as important as providing a sense of home. In either case, the single objective is what it takes to put a winning ballclub on the field. The Latins, in management's eyes, are not a group apart but the solid center of the larger unit. Their sense of oneness and sharing is meant to be a standard by which the game itself can be played to its maximum.

"The main thing on this club is we don't have any superstars," said Garcia. "And when the Spanish-speaking players come here, they feel right at home. They're part of the group. They don't have to have a big name or anything. We all grew up together, they feel like they belong here. When I was in the Yankee organization, they had a lot of superstars. When you were there, you just went to a corner and sat down and said, 'Wow.' But here, you know. . . ." Garcia broke off, laughing. Bill Caudill had stolen up to him with a stick in his hand. "You see, the thing is, everybody's crazy here," Garcia finally said. "Like this guy who's about to belt me in the shins—he's the worst, you know. I mean, he's really crazy."

It was certainly true that Caudill, by baseball and perhaps other standards, was a bona fide oddball, as well as being one of the game's new millionaires. He gained the name "Inspector" (shortened from "Bat Inspector") by showing up for work wearing a Sherlock Holmes–style cap when he labored for the Mariners. When the Mariners were not hitting during the early part of one season, Caudill removed ten or so bats from the bat rack and deposited them in a refuse bin. The team responded that night, according to Caudill, by amassing eighteen hits during a game and thereafter referring to him by the sobriquet by which he is still known. Over his locker at Grant Field was a nameplate that read "Tubby II." On a shelf in his locker was a cage containing a small white mouse. The mouse's name, he said, was Ian II, named after a clubhouse attendant who had fashioned Caudill's nameplate. The problem of getting Ian II out of Florida and into Canada, he said, would be "squeaky," but he thought the clubhouse man, Ian, would be able to sneak him through. Given Caudill's prominence and the apparently prominent need he felt to be at a tilt, the way he viewed his role on the Blue Jays was intriguing.

"I don't consider myself a superstar by any means," he said. "I'm only going to be as successful as this club is going to make me. I can't do it myself. They've got to play well for me to have a chance to save a game. My success and failure depends deeply on them and vice versa. You can't single out one individual here. Even the bullpen's a unit. It's almost like a dream to play on a winning team, to be with a team that has a legitimate chance to go to the World Series. You can feel the winning attitude on this ballclub, it's in the air, you can taste it."

Or as Garcia put it: "Superstar? No, no, no he's not. We don't have that here. We don't believe in that. We all the same. In my point of view, Caudill is like Manrique [utility infielder Reyes Manrique], and [pitcher Dave] Stieb is like Manrique—he's just one of the group. Because when you start to have superstars, things are no good. I see that on a lot of clubs. This club, anybody can say anything to anybody. Everybody is allowed to laugh here. It's good."

PART THREE

SPRING GAMES

CHAPTER SEVEN

Spring Games

> The effort really to see and really to represent is no idle business in face of the *constant* force that makes for muddlement. The great thing is indeed that the muddled state too is one of the very sharpest realities.
> —Henry James, Preface, *What Maisie Knew*

There is nothing quite like a spring training game. On the one hand it seems closest to the sort of baseball one is accustomed to at country picnics or office outings. It is a balance between leisure and intensity, putting out and simply being out for fun. On the other hand, it is nothing of the sort. The games may look like little vacations from the real thing but they are not. What they are is different. For a young player trying to impress his way onto the team, the games are as crucial as any he will play. For a veteran with an assured position, they are to be endured or enjoyed en route to opening day. For still others, Grapefruit League games are so many laboratory hours for experimenting with new potencies. For fans, the matter is not quite so clear-cut.

We come to these games in all innocence, looking to have our fill at an old banquet table. And to be sure the familiar food is piled there. All of the stars, unsung heroes, psalm-singing magicians, crafty managers, nasty umpires, busy newsmen are there—but the meal is not the one we expect. The games seem to have no rhythm. The slowly building tension of a close game is broken in an instant by wholesale replacements in the lineup. A big hitter in a game breaking situation is just as likely to give way to an untested rookie and will wind up watching the result from the outfield as he takes his wind sprints before going in to shower. A few innings of effective work by a favorite pitcher will be followed by horrendous innings done by a pitcher who has little or no chance of following the big team north—or vice versa. In reality, however, there is a sort of rhythm to it all, one that is a little like trying to catch a distant radio station at night. The broadcast goes under a surf of static for a time only to emerge clearly once again. The games seem to have these moments in them: a single at-bat, an inning, half a game in which intense interest and excitement are sustained until the static of differing motives takes over once more. There is superb baseball alongside baseball that is seemingly performed at half-speed. There is an opportunity to see things highlighted rather than whole, to experience what amounts to epiphanies of skill or excitement while at the same time being able to take in the palpably present atmosphere of a country picnic. For myself, there was a certain *déjà vu* in all this: Baseball and Ballantine. Or as Edward Bennett Williams told me, "You have a chance to sit and talk without missing important things." Spring baseball invites your eyes and ears to many places. In these games, Mickey is always grounding to short while there is always life on the decks of the yachts.

Dodgertown is a two-hour drive from Winter Haven along a high-speed but narrow two-lane road straight across the midsection of Florida. Cars come toward you with their lights on out of the shimmering waves of highway heat. You're never too sure whether you're speeding toward a head-on collision or the open road. Coming from baseball's Plymouth Rock to baseball's Disneyland for a day's diversion on the decks should, morally speaking, have this sense of difficulty and danger built into it—

but here's to tax dollars eventually fixing the roads. Spending our way out of trouble has been an even stronger American idea than having to pay for joy. Or as Cuthbert Cuthbertson, one of the early Pilgrim arrivals in this country said, "I believe in God and a profit."

I went to Dodgertown ostensibly to see the opening game of the spring season between the Dodgers and a team from Korea called the Samsung Lions, one of six professional teams in a league that was entering its fifth year of play. The Lions had come to Dodgertown, as the Tokyo Giants had on earlier occasions, to train with the Dodgers in warm weather (the Koreans, like the Japanese, begin spring training in the dead of winter, running hard in January but holding off on actual baseball drills till the weather warms to the twenties in February). I was mainly interested in seeing how totally different cultures could come together on either side of the single game of baseball, as though two sides of a mountain were two different worlds made single by the common ground of a ballpark at the top. I was not disappointed. The Koreans at work were extraordinary. They approached the game as though it were an extension of village life from the mists of history. They worked communally and relentlessly, from dawn till dusk, with meetings lasting into the late night. The Lions' most celebrated player, Lee Man Soo, league MVP in 1983 and Triple Crown Winner in 1984, regularly began his day at 6 A.M. by taking two hundred swings.

Lovers of irony, too, would have appreciated the Koreans' attitude toward the Japanese who had come to Korea to play. It was roughly equivalent to the common Japanese complaint about American ballplayers playing in Japan. "The Japanese have a hard time adjusting," I was told through an interpreter. "They don't speak the language and they have a problem with food. Korean food, as you know, is hot and spicy, and they basically eat rice and bean-paste soup. But they can afford to buy Japanese food in Korea. They have their own schools, they can afford to hire a maid and have a chauffeur. They are very fortunate to be in Korea. They have nothing to complain about. Unfortunately, the Koreans can't do this."

Korean food was also a topic of discussion among the surprisingly many Korean-American fans who came to Holman Stadium to cheer their team on. In fact, word of the Koreans' Florida engagement with the Dodgers had been spread largely by the proprieters of a Korean grocery store in Melbourne, forty miles to the north of Dodgertown. It seemed that the Lions' team, homesick and languishing on the blandness of American food, ventured to this spot in Melbourne to search out some fellowship along with the ingredients for *kimch'i*, a flamingly spicy national dish. The Melbournians turned out in numbers, as did other Korean-Americans from across the state who had been alerted by the regional Korean-American associations.

"They were very happy to find us," Jae Noe, the 16-year-old son of the Melbourne proprietor, told me. "They asked us to come down and cheer them on. One of them bought some toys for his children, another one wanted breath freshener, you know, a spray, because *kimch'i* is very smelly and they were embarrassed being around Americans."

Jung Su Yang, an expatriate of fifteen years, along with a friend of his from Taegu, their old hometown, had come to see Lee Man Soo and other Taeguians on the Lions, players who, these gentlemen said, had actually been classmates of theirs once, friends they had played with and had completely forgotten about till the Lions' visit to Dodgertown.

The Dodgers, amid the festivities of an internationally flavored opening-day ceremony, beat the Koreans easily. Jerry Reuss pitched the first innings of a 7–0 game and also hit a two-run opposite-field home run, observed without comment by the new commissioner, Peter Ueberroth, who was then still carrying on the fiction of determining whether or not the designated hitter rule should be retained or abolished.

But by far the main attraction of the day took place beyond the natural grass-bank fences of Holman Stadium. Dodgertown, like Tigertown, was a converted World War II air base. But where Tigertown was strictly blue-color, Dodgertown really was another one of those Sunbelt fantasy extravaganzas. As you turn into the place from outside, signs lead you this way and that to the Dodger Pines Country Club, to the Dodgertown Landscaping and Nursery Center, to swimming pools, golf courses, conference centers, villas, practice fields with more facilities than are dreamed of in the philosophies of sporting goods companies, to theater and recreation facilities and to a dining room that is in reality a four-state restaurant and that, to any passing media person with a pass, will be glad to serve lobster or pheasant under glass for lunch—gratis. It is hard, nearly impossible, to imagine, when driving or walking along Sandy Koufax Lane or Walter Alston Drive or Jackie Robinson Avenue, that the roots of this place really do *not* go back to the brainstem of Walt Disney. Behind the facade of baseball paradise lie not one but two wars. The first was actual, the other social. Dodgertown came into being in 1948 principally to provide a training facility free from segregation.

"Dodgertown was originally the Vero Beach Naval Air Station," Roy Campanella told me. He knew Dodgertown as the young ad writers who sanforized the Disney prose for all Dodgertown literature would never know it. "And it was very interesting—a two-story barracks, not what you see today. We came here in '48, the first year of Dodgertown. Mr. O'Malley made special arrangements for Jackie and me and the other black players to get around to the different cities where we played. But staying here in Dodgertown, and living here, we were able to eat with our teammates, stay with our teammates, always be together."

Campy's age and his paralysis of nearly three decades disguise what a wonderful and special player he was. There will always be the picture of him in the baseball histories leaping upon Johnny Podres after the final out of the 1955 World Series. But unless you had actually seen him play, there is scant record of the special everyday image of the man standing at the plate, as round as he was tall, pumping his bat windmill fashion toward the pitcher; nor will you see the myriad of little strategies of communication that do not show up in box scores but that held together a gorgeously tragic pitching staff. He was, when be broke in, a different sort, and so he remains today. "I may not walk," he said in his soft, faraway voice, "but I haven't forgot how to hit or play baseball." Campy, after all these years, remains very much a man of the present, a spring-training coach and adviser to current Dodger catchers.

"To tell you the truth, the business of being one of the first black ballplayers was fine with me," Campanella remembered. "All I wanted to do was what I did, which was to get the opportunity to play in the major leagues. And I was not going to let anything get in my way. The slurs and remarks didn't bother me a bit. As they say in baseball, I didn't have rabbit ears. I was concentrating on what I was doing."

His first year in Dodgertown was especially memorable. Jackie Robinson had broken in the year before, but because the Dodgers did not place him on the major-league roster until the day before the season began, spring training that year was uneventful. Not so in 1948. The incidents—including death threats—were there from the start. "It was all right when we were in Dodgertown but it was difficult when we went out from here," Campy said. I asked him about a gun threat that had been reported that spring. "I remember it," he said. "There was a weekend series in Atlanta. Atlanta was in the Southern Association then. There was a telegram to Jackie and me from the Ku Klux Klan, saying that if we came to Atlanta we were going to be killed. Now the FBI was with us when we finally went to Atlanta, and we had received a wire from the NAACP to please come, do not be disturbed by the threats. We met Dr. Martin Luther King then for the first time. We had dinner at his home and we stayed at a black hotel and I think Jackie and I had the best series you could imagine. But anyway, when we got out on the ballfield, Jackie was at second base, of course, and I was catching. Now all the black people were sitting behind the fences in the outfield because there was segregation then. So Jackie started in teasing me, sayin', 'I'm closer to the black folks if anything happens. If they start gunning for us, I'm gonna run right out to center field; you're behind home plate—you have a much longer way to get to center field.' He laughed about it. But nothing happened, and we swept the Crackers that weekend. We won all the games."

Campanella's view of the game in 1985 is very much bound up with his gratitude to the Dodgers and to the O'Malley family for first giving him the opportunity to play and then never abandoning him when his playing days were done. He lives in Los Angeles now, represents the Dodgers in a variety of capacities throughout the year, and probably comes closer to bleeding Dodger blue than certain well-advertised Dodger blood donors. But Campy has something to offer the game today that goes well beyond his days as a Dodger or as a pioneer. It is experience, growing out of his having lived through one of the most tumultuous eras in the game's—and the nation's—history. It affects everything he sees today, including spring training.

"I played in the Negro National League for the Baltimore Elite Giants," He reminded me, "and going to spring training with the Elite Giants there was just no comparison with a big-league club. You started playing games practically from the first day of spring training. And number one, you didn't have any training facilities or trainer or training room. We didn't do any fancy exercising. We would have to run and run and run. There were no machines to help you condition yourself, there was no whirlpool. And I always, as a result, believed in this: that the more you ran, the better your body would be. That, and playing baseball every day. See, I never did get hurt. We never even heard of disabled lists. If you were out, somebody behind you would take your position. We usually trained in Nashville, Tennessee. Sometimes New Orleans. The owner of the Elite Giants,

Tom Wilson, his house was in Nashville and he had a ballpark in Nashville. We started training the same time as the big-league clubs and we played anybody, including semipro teams. We traveled by bus and lived in black hotels and sometimes would go three, four, five hundred miles a day for an exhibition. We'd play in Nashville one day, Memphis the next, down into Mississippi the next. Don't worry, they scheduled us so that we were active every single day."

I met Campanella this one spring day over lunch in the Dodger dining room. He was with his wife, and he sat in his motorized wheelchair. In a while, he would drive himself to the practice field and then to Holman Stadium for the game with the Lions. He would move along walks and ramps that had over the years been unobtrusively altered to ease his comings and goings; he would move in and out of rooms and areas that bore his name, among people who knew him when he played and among those who were not yet conceived when the 1958 car crash robbed him of his body. He yet defined—by his still undiminished presence—what it was to be a man of baseball. He was in Verso Beach not because his name was a decoration but because his word was still valued. Dodger management believed he could help their talented young catcher, Mike Scioscia. So did Campy. "There are things you can point out," he said, "like how you block the plate or the way you communicate with a pitcher that come from experience. You don't need a body for that," he added with a smile that reached beyond the years, beyond suffering.

In Tigertown, 150 miles to the west, the exhibition opener was between the Tigers and the Red Sox, the champs and—said some, including Sparky—their most likely challenger in the American League East. None of the international gilding attended upon this opening, but it had its own distinctly Central Florida flavor. "Welcome to the center of citrus country," declared the mayor of Lakeland to the capacity crowd. The occasion, aside from the World Champions' opening spring game, was the centennial of the town. The mayor and the president of the chamber of commerce gave their speeches. The late illustrious Joker Marchant was recalled. On the day the stadium that bore his name officially opened he, the genie of the place, with strong voice and clear eye, tongue invisible in his cheek, ordered each and every one of the 6,194 paying customers to make sure they took home all their peanut shells as historic souvenirs.

The small, single-decked concrete stadium filled to capacity was as picturesque as any Norman Rockwell country setting. Down the left-field line, behind a low chain-link fence, there was a grass bank filled with people on blankets, with picnic baskets, beach chairs, radios. Far beyond the right-field fence, plainly visible, were the minor-league practice fields and then a large, picturesque lake marred only by a huge power plant—a compromise with nature and beauty that old Joker had been powerless to stop by jest or legislation. The crowd rose to its feet for the national anthem, and everyone there seemed to join in its singing. A gentleman in the press box made sure that the hats of all working media were properly removed.

The most attractive feature of the day's game was the sense of anticipation and eagerness it generated. The players, knowing the game was the earliest of a slate of games that did not count, approached the opening moment as though it really meant something. "I always feel this way for every opener, whether it's down here, up there, or anywhere—you can't help it," Dwight Evans said. "I'm nervous before every game," Alan Trammel said, "it's exciting. The day it isn't is the day you hang it up."

The home side's crowd had barely finished singing the anthem when the Red Sox put two runs on the board thanks to an error, a passed ball, a double by Tony Armas and a single by Mike Easler, who was cut down trying to stretch the hit by Kirk Gibson. The Tigers did not answer this opening flurry nor did the Red Sox have anything more to offer against the oddly off-speed

pitching of Jack Morris, who was apparently using the occasion
to work on his straight change to the point of distorting his usual
championship season style. In the 4th innning, the crowd, enjoying the cloudless 80-degree weather no matter what, had something to cheer about. It was one of those spring moments. Lance
Parrish homered. This was, given Parrish's long-ball habit in far
more meaningful situations, not unusual. But each spring training at-bat by a commanding player offers a chance to isolate
what it is he does, how he does it. You have time to appreciate—
and to see. Parrish, of course, is big. His six-foot-three-inch,
220-pound frame, solidly and thickly muscled, gives him the obvious look of a home run hitter. But what I most noticed in this
at-bat was, curiously, his uniform. Unlike most players, Parrish
wore his knickertops at his knees. The stirrups of his socks were
low and conservative-looking, and far more blue than white
showed. I wondered if this was merely Sparky's influence, a
holdover from his days with the Big Red Machine when high
stirrups and long hair were regarded as an affront to the flag.
Then I noticed something else. It was hard to throw this man a
low strike. Parrish, in fact, homered off a pitch that was on the
outside part of the plate but was belt-high. With his great power,
he had no trouble steering the ball around toward left field,
while at the same time *keeping it in the air.* Conclusion? Lance
Parrish may or may not be the Republican National Committee
in baseball flannels, but he surely is helped in rearranging the
strike zone by the arrangement of his britches.

Tiger substitutes scored another run in the 7th inning while
Tiger regulars, stripped to their uniform undershirts, did wind-
sprints in the outfield. At the time, the run tied the game. The
crowd clapped and cheered, but there were yachts beyond the
outfield fence. The Red Sox, with their substitutes, scored a run
in the 8th and won the game. Mark Clear, the Red Sox Jekyll-
and-Hyde reliever, staggered through the 8th but pitched effec-
tively in the 9th. Beyond the right-field wall, the secondary
diamonds were filled with players. Out on the lake, a seaplane

was practicing takeoffs and landings. It hardly seemed to matter that the Tiger pitcher in the top of the 9th was Willie Hernandez. Or that Lou Whitaker was replaced in the 6th inning by an unknown rookie, Chris Pittaro.

Two weeks later, I watched a game at Tigertown between the Tigers and Dodgers. The champions also lost this one, again by one run, 8–7. The tempo and the mood of this game were different, however. Between the early and late games of the exhibition season, the machinery is slowly tightened, the springs and levers given torque and tension by the pressures of the nearing season. This is a subtle rather than a dramatic process but as nearly all baseball people will tell you, the ten games or so before the opening of the real season are the test.

Through the first two innings of the game, it appeared that the outcome would be dominated by the starting pitchers, Jerry Reuss and Dan Petry. Having seen Reuss for a few innings against the Samsung Lions, he looked superb once again in striking out the side in the opening inning. Dan Petry was shakier, yielding a run on a couple of hits in the 1st, but he gradually worked his way toward effectiveness by the 3rd inning. In the Tiger half of the third, the game suddenly and dramatically shifted. Reuss, who had seemed to be throwing so easily, gave up a couple of hits, walked three batters, surrendered yet another hit and left the mound at inning's end with five runs scored. Petry in the very next inning gave up four runs. By the 6th inning, the starters were gone—having both, in their ineffectiveness, fulfilled the perhaps more important spring requirement of sufficient pitches thrown. Willie Hernandez pitched two closing, scoreless innings in this game. The Tigers rallied in the bottom of the ninth with a single run but it was not enough. Once again, the rookie Pittaro replaced Whitaker at second, but this time the move turned out to be significant. Later in the day, Sparky announced that Whitaker would be permanently moved to third base to make room at second for Pittaro. A .280 hitter in Double A the previous year, Pittaro—for the next four days, at any rate—became the man who broke up the game's most successful middle infield combination. Within the week, however, Sparky shelved the decision he had said "would not be an experiment for a day or two." Conclusion? Sparky's pipe, while he would never treat it like the one Captain Ahab pitched into the sea, was no symbol of serenity after all. This little seriocomic roster move, more than anything else I saw in Lakeland, roused the suspicion that the Tigers were mortal enough to go the way of other recent champions and fall back into the hungry pack of "Baseball's Best Division."

Nevertheless, only a fool, a seer, or the baseball equivalent of Scrooge would have looked meanly upon this Tiger team in the spring of 1985. "We've got more superstars on this club than the Yankees have on theirs," Bill Freehan, the ex-Tiger catcher said. "The problem is our guys play in Detroit and not in New York. That's a media thing. I mean, Alan Trammell is the best shortstop in Tiger history. Lou Whitaker is simply outstanding. We've got three gold gloves guys, and Chet Lemon should have been a fourth. Gibson may be one of *the* most exciting guys in baseball. You put those guys in New York and you have a whole flock of superstars. We just don't pay them two million dollars a year—yet. How about Dan Petry, Jack Morris, and Willie Hernandez? They're not superstars? Look what they've done since '79. Jack Morris has won more games than any other right-handed pitcher in the game in the last decade. Only people who don't know baseball will say this is a team without superstars."

Was Willie Hernandez a fluke? He does not talk about his amazing 1984 record, in which he saved thirty-two games in thirty-three save situations. Rather, he recalls how his out-pitch, the screwball, was acquired only in 1983, when he learned it from Mike Cuellar playing catch in Puerto Rico. There is nothing accidental about Hernandez and the art of the save. "When the game's over," he said, his disturbingly atypical gray eyes staring at nothing in particular, "I leave everything right there. For years I learned what kind of mistakes I made, but now I can't afford to make too many mistakes. I make them, I remember them, and I leave them behind in the ninth inning. I lay down and meditate before a game. I go blank and think a little bit about game situations, how to handle it. Because if I'm going to pitch to a left-handed hitter and they're going to change to a right-handed batter, I want to really concentrate on knowing who that right-handed hitter will be in that spot. I put a towel on my face in the training room and I lie there concentrating."

It is the work habits and not the words of these Tigers, however, that leave the most lasting impression. Despite what happened to them in the season that followed, their principal blessing was not a championship flag flying over Tiger Stadium in 1985 but the way they had learned to take on the game. Their brand of professionalism, as they headed into the new season, was a delicate balance between hard labor and pure joy. Every morning, hours before the day's exhibition, the Tigers played what they called their "morning game." This consisted of two pitchers, four batters, and a host of fielders going through a simulated game in which all of the players, under game conditions, would perform. It enabled hitters to accumulate over two hundred extra at-bats before the opening of the season; it gave pitchers, particularly those who where not in the rotation, additional needed innings of work and fielders a chance to work on fundamentals under game conditions.

Each day, as well, Sparky took his pitchers to the outfield and played another sort of game with them. The pitchers gathered in left center field, ran toward Sparky, who was standing alone in right center, flipped a ball to him as they went past, and then went out as if for a touchdown pass, which enabled Captain Hook to keep his throwing arm in shape and the boys happy in making a game out of the labor of running. Unlike the Red Sox Easter egg roll, this one was simple, pleasurable, and efficient— even if it did leave Sparky in a bit of a sweat afterward.

I was also fortunate to have a spy on the premises. Not everyone who makes a business of seeing the game can count on such a resource, but during my stay in central Florida luck was with me. Diane Yost, groundskeeper extraordinaire, reported to me regularly in the shadows and eaves of Joker Marchant. "I watched Mr. Muffett [the new Tiger pitching coach] today. He is such a responsible man," she informed me one afternoon, "he stayed behind long after everyone went to make sure the dirt on the mound was filled in correctly." This seemingly gratuitous bit of information led me to wonder what loss, if any, the team might have suffered when Roger Craig, the former pitching coach (credited by many for the success of the Tiger staff in 1984), resigned his post. Thanks to Ms. Yost and Billy Muffett himself, an intimate of Craig's, a believer along with Ray Miller in the efficacy of changing speeds, and a man obviously skilled in understanding both pitching mechanics and human beings, I concluded—prematurely perhaps—that Tiger pitching, even if the forkball (a "slip" pitch which always carried with it the risk of arm injury) was not regularly invoked, would not rise or fall with the change of pitching coaches.

Ms. Yost was not a baseball fan. She was utterly uncontaminated by partisanship of any sort. She was the kind of innocent you hope for in a pastoral, honestly believing in the evidence of her own eyes. She wondered why there weren't more black players on the field or black fans in the grandstand; she noted an absence of both young people (they were out working) and old people (management made no provision to accommodate them) at the ballpark. She believed "baseball was a good fair game." She said she "watched how they think on plays, how they slide, how they listen to the first base coach. I can see," she added, "when the guy on first isn't listening, he'll be daydreaming or something—you can pick that up—you can see that he should have been farther off the base or that he didn't see a signal. . . . I can see where a lot even have to learn how to run."

But above all, because she was there every day, she kept a steady eye on the Detroit Tigers and she liked what she saw. "All of these players work hard. The younger ones, some of them, are louder than the older ones, but they all work very hard, they are all very much into what they're doing. They're very well composed whether they win or lose. A couple of years ago, somebody tore up a water cooler—but not this team. I think I like Chet Lemon best," she said, pausing to think it out. "Yes. He gives his whole body all the time, he runs on everything. And I'll tell you something else. I watch from the other side of the wall and I see that both teams, the Tigers and their opponents, converse, that a lot of them are buddy-buddy—and that," she said, unaware of league rules that prohibit fraternization, "shows good sportsmanship."

The Red Sox camp was also noticeably free of tension when the games began, and seemed to remain that way as the weeks passed. The team won and lost with no particular urgency. No conclusions would be drawn about any of the pitchers, John McNamara told the media, until they'd had at least three outings, and the hitters, as everyone knew, were a proven commodity no matter what they did in Florida. There was concern for one of the team's young pitchers, Al Nipper, who turned up a case of ulcers that was at first thought to be leukemia. McNamara's hope was that the young staff would come around and that the bullpen would improve. The previous year, none of the young pitchers had more than twelve starts, and the bullpen tandem of Stanley and Clear had been off. Nothing new. Red Sox hopes since 1918 were always that the pitching would somehow come around.

What set the tone for these games, which seemed to move back and forth between victory and defeat with the slow and impartial beat of a metronome, was the postgame press conference, which was, apparently, a regular feature of camp life at Winter Haven. These conferences were somber, quiet affairs—in victory or defeat—silence reigning in the room until manager McNamara entered the room and sat down at one of the com-

missary tables with the writers. Invariably, an additional length
of time passed before someone broke the silence with a question.
Something like: "What did you think of Kison today?" Answer:
"Kison had no rhythm today. He feels all right, though. [Long
pause.] Brown and Clear threw well. [Longer pause.] Fuson
threw well." That particular exchange took place on the day of a
defeat. On a victorious afternoon, however, there was the same
sense of lugubriousness and deep silence—punctuated by rou-
sers like: "Rice swung the bat pretty good today. [Long pause.]
He wants to get at least two at-bats from now on. [Longer
pause.] Boyd threw well."

It was hard to tell just what it was that made MacNamara so
unhappy. Perhaps it was something simple like knowing that
when the regular season came, he would have to go with one or
two pitchers who every two or three days would send him running for the Pepto-Bismol; or perhaps it was something even
simpler like not wanting to go through these ritual press conferences that had been established in the days of an earlier regime.
Whatever, dropping in on one of these get-togethers was a little
like being an interloper in a consultation room when someone
has gotten the bad news. The desire to get out of there and allow
the family to grieve in private was overwhelming. The only
problem was that the mood of these meetings seemed to be on
the field when the Red Sox played.

Nowhere was this more apparent than when the Yankees
came to town. Over the years, this northeastern rivalry was one
of the most intense in sports, a contrast in different life-styles,
culture, history, and world outlook, good for madness and menace whenever and wherever the teams met. No longer. Even the
presence of George Steinbrenner, sitting behind the dugout at
third base, could not convert what took place on the field to the
semblance of lifelikeness. As though the heavens themselves
were indifferent to Steinbrenner and his ministrations to make
things crucial, a 7th-inning rain drove him from his box and the
premises. The Yankees won the first of two successive games,

9–6. A six-run Yankee 2nd inning, featuring several infield hits, and a five-run Red Sox rally in the 3rd highlighted by a home run by Mike Easler should normally have lent excitement to this game. It did not. On the field and in the stands, it was just another day's outing. Years ago, the follies of the Producer on one side and of Sullivan and Leroux (occasionally referred to as Dumwood and Shoddy by the regulars in the commissary) on the other, had removed all menace and life from the Great Rivalry. On this Saint Patrick's Day, the event of the game was a half-slide by Rickey Henderson into third base, in which he nearly broke his ankle.

The Yankees won the next day's game as well, 2–1. This, too, was a game that had its moments and that might, in earlier years, have produced a genuine round or two of bragging rights. In contrast to the previous day's game, this one featured strong pitching by Bobby Ojeda and Dennis Rasmussen. Both left the game by the middle innings with the score tied at one. The Yankees' decisive run came in the 8th inning on an opposite-field home run by the normally weak-hitting Andre Robertson. But there seemed to be neither dismay nor joy in the stands or among the players. For me, there were individually absorbing moments in the game: a single by Dwight Evans lined slightly to the right of second base into center field—disciplined hitting at its best; Dennis Rasmussen striking out Bill Buckner and Mike Easler in succession; Sam Horn, a young, enormously gifted power hitter with no chance of winning a place on the current Red Sox team, making a late-inning appearance at first base.

Beyond the left-field fence was the orange dome of the Florida Citrus Grower's Association. Beyond the right-field fence, where once a beautiful stand of dark evergreen trees stood, a condo complex rose on land once owned by the Red Sox. It was as though the team itself was hemmed in, narrowed to ever smaller zones of play. The Red Sox clubhouse, from what I could tell, was a quiet but not an easy place. One day, a young and perfectly polite reporter doing a magazine piece on baseball gloves incurred the wrath of Jim Rice, who had the fellow ejected from the clubhouse under a hail of oaths. It was hard to tell what Rice was thinking, except that later, in reviewing his team's prospects for the coming season, there was an obvious edge about him:

"The season hasn't started yet," he said, "you can still trade. You can't say, because you still have trading deadlines. Rupert Jones was released by Pittsburgh last year—all of a sudden he comes up with Detroit—so I can't say what we're going to do. A key guy may get injured. Jerry had an operation last year, Stapleton had an operation last year—we missed a lot of guys, so you can't say and I'm not going to put myself in a position like that. I don't know who's going to be released, who we might get in a trade—we've got 162 games to worry about."

Over the years, Rice has labored under the Boston area's not-so-invisible cloud of poisoned race relations. En route to his record two-million-plus-dollars-a-year long-term contract with the club, he was the subject of a *Sport* magazine article (which he disowned), criticizing the team's and the city's racial attitudes, attitudes that many people other than Rice believe were somehow bound up with the team's willingness to trade players such as Earl Wilson, Reggie Smith, and Cecil Cooper—black players who had not reached their potential with the Red Sox but who went on to become stars elsewhere.

Rice acknowledges that it indeed matters to him that he is the left fielder in the line of succession from Ted Williams and Carl Yastrzemski. "You can say that is part of why I signed," he said, "because I've been in this organization for fifteen years and I just wanted to stay in it." But if there are scars, as *Globe* writer Larry Whiteside believes, for having endured and triumphed over the system in Boston, it has driven Rice more deeply within himself, to a point of even greater concentration upon what he does on the field. "He came to me at one point and said he wanted to go on a weight program," trainer Charley Moss told me. "I told him with his strength he didn't need to and I asked him why he wanted to. He said because he wanted to hit sixty home runs."

One of the few players on the team to whom Rice has reached out is Oil Can Boyd. (Later in the season that followed, their friendship flew apart in an ugly but well-reported confrontation in the Boston clubhouse.) Boyd is not only young, talented, black, and a pitcher—he is also irrepressible to the point of flamboyance. He is a storm of nervous energy. His enthusiasm and eccentricity in the quietude of the clubhouse must, at times, have seemed downright unsettling. Though he moved through the Red Sox minor-league system rapidly, he was not initially successful in the majors. He was sent back down in 1984 before being recalled permanently later in the year. His style, he said, made it hard for him. "I used to get a little sarcasm, things like 'You're afraid to be on time'—but I wasn't late. It was just a thing where the other guys were so uniform about bein' there at four o'clock in the evening on the days when they were goin' to pitch, you know, and I took it hard. 'Cause I said this is the way I gotta be on the day when I perform, when I pitch. I don't care how you gotta be on your day, you do anything you want to . . . but I wasn't gettin' them out, so I was accused of being flamboyant."

Fellow pitcher Bob Stanley and Rice alone among his teammates took Boyd in tow long before winning in the big leagues smoothed his way. "Jim and Bob respect you and understand you," he said. "Jim would take me into the outfield and say, 'Do the job you have to do, and then do anything you want. If you don't do the job, it doesn't matter anyway—that goes for everybody.' . . . Bobby's around me all the time, he knows me as good as any pitcher on the staff, he takes time out to talk to me, B.S. around with me, the whole thing."

Success has enabled Boyd to become the movable feast he really is. The media regularly seek him out, and he usually obliges them with an improvisational and original élan, which they love. Boyd pumps his fist in the air when he records a strikeout, congratulates fielders on good defensive plays, talks to himself on the mound regularly and loudly enough to seem somehow that he is a black reincarnation of Mark "The Bird" Fidrych. This he is not, nor is he, as the media have sometimes suggested, another Satchel Paige. He is, it is true, skinny and eminently quotable, but he is a duplicate of no one. Here he is on the question of the DH (Boyd apparently feels personally done in by its use in the American League):

"I can hit and I can run. I led off in college my freshman year. I know what it's like to put the ball on the bat and run and drag, turn double plays, and break 'em up—you know, I love base-ball. Fuck, I still feel like I can go out there and pitch nine in-nings and still stay in the ballgame because if he asks me to move a runner over I can hit it to right field. I can feel what a guy's gonna throw me . . . just by bein' a pitcher you have that in-stinct. I wanna show 'em in the spring I can slug, oh yeah. When I go home after the year, all I do is swing the bat—I get with my brothers and we go s-l-u-g! That's how I get in shape. Other guys go home and lift weights and do Nautilus, I stay at the ballpark all day, runnin' and throwin' and shaggin', and sluggin'. It's hot in Mississippi. I played ball on Christmas Day, they had to come to take me home to the tree. Thanksgiving, too. I'm too old to play with toys, but I ain't too old to play the game. Yeah, every-body else, snow in the North, down here my friends and I live it up and go to the ballpark and just hit. I miss it. Yeah. I miss it."

But this whirlwind of energy, which seems to compensate for the missing pounds on his frame, is misunderstood if it is some-how seen apart from how he "performs," what it is he puts into his game. On the day he pitches, he works himself into a jittery, almost nasty frenzy. He will get into arguments with his fiancée or a friend or a fellow player or a clubhouse attendant. If no one will argue with him, he will take out his shoes and get angry in polishing them. This energy, which seems so flamboyant and attention-grabbing, is, in reality, neither. It is what has enabled him to triumph over the system where others might have fallen by the wayside.

"I was a bit scared in the minor leagues," he said, "because I heard about the organization being racial, but then as time passed and the managers and I talked about that and what it was like, they would say, 'When you can throw the ball like you can, you're gonna be able to play anywhere.' That took it away right there. My talent. Goin' out there and doin' my job—I can play as good as anybody, and I got to play somewhere. Some of the black ballplayers in the minor leagues, they say they experienced discrimination, but I didn't in the Red Sox organization. The players said, 'Well, the city is racial.' And I said it might be, but I haven't experienced it . . . see, I grew up in a racial atmosphere. I was born in Meridian, Mississippi. Where I came from, it was automatic. You know, to play here is really special for me. To pitch here. You know, I say, yeah, yeah, I'm really high on that. You better believe when I go out there I'm gonna be ready to do my job."

Oil Can Boyd did not make an appearance during the Yankee series. Instead he prowled around in the area off the right-field foul line among a group of players, reporters, sporting goods salesmen, and park attendants. For a while he had a bat in his hands, and from time to time he would pause, get into hitting position, and take a cut. Then he disappeared only to return later with an enormous glove. He pantomimed pitching with it. The glove covered the upper half of his body like a tent. You could see only his knees and elbows poking out from the huge blob of tan leather before he spun down into his follow-through. If it came to choosing between what was taking place on the field and off, there was no contest.

At a display set up by Mizuno, the sporting goods company, salesmen were running a demonstration of some sort of miracle padding for mitts. Every half hour or so, as though they had the shell-game concession at a country circus, they arranged these two slabs of glass—one covered with ordinary padding, the other with the new magic stuffing. Then, pressing a couple of buttons, they released baseballs that crashed against them at high speeds. Invariably, shattered glass lay behind one panel, intact baby smoothness behind the other. It was a good show.

When I watched it, Yankee pitcher Joe Cowley fell for it as though he had been watching Mark Twain's Royal Nonesuch. The black glove Cowley wears today is Magicstuff or Permashock or whatever they were selling that day.

The nearest thing to a spy I turned up in the Red Sox camp was another innocent, the ballpark organist. This chap bore an uncanny resemblance to Ringo Starr (he didn't see it, he said the look was more Tony Orlando), was a Winter Haven resident, and had for years—till he was let go—been the regular organist for an establishment called J. Riley's Pizza and Pipes. He was fired, he said, because management, well aware of the median age of their clientele, wanted something more up-to-date than thirties and forties Wurlitzer theater organ music. For the Red Sox, however, this was just fine. And so for these few weeks of spring training, before he went back to his year-round work delivering pizzas for a rival firm, he played for spring-training crowds in Winter Haven.

"It was kind of funny how I got this job," he told me. "I was told the Red Sox were looking for an organist and I was given a name to call at the Holiday Inn. Well, I called this guy and said, 'I hear you're looking for someone to play for you.' He must have thought I was crazy, that I was a pitcher looking for a tryout on the field or something, until I explained. Then he said, 'Oh yes, yes, yes, come down and play for us.' I did, and this is now my fourth season behind home plate. I have aspirations of someday going out to California and working for the Yamaha corporation as a traveling artist."

The organist—Tom Hoehn—kept things going. Red Sox management wanted everything he played to be upbeat and with a beat—but only before and after the games and between innings, in keeping with the team's traditional family image. This was all right with Hoehn, whose eighteen years of study on theater organ had left him with little taste for music any flashier than Glenn Miller or Tommy Dorsey. "I always play Scott Joplin's 'Organ Rag,'" he said. "I usually open with that shortly before one o'clock. I do 'Twelfth Street Rag' and 'Tico, Tico' quite a bit and, of course, 'Take Me Out to the Ballgame.'"

In fact, Hoehn's inclinations ran according to weather conditions. The colder the weather, the faster the beat; slow hands and pedals all the way around for stickier days. None of it, however, had much to do with what was going on on the field. Though he was perfectly cheerful—and grateful—in performing his work, Red Sox baseball simply did not catch his fancy. Once he was an organist for the Tampa Bay Rowdies. He knew nothing about soccer, but the Rowdies ignited his passions. "I played through the whole game in this air-conditioned, glassed-in room where the mike picked up every single sound. If I was to sneeze you'd hear it over the whole stadium and the north side of Tampa. And I got so excited one day, I yelled at Rodney Marsh, 'Come on, get your ass in gear! Get your ass in gear!' Next thing I knew there was a knock on the door. Management. That was it."

Hoehn played from his perch in Chain O'Lakes Park, worn souvenir Red Sox cap sitting incongruously on his mop of dark, long hair, a cigarette dangling from the corner of his mouth, his Ringo Starr mustache drooping. For forty-five seconds between innings, people beat their feet along with him, and then the music and the foot stomping stopped. The people in the grandstand turned their attention back toward Red Sox baseball. Hoehn usually turned his back and headed for the catwalks or refreshment booths behind the stands.

"Oh, I like baseball all right," he explained, "but I think I liked it better a few years ago." The Red Sox, he assured me, were okay, but they were really a little old-fashioned. Chicago was more his style. He was talking about the musical group, which reminded him of Glenn Miller.

The Toronto Blue Jays, though no one was quite willing to say it, played their spring games as though they were interested in winning them. "Oh, yes," Jesse Barfield said, after the Blue Jays compiled the best spring record in the majors, "when you take the field, you take the field to win. Winning in the spring can give you a winning attitude going into the season. I'll admit it. We were out there trying to win." The Blue Jays, for the first time in their history, turned up in Florida with a good portion of the national media picking them as favorites in the American League East.

When they appeared in Kissimmee for a game against the Astros in mid-March, they might have been any team that had made a three-hour bus trip in order to complete an afternoon's work. Only a portion of the squad had come. They straggled across the field carrying their equipment bags, lingering to talk with players on the Astros they may not have seen for a while. The center of attention for the Jays, as well as for fans and media visiting Kissimmee, seemed to be Dickie Thon, the Astro shortstop who was trying to make a comeback from a beaning injury that nearly cost him the use of one eye. Each day, Thon patiently held court with writers, answering the same questions again and again—that he had good days and bad days, that he had been working out for six months now, and that, yes, even though it had been slow, there had been improvement. He was doing only what other players were doing now, taking ground balls and hitting—and playing exhibition games. So far, so good.

But to the Blue Jay players who chatted with him in his native Spanish, the answers were somewhat different. He still was not able to pick up the spin of the ball. He could see it but he couldn't see the spin. There was, if you listened closely enough, the kind of shared concern in the players' language that went beyond the game itself. These players in the rival uniforms, perhaps better than anyone, could understand just what measure of life's opportunity was riding on Thon's recovery. Over near the dugout, Astro manager Bob Lillis explained that Thon, healthy, "was the engine that made us go: he lifted everyone; when we were out of a ballgame, he could get us going; when we were in a tight game, he could hit one out or bring home the key run." He sounded more like a concerned relative than Thon's manager.

The Jays' lineup that day was filled with reserves, so it was almost impossible to make sense of manager Bobby Cox's assertion that the biggest thing he was trying to accomplish during the spring campaign was "to get my guys to come out with confidence." Winning the game really did not seem to be a priority.

For a few innings the game proceeded in desultory fashion. Luis Leal at the outset of his afternoon's work seemed strong. Normally, the first pitches thrown don't, by themselves, touch the spine of tension that secretly runs through every game. But Dickie Thon was the Astros' first batter, and so Leal's pitches to him had the quality of framing a small, self-enclosed drama. Thon grounded routinely to shortstop. In Thon's next time at bat, Leal got two strikes on him, came in tight with a pitch, and then, in a thirty-two-vertebrae head-and-body fake reminiscent of Luis Tiant, buzzed a third strike past him. There were some in the stands who thought unfair advantage had been taken. It was not so. Leal, genuinely warmhearted and as understanding of Thon as anyone off the field, had dueled with him as professional pitcher to professional batter, a gesture of respect. The Tiant fake, for Leal, was something he needed to sharpen in a repertoire that was not yet complete enough to guarantee continued major-league employment. "I don't do it too much," he explained afterward, "just sometimes. So they won't know what pitch I'm throwing, fastball or, sometimes, hard slider. When I saw Tiant have that success, I'm pitching like that after I saw him."

Thon remained in the game long enough to drive a run-scoring double into the left-field corner, a hit typical of his pre-injury days, and one that tied the game at 2–2. The Jays moved back in front again when a reserve outfielder, Lou Thornton, homered in the sixth. Then, in the 7th inning, Bobby Cox brought Bill Caudill into the game. This was, to be sure, a routine move in a routine spring game. But no one who had followed the fortunes of the Blue Jays the year before could fail to understand the importance of Cox simply being able to make this move. Relief pitching, pure and simple—first-rate, nasty, unhittable relief pitching—more than anything else was the instrument that would enable the Blue Jays to leave camp with the confidence Cox hoped would carry them to a pennant. They had finished second to the Tigers in 1984, but, most important, their relief pitching was the worst in the American League. Fifteen times they had blown leads going into the 8th inning (the Tigers, by contrast, had surrendered three; the Brewers, with the second-worst record, lost ten 8th-inning leads). Caudill and Gary Lavelle were the missing pieces in the pennant puzzle that had taken so many years of patience and losing to piece together.

But on this afternoon, Caudill, in that briefly intense and curious spotlight typical of spring baseball, struggled through two late innings' work, yielding a pair of runs and a comfortable lead. The Jays held on to win, 5–4. It would have been foolhardy indeed to draw any sort of conclusion from this or any single game, but it provided just enough to force one back to the realization that baseball is, after all, a game of possibility, not certainty. And surely, one of the most intriguing possibilities over the years has been the one where free agents and big-trade players take to their big contracts in the manner of Faust signing on with the devil. I suspect that all baseball fans, whether or not they have ever articulated it, wonder if there isn't some heavenly antagonism at work in all this—to the point where some of the game's millionaires, as though their own subconscious demanded it, just have their arms go dead on them. In light of the non-season Caudill wound up having in '85, it is a notion hard to put to rest.

The very next day, the Jays returned to their spring home in Dunedin and a game against the Chicago White Sox. This game, too, was a close one, and one that, in the end, featured Toronto's newly acquired bullpen. If he had done it by actual design, Cox could not have more clearly demonstrated to his team what he had in mind when he talked about coming out of spring training with confidence. That afternoon the Jays had a taste of bona fide American League competition. Floyd Bannister worked the first four innings for the White Sox and looked very sharp. A 1st-inning run, manufactured by a walk and a robust double to the right-center-field fence by Greg Walker, held into the 4th inning, when the Jays tied the score on an RBI double by Jesse Barfield. In the 6th inning, with the White Sox having moved out in front by a single run, the Blue Jays showed a bit of what is probably the most overlooked aspect of their game—power. A single to left by Damaso Garcia was followed by consecutive home runs—one by Lloyd Moseby to right center field and then another, by George Bell, far over the fence in left, in the general direction of Moose Bay. By then, starter Jim Clancy, recovering from an appendectomy, had given way to two minor-league pitchers, who handed over a 4–2 save possibility to Gary Lavelle, the left-hander acquired over the winter from the San Francisco Giants. Lavelle, a soft-spoken, courteous man, possessor of a good fastball, better slider, and even more potent sense of mound savvy, disposed of the White Sox in order in the 9th, striking two of them out. It was just the sort of work first-rate relief specialists are expected to do, rendering routine what is actually fraught with danger and potential for misery.

I was curious, though by this time somewhat able to anticipate, what Lavelle's attitude toward his new team might be. He had no problem with the prevailing "no stars" climate in the clubhouse, because, he said, he had always been a team player, He did need the spring for work, of course, but what was equally important, what was special during the spring, was that there was time to become assimilated, to settle in and acquire the sense that he truly belonged. "These six weeks," he said, "are not just for my arm."

The dimensions and distractions of Grant Field, surely one of spring training's coziest stadia, promoted family feeling every-

where. Picnic tables were just beyond the grandstand, and La-
batt's and other signs of the north abounded; the separation of
field and spectators' areas was so minimal that it was not altogether clear where one began and the other ended. When the
national anthem was played, everyone—including some of the
Latin players—sang "O Canada."

And yet, though none of this seemed forced, it was perhaps a
little too easy to mistake the easy mood of togetherness—winning teams often provide that—for the carefully sculptured balance that this team really represented. Jim Clancy, the Jays'
starting pitcher for the afternoon, was, at 29, one of three original members of the expansion team. He is a quiet and sensitive
man with a penchant for the classical guitar, which he has
taught himself to play. He brings his instrument with him
throughout the season and will go off by himself before he
pitches to play it. Because it is classical music he plays, he is
reluctant to be heard within earshot of his teammates; it is a
solitary but satisfying activity for him, important for his preparation in pitching, but otherwise having little to do with the precise way in which he fits on the team.

As an original Blue Jay, he knew something important.
"When I was first drafted by Toronto in the expansion draft, it
was a big break for me," he said. "Losing was expected back
then, but that's changed slowly here to where we're now expected to win." Clancy, youthful but nevertheless senior in experience, approached his work with a sort of acquired mental
toughness that was both exemplary and mandatory in enduring
the vagrant fortunes of any championship season. "The way I
look at it," he told me, "a win and a loss are the same. An hour
or two after it's over, it's over. You can't go back to it. There's
nothing I—or anyone—can do about it."

Barfield, like many of the Blue Jays, was also a young veteran. A utility player for most of the four full seasons he spent
with the Blue Jays, he was the reason the team felt secure in
surrendering outfielder Dave Collins in the trade that brought

them Bill Caudill. In 1985 Barfield became the newest member of an outfield trio, all of whom were all born within sixteen days of each other in 1959. "I don't feel any pressure personally," he said, "for the simple fact that I know we have a good team and are capable of winning." Barfield's strength, apart from an ability to hit for distance and to throw with power and accuracy from right field, was that he had been in the Blue Jays' organization since he began as a pro in 1977. He knew something about his own ability and, just as important, something about the abilities of his teammates. "Oh, the pressure's there for the team, no doubt about it," he acknowledged. "Everybody feels it—and you've got to be able to deal with it. But we play well together, especially being as young as we are. The thing is, we learned how to lose together, and then we turned around and learned how to win together. People said we might have lost morale when we lost Collins and Griffin, but I don't think so. Because we're a young ballclub and we stick together and we have a few veterans who keep us glued together."

On the day of this particular spring game, Barfield was sick. He had had what he thought was food poisoning the night before and could easily have taken the day off. He chose not to. "It may sound foolish," he said, "but I know once you're up here you have to work hard to keep it. So I'm not gonna go home and go to bed, I'm gonna came out here and play. . . . I told myself from the start that I was gonna work that much harder in spring training. They showed a lot of confidence in me. They said, 'Here, this is yours,' and I'm gonna give them something in return."

Barfield had specific tasks to accomplish in the spring. He wanted to work on making an adjustment in his hitting that would allow him to have a somewhat shorter stroke. He had been accustomed to wrapping the bat almost behind his ear while waiting for a pitch. By dropping his hands slightly as the pitcher came forward to release the ball, he would set himself in a "launch position" in such a manner as to cut down the distance between the point where he started his swing and the point where he made contact with the ball. After trying and rejecting a number of changes in his stance, he settled finally on what seemed to be only the slightest of adjustments.

As well as holding down a regular outfield position, Barfield was also expected to provide much of the team's home run production that might have been lost with Cliff Johnson's departure to free agency (Johnson returned to the Jays in mid-season). He approached the double challenge as though he had been at it all along. "I've got a wife and two kids now," the 25-year-old veteran said, "and if I go oh for four, I don't take it out on them, that's for sure. But I'll tell you, a lot of guys go out there and say let the chips fall where they may. I don't take that kind of attitude either. I like to say I'll be the one to go out there and make the chips fall. I'm gonna go out there—like today—and push myself." There was not the least trace of cockiness or overconfidence in this. Just that blend of youth and experience that seemed to epitomize the entire team. It was as though in Barfield and his teammates, the Blue Jays had learned to successfully concoct, as centuries of alchemists had not, a single mixture of fire and ice.

I saw the Baltimore Orioles play both early and late. I was particularly intrigued to watch them in their spring games, because more than any other team in the American League East their fortunes in the coming campaign seemed to hang on question marks. I had seen them over the years and, like any fan, been more than impressed by their consistent success—to the point where I was surprised by their abrupt departure from significance in 1984. The Tigers had not only buried their opposition, they mandated coroners' reports on them. This was particularly true for the Orioles. Champions the year before, they had been unusually savaged. Old age seemed to catch them all at once. By the end of the 1984 campaign, they had let go three mainstays from the championship years: Jim Palmer, Ken Singleton, and

Al Bumbry. The farm system, which formerly had been able to provide replacements, was not able to this time, thus forcing the club to a seeming break with tradition in acquiring free agents over the winter. The pitching staff, long the bullion reserve of the organization, seemed suddenly to have been converted to questionable scrip. The time I had spent with the team in early camp had surely been eye-opening, but not to the point where I could say with any certainty that I had seen more than what the Orioles once were rather than what they had become.

I caught up with the O's one afternoon in Tampa, where they had come to play the Reds at Al Lang Field, an old and peeling single-deck ballpark not unlike Miami Stadium. This, I realized, was not the optimal occasion to view the Orioles. Not only were the Reds professional baseball's fountainhead organization, dating back to 1869, and the club longest in residence at one spring-training site (save for three war years, they had been in Tampa since 1931), but they were also the employers of Pete Rose. The gods might have deserted Cincinnati in the seventies, but the Reds, in 1984, had managed to sign Rose on once again. Rose originally signed with the Reds when Jesse Barfield was 9 months old. He won his first batting title when Barfield was 11. He collected his three thousandth hit and set a National League record by hitting in forty-four straight games before Barfield turned 21. Spending any time around him at all leaves the distinct impression that he may be there and playing after Barfield finally retires, sometime around the beginning of the twenty-first century.

Watching the Orioles and the Reds prepare for their game was actually instructive because, try as I might, I found it hard to resist observing a team on the one hand and an individual on the other. Cal Ripken, Jr., was surely a prime candidate to play his way into the record books, but it was hard to watch him independent of the things the Orioles did together. At the batting cage, Ripken was just one in a group of Oriole players whose turn it was to hit. In fielding practice, you noticed the way he moved and threw because there was an entire infield around him. At one point, I became engrossed in watching Ripken in a game of pepper, surely not one of baseball's feature attractions for spectators. But something was different here.

Ripken's teammates did what most pepper hitters do—they lightly tapped down at the balls thrown toward them, hitting one-hoppers back to the other players. Ripken did not hit down on the ball. He tried to keep his stroke level and to line the ball directly back to his teammates.

In the way the Orioles played pepper, this was risky. The group good-naturedly played for points among themselves. Each batter picked up a single point when he successfully bounced a ball back to a fielder. He got two points for hitting a catchable ball on the fly. He was automatically out, however, if a ball hit on the fly went past or over the head of a fielder. Bat control being as difficult as it was, the hitter of bounders had a decided advantage.

In his turns, however, Ripken, who easily won the pepper sets, hit drive after drive straight into the fielders' gloves. Two points, two points, two points—the hitting followed in machine-gun fashion until the skill of what he was doing became apparent. Of course he was having fun, he said, but he acknowledged that he used the exercise to work on bat control, to work in that traditional Oriole slow-motion way, for the feel of a level swing.

Sometime later, while the Reds were taking batting practice, my eye inevitably sought out Pete Rose, who, wearing his manager's cap (and jacket—it was a chilly day), was standing off to one side hitting ground balls to Davey Concepcion at shortstop. Now this, too, should not have been a source of unusual interest, save for the pairing of two great fading veterans of the Big Red Machine in the casual circumstance of a routine infield drill. But it was.

For a few moments, what seemed to be going on was this dual activity of batting practice and a manager hitting ground balls to his shortstop. Rose put his fungo tosses up and tapped out

relatively easy changes for Concepcion. What struck me immediately, however, was the ease and grace of Concepcion's movements. There is a special, almost balletic coordination in picking
up grounders that has always, for me, been a barometer of the
difference between professional and amateur infielders, but I
don't remember ever being quite so riveted by the ordinary practice movements of a fielder. Again and again, Concepcion
moved as though his body and glove were performing a single
effortless motion from the time the ball left Rose's bat to the
moment when it was thrown back in. If the ball was hit left,
right, directly at him, if he had to short-hop it, backhand it, field
it at his shoetops, it made no difference whatsoever. So easy
were Concepcion's movements, they seemed entirely devoid of
the motor task of response, as though he were merely pantomim-
ing. Rose then began hitting the ball harder. There was nothing
sudden or dramatic in this, but the tempo and intensity of the
drill had picked up. It did not matter. Concepcion handled balls
that were rocketed toward him as effortlessly as the ones that
had been gently tapped. Activity around the batting cage slowed
as more people began to watch. Rose smashed the ball harder
and harder. Concepcion seemed, if anything, smoother and
smoother. What had happened was this good-spirited *mano a
mano*. Concepcion had not bobbled a single ball. No matter how
hard Rose tried, he could not get a single catchable ball past
him. The errors belonged to Rose in the energy of his effort. He
hit occasional line drives to the middle of the outfield or balls
that squibbed a few feet away, and often he hit shots along the
ground or which exploded on a short single hop that no mortal
should have been able to handle with such ease. Concepcion
made one spectacular play after another, never breaking a
sweat, never once doing anything more than seeming to continue
a program of pantomimed routines. Rose finally got one through
Concepcion's legs. But he had moved from the fungo circle almost to the middle of the infield grass to do it. Concepcion
laughed and waved a hand at Rose. A noise—something like a

gasp of disbelief coupled with a cheer for what had just taken place—came from the field and the stands. But it was Rose, the manager and the player bound eternally to his Boy Soul, who expressed it best. He took one look at Concepcion, tossed his bat high in the air, and walked away, performing his own pantomime of Oliver Hardy thinking he has just gotten the better of Stan Laurel.

"Everything about this game is fun," Rose said, surrounded in the dugout by the horde of reporters who would be with him every day until he finally passed Ty Cobb's record and who would always be looking for him to reveal, by word or gesture, that playing baseball could have no further meaning for him than Cobb's mark.

As Rose was not in the lineup that day, the game focused on the Orioles. They proceeded to handle the Reds as though they were a minor-league team. And they did so calling attention to some of the very questions Bird watchers might have had about them. Two of their free agent acquisitions, Lee Lacy and Fred Lynn, contributed big hits early and, in Lynn's case at any rate, promised an outfield defense that would be stronger than in the recent past.

A couple of Oriole minor-leaguers lit up the day as well. Jim Traber, whose debut with the Orioles the previous fall included his singing the national anthem at Memorial Stadium, hit a two-run homer in the 7th inning, and Fritz Connolly, an overlooked player when camp opened, hit a pair of key doubles and had veterans in the press box talking about the Orioles' basketball team. Connolly played third base, was six-foot-five and, with Ripken alongside him at short and Gary Roenicke hulking behind him in the outfield, gave the left side of the Oriole defense the appearance of an NBA forward wall. More important, Connolly raised the hope that the Orioles might have solved a chronic problem at third base without having to go outside their organization. In the short season all things seemed possible.

By far the most critical component in measuring the Orioles' chances was their pitching. In this game, the successive mound appearances of Storm Davis and Dennis Martinez seemed, somehow, important. Both were key pitchers in the Oriole plans to regain supremacy in the American League East, and both had become uncertain contributors. Davis, although posting respectable numbers for the previous season, had slumped badly in the second half, and Dennis Martinez, two years past treatment for alcoholism, was also two years past his last effective season of pitching. Both pitchers seemed impressive if not overpowering in their three-inning appearances.

"It was a little difficult today," Davis said later, "because we were playing a National League team, and there was just no way of really knowing the hitters. But I was satisfied with what I did." Davis explained that he approached pitching the Reds as he might the Minnesota Twins in the Metrodome. "If you just beat the Yankees, say, and you threw ninety percent fastballs, and then you come up against the Twins in the Metrodome and you know that they're primarily a fastball-hitting team, you throw differently. Today was one of those situations. The National League is primarily a fastball-hitting league, and so I threw the way I would to the Twins. This was one of those situations where you work on getting your breaking ball over and changing speeds with it." Good sound Oriole thinking—though Davis was primarily a power pitcher.

Davis, remarking on this, said that he had learned a lot in his short time in the majors from fellow pitchers Scott McGregor and Mike Boddiker. The Orioles' staff, from the days of Jim Palmer, had always thought of itself as a unit, and this remained the case in the spring of 1985. Davis was still in the process of learning. "Last season," he said, "I started to learn much more about changing speeds and pitching in situations. A lot of people were second-guessing me because of the fastball I have, but I had to learn to pitch my game. I'm part of a staff and we really learn from each other and help each other. Scott and Boddiker communicate a lot with each other, and Flanny and Dennis and

I do because we're primarily fastball pitchers. Now with Flanny out, I've been relying more heavily on Scott and Mike, learning what to do and what not to do, how to approach hitters. Listening to them talk about hitters is different. I learn from them and I like to think they pick up things from me, too. We've pushed each other hard this spring. We're running harder, running more. We're all working out, in the trainer's room, in our drills; mentally we're trying to keep each other up. We all know we can have a good season, a lot better than people expect."

Dennis Martinez's outing seemed even more critical. In 1982, his last effective season, he won sixteen games. In the strike-shortened season the year before, he had led the league with fourteen wins. But Martinez lost his effectiveness and, he said, nearly everything else in the period following. Over a period of years that included the pressures of pitching, political upheavals in his native Nicaragua, and his father's alcoholism and subsequent death in a fatal accident, Martinez drank more and more heavily. By the time the Orioles reached the World Series in 1983, he was a forgotten man in the bullpen—and an alcoholic. When Joe Morgan, then on the Phillies, came to the victorious Orioles' locker room after the last game of the series, Martinez, sitting sullenly at his locker, suddenly lashed out and spilled a drink on Morgan. Two months later, he was in a minor automobile accident that resulted in his arrest for drunken driving.

Martinez's rehabilitation began immediately. Told by the Orioles that he would be released unless he received treatment, he entered a program at the Sheppard-Pratt Institute in Baltimore, administered by its director, the consulting psychiatrist for the team, Dr. James McGee. The eight-week program there and subsequent—and continuing—involvement with Alcoholics Anonymous restored Martinez's health. But not his pitching effectiveness. He labored through the 1984 season a shadow of the pitcher he once was. It was as though some vital competitive component in his makeup had been cut out of him in the process of his rehabilitation. "He changed his entire metabolism," Ray

Miller explained. "He tried to crash-course it in one season, and I don't think he could do that. . . . I don't know how to explain it—it's just experience—but you see a glint in a guy's eyes."

Martinez himself seemed painfully aware of this dilemma. "Every day is different," he said. "It's only what I do today that counts. . . . Last year my recovery was my priority. Baseball was still my job and my life, but my recovery came first."

Vida Blue, who went through a similar period of recovery from addiction, understood something that Martinez's teammates and possibly Martinez himself may not have fully grasped —and that, if true, surely was a key to his eventual ability to perform again. When I met him in Arizona, Blue described the personality change he had experienced.

"What happens, medically speaking, from what I've been told, you're mourning for the loss of your beloved, what it is you've been so dependent on. That's only a stage, but it affects how you see yourself, even your job. Religion does that—for the better. . . . I went through a mourning period. I've had a year and seven months of sobriety, it's nothing to brag about, it's just a fact. There was this period of mourning when I couldn't sit down and drink my Heineken or Beck's or whatever it was. But what happened is that it made me simplify my life. Just a minute here, do I need a six-room house? I'm a single parent, do I need three cars? . . . I don't know yet if I'll make the baseball team but I know that I've learned to deal with life on life's terms."

It is hard to put oneself inside someone else's head. Martinez is a man who comes from desperate poverty, who remains mum but obviously not unfeeling about the troubles tormenting Nicaragua, where members of his family still reside. His eyes light up when he speaks of a recent movie depicting the last days of the Somozas, because in it one of the characters fighting against the dictatorship wears a Baltimore Orioles cap and instructs an American visitor to carry a baseball back to America for him and "give it to Dennis Martinez."

"When I saw that, I said, 'Wow, look at this!' I was surprised," Martinez explained. "It was something. I really enjoyed
that movie, even though I wasn't there when the Sandinistas
took over. But I asked a lot of people, and they said that's almost
the same way it happened down there. And the great thing was
that I saw the people, and all the things that made me feel I was
at home again. Yes, I want to see peace. Then I would be able to
go down there and take my kids; even though I brought them up
here, it's not the same. Nicaragua is my home."

Martinez is more aware than anyone of his own vulnerability
and what it is he must do. He says again and again—it is his
litany—that he will be an alcoholic all his life, and that he can
never delude himself that a cure can be permanent. "Every day
is different," he says. "It's what I do today that counts. It only
takes one drink to get back to where I was. . . . I want to be
honest with myself. If I tell people I'm okay and I'm not, I'm
only fooling myself. I'm the one who gets hurt."

Was the period of mourning over for Martinez? Miller believed the glint had come back in Dennis' eye. Martinez himself
now said, "I have to be responsible for what my job is. And what
that is is to go out there every fourth game and win it, game by
game, pitch by pitch. I can't let the last game or the last pitch get
to me, and I can't be thinking about the game after the one I'm in
right now. I know that Scotty and Mike and Storm have to do
the same. . . . I don't think my career is over yet, and if I said I
was adjusted to the idea that it might be, I wouldn't be honest
with you or myself. . . . I know one thing. I haven't lost my wife
and my kids. I haven't lost my house or my job. And I know that
there is a higher power which is God and that can never be taken
away. . . . What can I do? There's nothing I can do except to do
what I have to do. If I have to leave, I have to do it, if I have to
pitch with pain out there, I have to do it. When I can't handle it
anymore, I'll quit."

It is very difficult in the fraternity of professional baseball
players to separate personal caring from the shared will to win

games. Friendships, close friendships, are not common on baseball teams. And it is never certain that the fate of any one
player—even one like Martinez—ever compels great personal
concern beyond the days or weeks following a leavetaking. But I
am certain that in the peculiar family that is the Orioles, the
concern for Martinez has become both professional and personal. I listened to a conversation between Martinez and his
catcher for the afternoon, Rick Dempsey. Shop talk, it was,
surely, but the last time I listened quite so intently to what was
said between a pitcher and catcher was when I read *Bang the
Drum Slowly*. I had asked Martinez, with Dempsey standing
alongside him, how well he thought he had done that afternoon.
This is some of what followed:

MARTINEZ: I was no good today.

Q: How come?

MARTINEZ: Because Dempsey was dead.

DEMPSEY: When he doesn't like me behind home plate, you
know we're gonna win. (*Pause*) He changed speeds well
today.

MARTINEZ: You have to be proud to have someone like him
behind the plate, right?

DEMPSEY: Right. Where are you going for dinner tonight? (*They
both laugh.*) He really did change speeds well today, but he
threw too many forkballs.

MARTINEZ: I'm working on this pitch. I'm trying to get my
confidence.

DEMPSEY: I knew that, that's why—

MARTINEZ: And you can call it early in the count, like the first
pitch, if I'm getting it over the plate.

DEMPSEY: That's what I'm thinkin' too because now you're
throwing it over the plate and I can call it—and I want to
do that because I don't like guys sittin' on your fastball, first
pitch, especially right-handers. So we'll see what happens.
Now's the time to experiment . . . but I wanted to start a

right-hander off with a slider, just throw it right down the middle and give him something to think about.

MARTINEZ: I've been trying to forget about the slider for a little while, but now that I'm working on the forkball, maybe I'll go more to the curve ball.

DEMPSEY: Oh, I'd much rather have your slider than a curve ball, because you can get to use it against right-handers.

MARTINEZ: Then we gotta go through with the forkball.

DEMPSEY: You might seriously think about keeping your slider and throwing that pitch hard to right-handers. Throw your curve ball like Scotty throws it—a real slow curve ball—to left-handers when you're ahead in the count. Real slow. Instead of trying to throw hard fastball, hard curve ball, hard slider. You just lob a curve ball up there—to a left-hander, not a right-hander—and it'll really keep 'em from looking hard stuff away. It'll really set up your good forkball and your good fastball.

MARTINEZ: How did I throw the forkball today? It dropped pretty good, didn't it?

DEMPSEY: One time it dropped so far it caught me right on the palm. Goddamn, Dennis, that's the best I've ever seen you throw it. *(To me)* You know, it takes about a good year, year and a half, before you really get control of that pitch— you can't just go out there and throw it.

Q: Why does it take so long?

DEMPSEY: Because your fingers have to get used to spreading out and you have to build muscles in those fingers and you have to have a perfect release point with it all the time. . . .

MARTINEZ: I feel very stiff between these two fingers right now.

DEMPSEY: He started throwing the pitch last year.

MARTINEZ: Yeah, I did last year, but I didn't throw too many. . . .

DEMPSEY: No.

MARTINEZ: I wasn't really ready . . . because last year I had no confidence at all.

DEMPSEY: You want ice for your arm?
MARTINEZ: No.
DEMPSEY: You threw the hell out of the ball today, Dennis.

Two days before the Orioles came north, Dennis Martinez pitched against the Yankees in Miami Stadium. He pitched seven strong innings and left the game with a 5–2 lead. He was not the focal point of the day's proceeding, however. Rather, it was the bullpen. In the preceding year, their ace Tippy Martinez had, for the first time in his career, come down with arm troubles, precipitating the acquisition of reliever Don Aase over the winter. Neither of them had performed with great consistency during the exhibition schedule, but this late spring game emphasized just how much hope was attached to their succeeding. Many of the writers had noted that the Orioles seemed unusually pressured to win in these final games, and the frequency with which manager Joe Altobelli went to his top relievers seemed to bear this out. When the Yankees closed to within a run at 5–4 in the 8th inning, Altobelli immediately went to Aase to keep the lid shut in the 9th. Aase was able to retire only one of the six batters he faced, and Tippy Martinez, who had pitched the night before, was hardly an improvement. The Yankees finished by scoring six runs, winning the game 10–5, and leaving everyone in and around the Orioles in more doubt about the upcoming season than the result of a single exhibition game warranted. Altobelli, later, seemed testier than I had ever seen him. He denied that any pressure to win was present, or that the current spring campaign was in any sense different from any other he had been involved with. But it was clear it was. "Take K.C.," he suddenly blurted out, seemingly in relation to nothing. "How many games did they win last year? A few over .500. And they win their division. We won eighty-five, more than they did, and we're down in shitsville."

PART FOUR

STARS

CHAPTER EIGHT

Three Just Men

I find one universal rule . . . and that is to avoid affectation to the uttermost and as it were a very sharp and dangerous rock; and to possibly use a new word, to practise in everything a certain nonchalance that shall conceal design and show that what is done and said is done without effort and almost without thought. From this I believe grace is in large measure derived because everybody knows the difficulty of those things that are rare and well done.

—Castiglione, *The Book of the Courtier*

In André Schwarz-Bart's book *The Last of the Just,* the well-being of the world is said to hinge on the existence of thirty-six Just Men. I have always believed that something of the same principle applies to the world of baseball. In every generation since I began observing, there have been players—not exclusively the era's superstars—who seemed to embody and support the game itself in the way they have had at it. Everyone has a list. Mine includes (in no particular order) Joe DiMaggio, Ted Williams, Stan Musial, Jackie Robinson, Willie Mays, Hank Aaron, Carl Yastrzemski, Al Kaline (among others)—but also, Tommy Henrich, Carl Furillo, Nellie Fox, Dick Groat, and Lee May (among others). Aside from obvious skill, the unifying bond among these players is a sort of steadiness and inner purpose larger than adversity. Stardom, for me, has always included this quality of intensity, present whether a player was making a few thousand or a million dollars. Great skill is not alone a guarantor of such play; witness the sometimes dramatic drop in productivity with occasional free-agent stars. Neither is simple determination. For me, baseball's Just Men—whether they meant to be or not—have always been an example to others, on and off the field. In the way they played the game over many years (six years minimum are a must), they have passed on a standard others strive for. This is not so much a matter of numbers as of a way of playing. Inherent in this is a sort of grace that preserves the game from the various forces (drugs, labor wars, dilution of talent, greed, and hucksterism) threatening to destroy it.

It so happens that within the American League East, my springtime grail, there were three certain Just Men working away at their trade. Each of them—apart from their having made my baseball-watching life so much more enjoyable over the years—illustrates a subtle counterpart that always exists between a star and a team.

It is one of the pleasures of the short season that players generally are so much more accessible than they will be later. In the spring, there is more leisure not only to watch games but also to spend time with players who normally reserve themselves for a few moments before locker-room stools or for brief conversations in hotel lobbies and airport lounges.

Spring training allowed me to be at leisure with many people in the game—but, in the spring of 1985, none more so than these three just men.

I saw them as I found them—on the field and off: in a quiet apartment in Key Biscayne, in the coolness of early morning in central Florida, riding along stretches of Florida's western coast. Each of the three, perhaps coincidentally, had largely kept aloof from the media during his playing career. But each of them, in my spring travels, was as inevitable as the fire and color of the season itself. They enabled me to see, as I never could have in the regular season, some of what was enduring and beautiful in our national game.

II

Eddie Murray has always had a reputation for disliking spring training. He denies it—almost. His hands are too soft for a lot of hitting early, he says, and the minor-league diamonds used in the exhibition season have nasty surprises hidden in their uneven surfaces. But in the spring of 1985, Murray, a latecomer to camp, showed up with his hands already toughened and his batting eye sharp. He acknowledged that for the first time in his career, he had been working out at home. He was getting older, he said, and the time had come to make adjustments.

No matter what his approach is in the early season, no one quarrels with what he has given the game. If you ask baseball people to name the game's preeminent players, the one person included on any list is Eddie Murray. And usually without hesitation. "He's the best there is, that's all—hands down," Sparky Anderson said. "If I were playin'," said Ted Williams, "he's the one guy I wouldn't let beat me. He'd be number one." If you are from Missouri or are suspicious of Sparky Anderson or somehow have been absent from the planet for the last decade and demand the cold evidence of numbers, there is plenty.

Since he began playing for the Orioles in 1977, Murray's batting average has hovered right around .300. He has at the same time driven in over 800 runs, hit over 220 home runs, is second only to Mike Schmidt in consecutive 20-home run seasons (Schmidt has 11; Murray, with 9, has played only nine years), and he ranks fourth in the history of the game in career homers by a switch hitter. Even more telling is his performance in the clutch. The Elias Sports Bureau came up with a category called "Late Inning Pressure Situations," defined by what a player does from the 7th inning on in games where two runs or less separate his team from the opposing one. This is their ranking of the game's top clutch hitters over the last decade (through 1984):

Player	Pressure Avg.	HR	(Overall Avg.)
Carlton Fisk	.263	28	.280
Steve Garvey	.312	32	.302
Keith Hernandez	.292	16	.300
Reggie Jackson	.268	39	.263
Thurman Munson	.309	3	.304
Eddie Murray	.323	40	.298
Tony Perez	.263	21	.271
Lou Piniella	.289	14	.293
Willie Stargell	.267	23	.278
Carl Yastrzemski	.266	24	.272

Steve Garvey, whose offensive statistics have been maligned elsewhere, clearly does well here, but it is Murray whose numbers simply outshine the rest. When you add to all this his outstanding defensive play at first (he won his third straight Gold Glove in 1984, and only two other first basemen in history have ever won more), his endurance (he has played in over 97 percent of his team's games), and his general value to his team, you have a reasonable statistical model of the best.

Curiously, save for the strike year of 1981, when he tied for the league lead in homers and led in runs batted in, Murray has never led the league in a major offensive category (he led in walks in 1984). In addition, though he has been an all-star four different times, 1985 marked the first time he was voted directly to the team (the other times were by managerial selection). He has never been named league MVP.

To have finished high but not at the top of the various batting departments over the years says only that Murray is a model of steadiness rather than a roman candle. This is borne out by the numbers, of course, but, more significantly, by the people who play with him. Murray in the lineup is like bullion in the treas-

194

ury. A glimpse of this noncomputable but essential quality came in the 1983 World Series. Through the first three games of the Series, Murray had only one hit. He got another in the fourth game but still went into the fifth game with only those two hits to show for sixteen times at bat. Without Murray hitting, the memory of the 1979 World Series, where the Pirates rallied from a three-games-to-one deficit to beat the Orioles, remained an uninvited clubhouse ghost. But Murray, arriving at the park that day, had figured something out. "National League pitchers," he said, "pitch a little backwards." By which he meant that the tendency to throw breaking balls early in the count, common in the American League, was reversed by the Phils' pitchers, who tended to come straight on from the first pitch, making Murray, in his own words, "overly aggressive." He had been swinging at too many first strikes. So he made an adjustment for himself. He decided to lay off the first pitch, to just look. In the fourth game, in his first at-bat, he nearly hit one out. A solid hit followed. "Uh-oh, he's back!" one of his teammates joked. They didn't really know.

When Murray walked into the clubhouse the next day, he did know. "It's guaranteed," he told Rich Dauer, the second baseman, in his characteristic half-kidding, half-serious manner, "I'm goin' out here today." Dauer was suddenly tuned into Sydney Omarr. "But is this game guaranteed?" he ventured. Murray nodded yes. Dauer, said Murray, "went skipping around the locker room yelling, 'He said it's guaranteed! He said it's guaranteed!'" When Murray hit the first of his two home runs on that final day, he carried his teammates one step further. "That's not it," he said. He hit his second home run. "That's not it, either," he said, coming back to the bench where his teammates, by now, were as believing as they were freed from whatever shades had been haunting them. On his last at-bat, the Phils brought in a left-handed pitcher to face Murray. He knew that because of an injured wrist, he had only one good swing in him batting right-handed. Murray signaled "maybe" to the bench and then proceeded, on the first pitch, to use up his magic buffalo hide and hit one out—foul. Murray laughed. "Oh boy, I know I'm lost now!" His teammates laughed. The championship was safely in their hands.

What is much harder to figure out than Murray's statistical steadiness is why the powerful and almost mystical hold he has on his teammates has not carried over to the general public— and to the media—whose votes determine Most Valuable Player awards. Murray could easily have won the award in 1983, more uncertainly in other years, but he did not. Cal Ripken, Jr., equally deserving, won in 1983, but many people close to the Orioles acknowledge that the determining factor in the vote had less to do with talent than personality. Over the years, Murray has shied away from the press, to the point where many have seen him as intimidating, uncooperative, and downright hostile. He has, in reality, done little to change anyone's opinion. He seems not to care in the least. The only thing at all at odds with this collective nonportrait of an angry loner is that it is dead wrong.

In fact, Murray does *look* angry—and intimidating. He is a large, barrel-chested man whose modified Afro, mutton-chop whiskers, and glowering looks lend to the coal blackness of his face an appearance of such menace that it comes as a shock to hear a voice escape from his body that is benignly soft and evenly modulated. You anticipate the basso of a roar and growl and instead receive something so nearly seraphic, you believe your senses have gone awry. This, too, is misleading. Murray's outward manner masks a personality that is original, command- ing, and complex. In the end, he is *exactly* what you see on the field. His game happens to be who he is. The surprise is that the public facade he maintains is generated neither by meanness nor deviousness. It is a covering for a largeness of spirit that makes everything about him and his game different and rare. It also makes his relationship with the press difficult and remote.

Murray, more often than not, will look or walk past a reporter who tries to initiate a conversation with him. Sometimes, particularly with local reporters—and provided the questions coming at him are less about himself than about baseball—he will be briefly obliging. None of this is exceptional in a professional athlete, and, as with other athletes who keep their reserve, his manner had tended either to offend people or to make them scour his career for explanations.

The usual one is a newspaper article that appeared during the 1979 World Series, depicting Murray and his family in unflattering terms. The gist of the article, by a writer who never bothered to corroborate what he wrote with any of the Murrays, was that the family had been hostile to white scouts interested in Eddie and that, therefore, player and family, far from being virtuous citizens, were, in reality, black racists.

The story, Murray knew, was blatantly false and malicious, and obviously it deeply offended him. But apart from pointing out that the falseness of what was written was apparent on its face, he has never sought to answer the article.

"If I bring it up, it's there to judge again," Murray said, "and I don't want to do it. Just let it die."

But the article did not cause Murray to go into a shell. He was reticent with the press before it was written and remains so today, not of suspiciousness nearly so much as out of a profound distaste for putting himself ahead of others, in the press or on the field. "I'm not a me-me-me, I-I-I person, and that's all interviews are about," he said. Murray was one of twelve brothers and sisters growing up. It was as though in the very accident of his birth he was confronted with the practical need to eschew self-importance. If it hasn't affected every pore of his being, it is nevertheless so pervasive that it influences even obscure areas of his life. Like Sir Laurence Olivier, he is ill at ease with his looks and the sound of his own voice. In conversation, his language often borders on the eccentric because of the ways in which he avoids the use of the word "I." If he is curt or short with the press, it is because he knows the energy put into talking about himself is taken directly from what he puts into playing baseball. And baseball has never been about himself alone. He learned that early and has never forgotten it.

It is commonly assumed that growing up in a family as large as Murray's meant, before anything else, excessive hardship. But that was not his experience. "I wouldn't have traded it for the world," he said. "It was great. Maybe that's where a lot of the 'us' comes into it. You sit there and it was never 'me' or 'I' . . . and it wasn't a tough ship to run, either. It was like a well-tuned Mercedes, believe me!"

The Murray children did things together. They went to the movies together, they marched into restaurants together, they went to picnics together, and there were enough of them to come close to forming their own baseball team. To hear him say it, you might have thought that Ludwig Bemelmans had really gotten his inspiration for the Madeline stories from the Murray family of Watts, California.

"I'll tell you this," Murray said, "it got to the point where you really didn't need any other friends—oh, I had 'em all right— but it was just all of us together could take care of our own needs. Even baseball. The girls played baseball too, and believe me, we had a few of them who were good."

The center of Murray's life—and of his family—was his mother. A powerful and generous woman, widely known and respected throughout the neighborhood, Carrie Murray was, in the hub of her own family, organizer, law-giver, judge, enforcer, teacher, adviser, confidante, philosopher, and logistics expert. She had, in Murray's words, "control of the whole situation." She could be dictatorial. Murray told the story of an older brother, Charles, forbidden to play on the high school baseball team. The baseball coach at Freemont High School happened to see Charles hit a softball during gym class and was so impressed he asked him to come out for the team.

"Now, you're talking about a boy nearly eighteen years old," Murray said, "and all he could do was say, 'You have to ask my mother!" The coach did ask Mrs. Murray. The boy had chores to do, she said testily, and that was all there was to it. Except that Charles wanted to play. Finally, an uncle interceded. He had his work cut out for him. "She was still sort of oppressive about it," Murray said, as though it happened only a day ago, "and my uncle listened to her for a while—about all the chores my brother had to do and the like—and then he just started to make her feel bad, I guess. 'Aw, let the kid have some fun, don't be so mean,' stuff like that. She wound up calling the coach back or sending him a note, and so Charles was allowed to play. He played one year of overhand and he was so good, Houston drafted him."

Murray attended a well-integrated junior high school in San Pedro, to which he was bused, and then went on to Locke High School in Los Angeles, where he starred in basketball (he was a center) and baseball, and from which he graduated in 1973. School was easy, he said, largely because of his mother. "None of us ever had to worry about school," he said. "We all did our work and there was no such thing as bringing home Cs. When we came home, we had to clean the yard, empty the trash, do the dishes—and then do the homework. All of it. And it had to be done right. If you rushed through it just to get it to school in time to get your grades back, you'd be in double trouble. So it got to be a thing to do it right before we were allowed to go out and play. And that was everything. Because we loved to go out and play with each other."

Even more important, Murray says, was his mother's influence on his temperament. He was by nature rambunctious and energetic, so much so that often, simply because he could not contain himself, he let fly without thinking. "We had a lot of trophies in the house," he recalled. "We'd be sitting around in the living room watching television, and then, during commercials, just because I needed to be in motion, I'd do something crazy like pick up a pillow and fire it across the room—wipe out three trophies! Well, she got sick and tired of that. When it finally got too much for her, she'd give me a beating and make me do extra chores. But never just to be punishing me. She finally installed it in me to just slow down, to think before I did things."

Murray also gives large credit to his mother for his distinctive playing style, a style marked by this dual quality of full intensity coupled with thoughtful restraint, which he calls "low-keying." Even when he was a rookie, taking the field before a full crowd at Memorial Stadium on his very first day, this ability to "low-key" gave him an advantage far beyond his years.

"I just wasn't that excited," Murray said, recalling the day. "I think it took so long for my mother to train me that way it had become second nature or something. It's definitely been to my advantage that she finally succeeded, because the payoff has been there in so many ways, like that first day. I went out there and I looked around and I looked up . . . and there was Memorial Stadium, packed. Sure it was special, but it was like it wasn't."

Murray is just as definite in crediting his brothers with developing this side of his personality. His oldest brother, Charles, after his initial season in the Astro organization, came back to Los Angeles and helped form a pickup team of other young professionals—including Bob Watson, Bobby Tolan, and Doc Ellis—called the Pittsburgh Rookies. Murray was their batboy (a fact Ellis still teases him about every time they meet). From his post on the sidelines, the child, unaware that anything special was going on, became the father of the man. "So many of these guys were in the major leagues, and I was rubbing shoulders with them every day," Murray said, "I just didn't pay attention to that part of it. It seemed natural. I learned from watching them. All of them seemed to be very cool about playing the game of baseball—and it was like I just patterned myself after them. I figured that there had to be something to it. All of these guys were good, and none of them overreacted to anything out there on the field. They would make a play, turn around, and throw the ball back. I was an eight-, nine-year-old kid, and I had a front-row view of just watching those guys play, and so I grew up wanting to play that way myself."

The picture of Murray growing up in Watts is at once familiar and unexpected. It is familiar in the sense that no matter how unique his own history, he was borne along by a social tidal wave. Murray was still in grade school when the 1968 riots broke out. Because his mother kept such tight reins on him, he was kept indoors through it all. Most of what he saw, save for the burned-out aftermath, he saw on television. But for the first and only time in his life he saw fear on his parents' faces. The memory of it has never left him. It is his memory of what for others who did not experience it remains an abstraction, a part of American history rather than of people's day-to-day lives:

"When you see your parents—people you believed in completely—when you see fear in their faces," Murray said, "then you get scared. And they definitely tried to be cool. You know, they knew that we knew so long as they were in control, we would know that everything was fine. But once you start to see the panic on their faces . . . we knew they had no control . . . there was stuff going on that they definitely had no control over, and so after a while it just became time to . . . panic."

But just as the Murray family conformed to no stereotype of large families, so life in this large black community, which had become almost a metaphor for black ghettoes everywhere, was unexpected and particular. As life was far from grim within the family, life without was diverse and challenging. Murray's experience in growing up was as much the ease with which he able to mix with whites at school as with blacks in his own neighborhood. The world he looked out on was not, and never would be, exclusively black or white.

"I enjoyed going to school, I really did," Murray said. "The learning part, the getting in and mixing . . . I just never experienced any differences between people. I made some tremendous friends there . . . and then when I went on to high school and wound up playing against my junior high school friends who had gone off to other schools, we'd sit down and talk about old times, just the way school kids do everywhere. 'Hey, what happened to so and so, did you hear about what happened to this one or that one'—all that was fun. And the other part, that I might have been green to, I don't know, I just didn't see."

From the time he was 8, Murray dreamed of being a major-league ballplayer. He had, in the classic fashion from which baseball legends are made, a childhood coach and a young boy's team. But this was not a small-town setting by Hallmark Cards, it was yet another example of life in an extraordinary urban community.

The coach was a man named Clifford Preelow. "He is," Murray said, "the best baseball person I know today." Preelow was a man whose devotion to the game and to the kids he coached was total. He ran and personally outfitted the Little League team Murray played on. He was more like Nadia Boulanger with a class of piano prodigies than like your typical recreation counselor with a group of noisy preteens. "He taught us—at eight and nine years old—to be fundamentally sound," Murray said. "Everyone didn't come around the same or at the same time. But he hung with those kids and he really taught them. It took a little longer with some of them, but you could see them come around," Murray remembered, and gradually this large, glowering man who low-keyed everything seemed to soften as memory took him, and once again he was in Will Rogers Park, listening and learning. . . .

"He taught us always to think ahead, to see the game before it happened . . . and that was hard to do when you're talking about nine- and ten-year-old kids. There definitely was no favoritism. When we went out there he would never lighten up. He always threw the ball with something on it—I mean, not real hard, because he never forgot we were kids, but he wanted things from us. He expected everybody to bunt the ball inside the foul lines. If you didn't, he made you run. Not everyone—just whoever didn't put the ball down between the lines. He'd say, 'You missed the boulevard'—and that meant we had to run. We ran one long lap around the field—and that was extra-long if you were eight or nine—and when you got back and it was time to pick up the bat again, somehow you were a little more ready to put the ball down. I mean it was tough to make that run, but as kids you found fun in it. I mean it was like you didn't want to make that run out there, but still we really had fun. And I'm not kidding, as kids, when he put down that bunt sign, you bunted the ball down there in the game. We did cutoffs and relays, we hit the right people when we threw, and we ran the bases; we went through all that as kids. It was just a lot of baseball sense—instinct—that was put in us by a man."

To be sure there was much that was distinctive—even then—in Preelow's pupil. He had a sense of himself as a 9-year-old that many professional players never have. With all his dreams of one day playing in the major leagues, he never saw himself apart from his team. "At the time," he said, "I didn't think I was all that great because I figured our whole team was that good. And playing with my younger and older brothers growing up, I just never considered myself that much better than anybody. It was just that that was something I loved and happened to pick out in life that I wanted to do." Preelow must have known that, also. When Murray was 11, Preelow nudged him a bit toward center stage. He gave him a team to run by himself.

"Of course, I had pride in what I did even when I was eight," he said. "I've always had it. We lost ballgames, and I knew how to lose—I mean, I knew the world wasn't going to end. It was tough as kids because as kids we didn't know very much. But it was a winning something . . . out there. Sometimes it might have come from breaking up a double play, sometimes it took getting hit by a pitch or pitching that last inning when your arm was hurting. It was something like . . . you just didn't want to put things on anyone else's shoulders."

But the dominant impression given by Murray of these boyhood years in which baseball became second nature to him is what he shared with his family. Murray and two of his brothers within near range of age became known on the sandlots of Los Angeles. Crowds turned out to see "the three brothers" as their reputation spread. Getting to and from different ballfields in widely separated areas of town was unflaggingly attended to by the children's parents. The picture of surviving summer in the city is not one of triumphing over deprivation but of personal and shared joy:

"Well, we all loved the Dodgers as kids," Murray remembered, "even though we couldn't go to see them much. We really didn't want to, because we were out there playing. There were times during the summer when we'd play three times a day. Every once in a while, we'd play in the same ballpark, but you know, on different teams. I'd be playing in one place and my brother would be on another field trying to hold things down. I'd pitch my game and then end up coming in to pitch the other one—winning both! Pulling off the uniforms, running across the field . . . and you know there were days when my parents . . . just took us everywhere we wanted to go . . . I mean they just took care of us. They saw this was something we were interested in, so they really took part in it. We could see that in them. It was never having to take the boys to play, it was always their going to watch a good ballgame. . . . We used to draw a lot of people to see us, to see the three boys—they never knew our names—but they found out we were brothers and they came out to see us. And one of us would wind up pitching while the other one was the catcher . . . it was something."

For the longest time, Murray has been sobered by the thought that he, not any of his brothers, became an established major-league ballplayer. This was, Murray remains convinced, not a question of talent so much as opportunity. He was in the right place at the right time, but his brothers were not. His brother Rich, still playing in the San Francisco organization, had, at one time, been touted as Willie McCovey's successor. But a serious injury aborted his major-league career before it ever really began. And Charles, Eddie said, was probably better than any of them. "There are people today, especially who grew up around the L.A. area, who knew all five of us, who still tell me that Charles definitely was the best. They'll say, 'Listen, you *know* you weren't the best.' And I'll say I know that. The way I look at it, I really got a break." Charles, for a time, played in the Houston organization, never made it to the major leagues, and today lives and works in Baltimore.

The break Eddie Murray got was that the Orioles had some idea of who he was. Other teams, apparently, did not. Murray's developed low-key style had thrown scouts off. Most mistook it for laziness and forgot about him when the 1973 amateur draft approached. The Orioles, armed with the results of a motivational test taken by Murray that showed something very different, drafted him in the third round. In *Dollar Sign on the Muscle,* a book on scouting by Kevin Kerrane, an Oriole official explained how the team came to secure Murray:

"All the scouting reports I'd seen on Murray stereotyped him as a big, lazy power hitter. I think most scouts, when they judge makeup, tend to value kids who remind them of themselves when they were players—and that's why you run into problems when white scouts look at black prospects. Here was Eddie Murray, younger than most of his classmates, and extremely composed, cool—to the point where scouts called him 'lackadaisical.' But then I read his motivational profile, which said his drive was well above professional average and his emotional control was off the charts. And it hit me that the emotional control was *masking* the drive."

Whatever, Murray's professional career from the first day has been marked by the same style, and the results have been nearly unwavering. He was a solid, not a spectacular, minor-league player. He did not have a single .300 season, nor did he ever have league-leading figures in any hitting category. He was a hard worker, a fundamentally sound player, a team player. And there was waiting for him in the minors an approach to the game that perfectly suited his "masked" drive. The Orioles' spring-training camp in those days was run by the big team's present third base coach, Cal Ripken, Sr. Ripken provided for Murray on the professional level what Preelow had in Little League.

"When we were down there," Murray recalled, "he even taught the game. I mean, not everybody really knew how to play the game of baseball. He taught it the Oriole way. We had booklets on cutoffs, relays, where to be on certain plays—everything. With men on this base, where did you go, what did you do? Men on that base, same thing. You wound up knowing what to do when a ball was hit and you were on the field. The fundamental Orioles came from this . . . and it produced a different breed."

Nothing better illustrates the intensity of Murray's approach to the game than his conversion to switch hitting. He has said little or nothing about it over the years, and yet it is the aspect of his game he possibly values most. Home runs by a switch hitter is one record he admits to paying attention to, although he is just as quick to add that the likelihood of his playing long enough to surpass Mickey Mantle is doubtful. Switch hitting, it turns out, is far more than a professional marker.

Murray arrived at this part of his game, he said, almost by chance. One day in 1975, when he was playing for Ashville in the Southern League, "it just came," he said. It started with his taking batting practice from the left side of the place in an effort to correct an error in his right-handed stride. "I had a tendency to overstride," he explained, "and I found that hitting left-handed shortened my stride and let me stay right on the ball. I hit the ball well, so every couple of days after that I started taking batting practice left-handed. Then it got to the point where I was hitting balls out of the ballpark and Cal and Shaefer [Jim Shaefer, present Kansas City bullpen coach] came up and asked if I could really hit that way, and I said sure, because we did it sometimes as kids, when we'd go three for four or four for four and then jump over to the other side of the plate. Then they said, 'Go ahead, do it'—and I did. First time up I doubled, and I've been doing it ever since."

But it is Murray's attitude toward switch hitting itself that is most revealing. He obviously did not polish this part of his game overnight. It was something that took time and, as nothing else, showed just how he approached his work. It took him about two months, he said, before he could consistently pull a ball from the left side. Along the way, he hit the ball hard and with power to the opposite field. As much as he could, he "went with the pitch." He started gradually. "Every now and then you'd pick a pitch," he said, "and you'd say to yourself, just try to hit the ball hard—and that's exactly what I did. You just start reacting to the ball. After a while, if the ball was in, I could really pull it. If the ball was away I hit it hard to left field. The coaches got to think I was a better hitter from the left side because I could hit it where it was pitched. From the right side, I was still basically a pull hitter."

Hitting left-handed, because it came so late, was a far more conscious process. From it, he learned a great deal about himself—and others—as hitters. To hit from the opposite side, Murray discovered, "you had to be hit by a pitched ball before you knew how to move. It was something entirely different. You've never had a ball thrown at you on that side, so it's just a natural instinct to stand there and freeze. You pray the ball that finally hits you won't be one coming directly at your head. But the big thing is just to accept the field. You have to do that, because at first everything you hit will be the other way. But the more you stay over there, the more swings, the more your confidence starts to come around. You stand in there and the field starts to open up—soon you'll hit the ball to short. From the line to short; from the line to center field. Till the whole field opens up."

This matter of having worked with his own self-confidence in an almost technical fashion taught him a great deal about the makeup of hitters generally. In the desire to become a switch hitter, Murray maintained, it was possible to see what a player actually thought of himself as a hitter. "The way you find that out," he said, "is you ask someone if they can hit right-handed—that is, if they are strictly right-handed to begin with. A lot is then determined by the answers you get. Some'll say, 'Yeah, I think so,' or you can get a definite yes. The thing is, if you don't think you can hit from your natural side, there's no need in getting on the other side. But if someone's got confidence and actually believes they can hit one way, then they can do it the other way. It's just that something in you, that competitor in you, will soon be over there on the other side."

In reviewing Murray's major-league career it is hard to think he was ever a rookie. The model of steadiness he presents—which on a graph might look like a straight line drawn with a ruler—again belies the passion that has always been there. To many in the Orioles camp, including Earl Weaver, Murray seemed large, quiet, menacing, and terribly efficient. Murray remembers that he and Weaver did not exchange a single word until July of that first year. Murray went out and played during spring training with no word from Weaver that he had actually made the team when they finally went north. The story was carried in the papers, but Murray, then as now, refused to read about himself. He played every day until July before Weaver spoke to him and then, Murray said, "It wasn't a conversation, it was just a 'hi.'" The episode reveals something about Murray's early relationship with Weaver but also something about what an unusual rookie he was:

"The way it came about was we were passing in the tunnel from the locker room to the dugout," Murray recalled with amusement. "He was going back to the locker room, and I was on my way to the dugout. The 'hi' happened just like that. He said 'hi,' and I said 'hi.' I didn't think anything of it and I just kept walking. But then you know how you hear spikes on cement. Well, I heard these spikes stop dead behind me. That was it. Later, he went to DeCinces, whose locker was next to mine, and he said, 'What about that kid, how come he doesn't talk?' Doug goes, 'What makes you think he talks to me?'"

But Murray was not as silent as all that, at least not in the beginning. He had enormous confidence in himself and even more in the team he came to play with. The Orioles of 1977, though they had finished second in the two previous seasons, were still one of the premier teams in baseball. Though Brooks Robinson was coming to the end of his career and though the Orioles, over the winter, had lost Reggie Jackson to free agency, there were still names abounding and enough new talent—the Yankee trade of 1976 brought them Rick Dempsey, Scott Mc-Gregor, Tippy Martinez (the Lord giveth and the Lord taketh away)—to guarantee good times in Birdland. The Orioles, as in the past, were loose, good-natured, fircely competitive, and very much a unit. The banter between players was sharp but familial in nature. And Murray, true to the spirit he found there, joined in. It was probably the first time since the days of erasing family trophies that he became so willing to let himself go. He paid for it.

The clubhouse leader then was another veteran reaching the end of his playing days—Lee May. In fact, Murray, though he initially played as a designated hitter, had been brought up to the team as May's eventual successor. He regarded the veteran player as most others on the team did, with a respect and affection that bordered on reverence. "When I came up, Lee May definitely was it," Murray said. "You know Earl would scream at some of the younger players and then maybe rap a little more, whatever, just making them feel really uncomfortable about going out to play, and Lee would come over and smooth things out."

May eventually befriended Murray, took him under his large and protective wing, and passed on to him so deep a sense of what it meant to belong to and take responsibility for a team that it had remained with Murray to this day. But in 1977, when he was "definitely it," Lee May had the sort of authority that could freeze a rookie in place, particularly one who worshiped him and who was not used to being talkative anyway. One day, said Murray, May passed by him while he was in a voluble mood. "Shut up, rookie, rookies aren't supposed to talk," he remembered May saying. "And the next time he looked up, I hadn't said a single word in four or five days. He came by and said not to take everything so personal, that it was just him needling as he always did."

What followed, in Murray's words, "was that we became real good friends." As he did with other young players, May saw to it that Murray's entry into the big leagues, with all its pressure and newness, would not have added to it the extra burden of isolation from those who already were secure in their place on the team. The veteran and the rookie often shared meals together—and the benefit of May's many years of experience as a ballplayer. "He definitely was one person you could open up to," Murray said. "And the thing I really admired about Lee and his family was that I took over first base maybe a year, two years, before he was ready to go. He still had some good years left in him, but the job was given to me, and neither he nor his wife ever held anything against me. Until today I try and visit him every winter in Cincinnati, when I take my little annual drive after the season ends. They're just good people, and I like being around good people."

But in the caring and direction he received from May, Murray learned how he, as an older player, might himself be helpful to younger players. Over the years, Murray has befriended freshman players such as John Shelby, Floyd Rayford, and Mike Young, to the point where, for period of time, he has had them live with him. Murray has never seen anything special in it. "That's only in turn, instilling in some of the guys something like confidence. You try to take the time to explain some things. The way I explain it to them is to point out that everyone out there on the field was a star somewhere—high school, college—and sometime that gets shattered. The physical ability is out there, but you try to point out that the difference in making it in the big leagues or not is how much belief you have in yourself. . . . You try to instill it in them that without that you're really not going to do too many things in life very well."

Mike Young, midway through a rookie season in which he became one of the first reasonably successful power hitters from within the Oriole farm system since Murray, was rarely playing and deeply discouraged. He moved in with Murray for three months. "He told me," Young said, "that if I wasn't able to play this game, I wouldn't be in this organization—this was when I was at a low, when I thought nothing was really ever going to go right. . . . I credit two people but especially Eddie Murray with helping me through that time. . . . He told me what he went through—it wasn't as dramatic as with me—but there were some things that were similar. He told me the one thing you always remember is that you don't give up. . . . I'm the oldest in my family. I have two sisters, and I always wished I had a brother. I can say Eddie is like a brother to me, an older brother. And I look up to him like a brother because I can say anything to him. I can talk to him. . . . There aren't too many like him anywhere."

But as May had done with him, Murray insists on the baseball side of this. It is part of what he must do, given his ability and the role he occupies on the team. He chooses his spots, but he points out young players' mistakes. He does it in a way where the players themselves trust his intent. "What I try to tell the younger players," Murray said, "is that I'm jumping on you because I'm trying to make you better and by making you better I'm making us better. That's just the way it is. I know definitely I can't win a pennant by myself."

But he plays the game as though that might, somehow, be possible. Murray has been described by many as a "natural," by which it is meant that his great ability seems almost instinctive—it is, assuredly, in Charlie Fox's sense of the word—rather than arrived at through a process of work. By his reluctance to dwell on his own accomplishments, he has probably done as much as anyone to foster that notion. In reality, it is another mask. Murray is the sort of complete player who is constantly looking for ways to improve his game and to help his team win. Even though he has been a prodigious hitter from the start, he is constantly looking for ways to improve himself.

Murray in his crouch, bat circling ominously above his shoulder, his glowering eye upon the pitcher, is, by his own admission, not a model of any theory of hitting. "Jim Frey once asked me my theory of hitting," Murray remembered. "I said the ball comes over the plate and I hit it. He said, 'Even if it's a curve ball?' I said, 'Yeah.' He said, 'What if it's a fastball?' I told him I swing at that one, too. I think to this day I've had two ballgames where actually home plate felt like there really was an inside or an outside or a middle part of the plate." But this rather classic picture of a free swinger is somewhat deceptive. Murray *is* an enormously selective hitter—as his league-leading total of 107 walks in 1984 attests—and he is so because the basis of his work is seeing the ball. His crouch, which he developed in part from watching Rod Carew, is designed to allow him to see all of the baseball—a straight-up hitter, he maintains, sees only the top half of the ball. He has learned, over the years, to "read" pitchers, that is, to study the different ways a pitch is delivered so that he can see the ball for as long as possible before it reaches the plate. While he does not "guess," he is so mentally alert that if a coach, say, were to signal him that a certain pitch was coming—something most batters would find distracting—he is instantly able to adjust. The presence on the staff of Frank Robinson, a master at "stealing" pitches, was welcomed by Murray for just that reason.

Murray has never found videotape, or weights or conditioning programs or any of the paraphernalia of training, helpful to him as a hitter. As his remarks about switch hitting indicate, he is as aware of the mechanics of swinging as he needs to be. He sometimes calls on Elrod Hendricks to help him if he is not going well because he feels Hendricks knows him as a hitter better than anyone. But mainly, Murray's effort is to keep things as simple as possible, to see the ball and to keep his mind riveted on the game before him. If he goes into a slump, his way out of it is sometimes to take extra batting practice, sometimes to lay off— but always to work on "hypnotizing" himself so that his level of confidence will remain high. (This he accomplishes, he says almost offhandedly, by plugging into a headset and listening to a particularly meaningful song over and over again—to the point where his teammates suspect he is half-crazy.) Beyond a birthright of obvious talent, there is his simply extraordinary ability to concentrate great mental power on what it is he has to do. It is there in every part of his game. It is his good angel and silent partner.

"Baseball is something where you can't go out there with a half-step," Murray said. "When you're out there, you've got to have everything together, I think. If you go out there and you're lackadaisical, there's a good chance you'll wind up injuring yourself—and I do try to avoid that. I told you I talk to myself. You have to talk to yourself about knowing what you want to do out there."

At the plate and in the field, this is no more esoteric than being alert to particular situations, to knowing contingencies so well that there will be no surprises, no time to clutter up plays with confused execution. Murray is *always* in the game, always seeking ways to stay a step ahead. In one spring game I happened to see, Murray speared a line drive with runners on first and second. The natural move for him would have been to double the runner off first himself. Instead he threw instantly to second. The reason was he had played this contingency out in his mind before it happened. He might have lost a footrace back to first base, but he had a chance at second because the runner there had taken a naturally bigger lead.

When he is at his position, he will joke with baserunners to distract them or lure them off-guard; with no one on base he plays as wide a first base as anyone in the league, allowing his second baseman to cover more of the middle of the diamond. So thorough and concentrated is Murray that he seems constantly to be mining new areas for his game. In 1984 he stole ten bases. He believes he is capable of stealing twenty. One time I observed Murray's pre-inning warmup routines in the field. Instead of throwing ground balls to each fielder, he tried—sometimes successfully—to hit the second base bag on the fly. It seemed like horseplay. It wasn't. Years ago, he said, he had begun doing this as an exercise to improve the accuracy of his throwing.

Murray, as he approaches 30, is in midcareer and yet at the top of his profession. Though still young, even by baseball standards, he has a bearing of years about him familiar in veteran stars, so that even peers somehow turn to him as an elder statesman. It is a load to carry for anyone—no less one of his years —but he carries it as though it is weightless. Because his own identity has always been so intimately yoked with others, it almost appears as if this side of himself is no less natural than breathing. He is the clutch hitter he is because he craves the responsibility. He *wants* to be in the middle of the big play in the big game. He is, on a team traditionally made up of role players, merely the ultimate role player.

In a perishable world of firsts, Murray secured what will be for a time the most lucrative contract in the game. If one of the characteristics of baseball's Just Men theory is a player's willingness to go through a brick wall whether pennies or millions in salary are at stake, then it is given certain legitimacy in Murray's case. "The only thing different about Eddie Murray today from the day he first broke in," said Oriole traveling secretary Phil Itzoe, "is the cut of his clothes."

Over the years, Murray has tended to treat money as he has everything else—his own advantage inevitably seems bound up with others. He has always actively and with an absolute absence of fanfare invested large amounts of time and money in local charities. Since 1977—his first year—he has bought fifty seats for underprivileged children for every Oriole home game. He helped establish a high school for poor children. With his new contract, he hopes to set up a summer youth camp like one that got him out of Los Angeles for a couple of weeks during his own childhood.

Because Murray himself is so reluctant to talk about it and because the notion of "charity" generally is so far distant in our day from the old Pauline sense of *"caritas,"* it is easy to dismiss or mistake the generating spirit that is involved. As he counterposes "I" to "we" in his vocabulary, so he genuinely believes that giving is the counterweight to taking. It is an article of faith that extends into seeing a world in which too many people go to bed hungry and too many resources are squandered elsewhere. "Money's not going to make you happy," Murray said, without guile, as though it was inconceivable that somewhere a jaded soul might actually smile in disbelief at such a familiar notion. "But it's nice to have it and maybe try to do something you care about. Everybody's not well off in the world. You just like to see what you can do with it, see if you can't put a smile on somebody's face. It's not always take, take—there's giving."

There is also in this large, powerful man who intimidates American League pitchers a quite genuine love of children. In the world of make-believe sports heroes, this is expected. In the mundane world of professional baseball, it is not. It is the sort of thing that went out with Babe Ruth. And in Murray's case, it is revealed only obliquely, through curtains of surprising shyness. And it might well be left to privacy, too—save that it sheds an even clearer light on what it is people are seeing when they watch Murray play what is, after all, a child's game.

Murray has been, it turns out, something of a babysitter for his married teammates. There has never been the least trace of obligation in this. Murray is an enormously playful man and is obviously comfortable with children, who are equally comfortable with him. "Sometimes I talk to them like they're grownups," Murray said. "I'll say—real poker-faced—'Who drove today?' The kids give you a look—you can read what they're thinking: 'He thinks we can drive—he's *crazy.*'" There is tremendous caring behind this. "Little kids are probably the ones you're always going to get the truth from," he said. "Sometimes they're so innocent they'll hurt your feelings without knowing it. I really do have fun with other players' kids—other kids, period. Kids are here in the world like everybody else, and it's a shame to know that parents sometimes don't care particularly where their kids are. And you know, from not caring here and not caring there, a kid can't help maybe leaning the wrong way—it makes you think that's why the world is in the shape it's in. It's a tough something out there when you, as a kid, are out there without anyone particularly caring about what you're doing."

Perhaps the most surprising discovery for me was that in the very power of Murray's personality he seemed so vulnerable. It was as though in life and on the field the very highest potential was, after all, packaged in a frame of common mortality. A family gave one person alone the strength of many. A team gave one player the only real chance he ever had to be in a World Series. Caring wasn't a Sunday school virtue nearly so much as what was mandatory to overcome odds and deficiencies that were obviously larger than oneself.

This particular spring was different for Murray. He was a late arrival in Miami because in the period just before the opening of camp, his mother died. It was only one of a series of family tragedies that have pursued him. In the weeks following, his father and youngest sister both fell gravely ill, and an older sister suddenly and unexpectedly died. Murray left the team for a few days when his sister died but returned soon afterward, and within a matter of weeks, though he acknowledged that the mental effort of playing was extreme, was performing along the ruler-line of his career averages. "You have in mind that none of us can live forever and that you too will die one day," he said, "so all you can do is what you do." The tremendous inner discipline that lay behind his entire career was stretched beyond any field of play—or was it? "I think I'm strong enough not to forget but to block out what I have to in order to go and do my job."

In the curious interplay that always is present between those things upon which our very existence seems to depend and those things we choose to do, the spring of 1985 marked an extraordinary confluence of forces for Murray. The year 1984 had marked the first time in his major-league career that he had ever experienced playing for a team out of contention. This also challenged his foundations. When September came around, the only motive for playing was his own average. He could not stand it. "It was tough to go out there and say, boy, just let me get mine. . . . I'd been there eight years . . . it was the first time . . . and the fans just knew this was the lowest I'd ever been or that we'd finished out."

Murray has strong and proprietary interest in the organization he plays for—the more so because of the cracks of age it has been showing. Almost all his thoughts about what is needed revolve around making sure that it is "the fundamental Orioles" that take the field. It is a problem beyond him and one that he feels he must answer to every time he goes out to play. It is part of a lifelong discipline that has brought him fame and wealth and joy and, in the middle of his journey through a world where success and duration itself are so severely foreshortened, greater uncertainty than he has ever known.

He knows that his career is finite and does not know what he will do once it is over. That is part of his future. He does know what it is he wants to leave behind. "If I'm able to go out there and play—having played with all kinds of injuries—that's it," he said. He thought about this for a moment and then added, in that strange syntax built on the avoidance of excessive use of the first person singular, "and to have been seen as just somebody who would go out there and play, and do the best he can knowing that you probably couldn't do anything but, it was just . . . sometimes . . . a little chemistry having you in the lineup."

Another part of the future is what Murray has yet to give to the game. The numbers can be guessed, handicapped, predicted from computer printouts, but they will not answer to what it is people sitting in the stands or playing alongside him will see. Of all the words I heard said about Murray, the most striking came from his friend, teammate, and costar, Cal Ripken, Jr. They will do as a preview of coming attractions:

"Eddie is what I suppose you'd call a team player. Except that that is a cliché. Everyone is a team player, or says he is. But then there are players, very few of them, that other players try to emulate. For me, that player has always been Eddie Murray."

For me, there is no better definition of a Just Man in baseball.

II

I don't remember the first time I saw Don Baylor get hit with a pitch. Going into the 1985 season, he had been hit 167 times in his career. The major-league record, held by Ron Hunt, is 250; the American League record is 189 and belongs to Minnie Minoso. If his employers allow him sufficient playing time, and if his career extends to an expected length, Hunt's record, which might normally be searched out in the annals of masochism, will be his. (Baylor surpassed Minoso's record late in the '85 season.)

Baylor is no masochist, and the actual number of times he has been hit is quite beside the point. What is unusual is the *way* he gets hit. Normally, when a pitch is thrown at or close to a batter, he leans back—or jumps—out of the way. Baylor *turns his body into the pitch.*

Watch him sometime. He stands almost straight up at the plate, crowding it as though somehow he was looking to bully it into submission. His bat suddenly tightens into a pattern of menacing, vertical arcs as the incoming pitch is about to be released. The pitcher—let us say, a good, nasty, intimidating headhunter with a powerful and proprietary interest in the sanctity of home plate—lets fly. As the ball approaches Baylor's body—provided it is not directly in line with his skull—he turns his front shoulder in toward the plate, at the same time tucking his elbow near his stomach. The ball strikes him. Baylor drops his bat and trots to first as casually as if he had drawn a base on balls. He acknowledges no pain. He will not even deign to look at the pitcher.

Baylor's move is so contrary, it almost seems like a violation of natural law. It would be the same if Rickey Henderson or Vince Coleman was actually able, somehow, to put aside the law of gravity. What Baylor's move really represents, of course, is very human and down-to-earth. It is the fruit of an extraordinary inner discipline.

"Getting hit is an art, no doubt about it," Baylor told me one spring day as though he had been waiting quietly for someone at long last to ask him about something he regarded as a legitimate part of his game. As he did with almost every other aspect of baseball statistics, Baylor knew numbers here exactly—he knew all about Ron Hunt and Minnie Minoso and where he fit in. He believed he would break their marks.

I am not sure Baylor initially understood my interest in the way he got whacked with the ball. For me, it was about his triumphing over his own nervous system. For him, it was related, almost exclusively, to his technique as a batsman.

"I stand on top of the plate," he explained. "And if you do that, it means they're going to pitch you inside a lot. If pitchers feel they can intimidate you by driving you off the plate, they're gonna do it. And if they can successfully do that, they're gonna throw that slider down and away, and you're going to look bad. When I was with the Angels, I talked to Drysdale about it. . . ."

Don Drysdale, the Angels' announcer, was a natural for such a consultation. One of the game's legendary nasty intimidators, Drysdale didn't talk with Baylor so much as exchange philosophies with him.

"He had a definite idea, a theory of pitching," Baylor said, "which was that he always wanted a hitter to give him one part of the plate, which would be his, absolutely. Okay, so as a hitter I know that I therefore will have one part of the plate, too. I want the inside half. That's my strong suit, and I'm not going to give it up. They want to waste a pitch with you inside—bang! If you've got control you can pitch inside in the big leagues and you can win. But if you miss you're going to get hurt. I'm going to stand on top of the plate and nobody's going to drive me off."

It wasn't that I was indifferent to technique. It was just that years of physical cowardice, in this instance, made me curious about how a fellow mortal could willingly let himself be hit with a hardball traveling at ninety miles an hour. How could you train the body to do that? Dave Winfield, Baylor's teammate and surely a rugged enough sort, did a reasonable approximation of St. Vitus's dance when a pitch was thrown close to him.

"You can hurt yourself more by doing that," Baylor said. "You can fall backward, fall on the bat, something," Still, Baylor saw it all in terms of the "idea" he had brought with him to home plate throughout his major-league career.

"Some hitters—Yaz used to be one—they want to stay back. That's their thing. Mine is—stay in. If you open, that means everything on your left side flies open, that is, if you're a right-handed hitter. If you open too quick, everything leaves you . . . so I'm always telling myself, like a refrain, 'Stay in, stay in.' I'm looking middle in, and I'm staying in."

It was odd, the more Baylor explained what it was he did at the plate, the clearer it became just how conscious a student of the game he was—but the more inexplicable was his ability to turn into rather than away from a pitched ball. He had done it as long as he could remember, he said. He did it in Baltimore when he broke into the major leagues in 1970, certainly, and probably before that. But he could not be precise. Then he said:

"I think it's just a mental toughness you have to have. When you walk up there, you cannot be afraid of the pitcher. Or the ball. I know when I first came up to the big leagues, I was overwhelmed by who was on the mound. Facing Gaylord Perry or Sam McDowell, Ryan, Catfish Hunter. I always gave them whatever they wanted. Before you knew it you were oh for three. Once you overcame that part of it—and only then—did you deserve to be here. Not till then."

Baylor probably got this mental toughness early. He grew up near Austin, Texas, one in a long line of churchgoing, God-fearing Baylors who, for more than a century, had kept the family's reputation spotless. Baylor gives special credit to his mother and to his grandfather, but to hear him tell it, it is a veritable army of Baylors reaching back to the beginning of the last century whose collective strength has endowed him with whatever inner fiber he possesses. "I have a large, large family," Baylor said. "My mom's side was five girls and two boys, my dad's was five boys. It's a growing thing. I can't keep up with it. They have a reunion in the summer when I'm off playing, and hundreds of people come from all over the state. One of my uncles comes from Atlanta and he's the only one from outside; everyone else is from Texas." Nearly all the Baylors known to this Baylor have been involved in the Baptist church. His mother was a secretary, and his father, his grandfather, his uncles all were deacons. Another Baylor was the church treasurer. And Don, for years, was the superintendent of the Sunday school.

Baylor says his grandfather's name alone carried the reputation of the family. "He worked for a hospital there in Austin for forty-five, fifty years. He never caused problems a day in his life, was never arrested for anything, did his hard work day after day, and that was it. He lived by keeping his name clean. And that's what I try to do, and that's what I try to teach my son to do. My brother, every one of us, is the same way. None of us was ever in the headlines—except for sports." But it was not sports that initially tested this power of anonymous uprightness. Don Baylor was one of three black children who integrated a formerly all-white junior high school.

"There were two boys and a girl," he said. "I had a choice to take a bus to the other side of town, but this school was on our side of town. You talk about toughness, those white kids had never gone to school with blacks and vice versa. And I would have to go in and ask for a uniform, and they were only going to give one of them away, and the other black kid got it because he was faster than I was."

This matter of securing a uniform became one kind of test (he was finally given one in the ninth grade). So, too, was the general and by now all too familiar climate of vituperation. "The words those kids used in the seventh, eighth, ninth grades. You had to bite your lip or stand your ground," Baylor recalled. "I stood my ground—and I made friends. It took a while, and it was only with the ones who would accept you. There were others who wouldn't and never would. Even the coaches were that way." Until Baylor's faster classmate went on to an all-black high school, he might have been Jesse Owens trying out for the S.S.

Ironically, it was a coach who helped ease Baylor's way. By the time Don got to high school he had already drawn some interest from scouts who had seen him play in the Pony and Babe Ruth leagues. But in high school—Stephen F. Austin, a prestigious and, until 1965, all-white school—Baylor found someone beyond his own family who was willing to stand by him. "I got the kind of support from this coach that you hope for. He turned out to be a lifetime friend. He's been to the playoffs with me, and he visits me for two weeks every summer. He was one of those people who simply stood his ground for his players, regardless of color. He named me captain of the baseball team. And believe me, there were pressures on him from the families of many of the wealthy kids on the club. There were a lot of doctors and lawyers and car dealers who were saying, 'Play my kid, my kid has to play,' and he didn't do it that way. He did it on ability. That's why I consider him a friend."

Baylor knew from the day he stepped out of high school that it was only his ability that guaranteed him anything. The pressure to produce was as enormous as any of the social pressures he had endured. And his high school coach, well aware of what the other side of this pressure might mean, warned his young friend. Baylor remembered, "One of his philosophies that I always think about is what you do to yourself on the days you don't come through in the clutch or drive in that run you needed to— he always told me I was too hard on myself, and he said that I had to learn to savor those days when I did well."

Baylor has become far too much the professional man of long seasons to take solace in a well-played game. It is gone in the playing, and there is only the next game. But seeing the game in which he doesn't produce in the same way has been a sort of existential challenge. Contrary to his public demeanor of evenness of disposition, Baylor's emotions run deep and at times can be volatile. The press widely reported his overturning a trash basket in the clubhouse when it was announced that Billy Martin was returning to manage the Yankees in the early days of the 1985 season. But he has always, from his high school days and before, been a man atop an emotional powder keg.

"You have to learn to forget the bad in this game," he said. "The sooner you do, the sooner you'll be able to continue playing. In '73, I made the last out in the playoffs. I saw Billy North jumping straight up in the air. They were going to the World Series, and I was going home to watch. We lost that game in our park, it was a day game in Baltimore. I thought that was the end of the world. I had made the last out and let Oakland go to the World Series. I stayed up most of the night with that, and then the next day, the sun was out and everything was going on as usual; I was still alive and I had my health and I could let myself think for the first time that it was a game and not life and death that I had just been through."

For the most part, the public has never seen anything other than the decorous professionalism that has been the hallmark of Baylor's entire career. The other side nearly always manifests itself privately. "Oh, there are times when I go up in the runway, where there's only me, the wall, and the bat," Baylor said. A hundred years of solid family deaconry have almost guaranteed private rather than public displays of feeling. But on one occasion, Baylor's temper nearly blew him out of a livelihood. In California, mired in a hideous batting slump, feeling leaned on by management for his role as union player representative, worried about a new contract, Baylor one day came across a derisive article about him by a local reporter, known by Angel players to be a mouthpiece for the front office. In the article, an Angel executive, critical of Baylor, was quoted directly.

"I was riding to the ballpark with my son, and we stopped to pick up a newspaper. There was that article, and I was furious. I took it the wrong way. I went to Buzzy's office [Angel GM Buzzy Bavasi], went right past his secretary and confronted him with it. He said, 'I only said that in jest.' I said that's not good enough. I told him that I came out and played hard for him every day, that I never asked to be out of the lineup, and that if he thought I was losing it, just to release me and see what other clubs would do. He said he couldn't do that because if he released me, he'd have to pay me. I said, 'Why don't you trade me?' and he said he couldn't do that either. I said, 'I'll tell you what, you can have your job, you don't have to pay me a thing. I'm done, I quit.' I left the office and they were screamin' after me, 'Stop him, stop him,' and I went and got my son, who was waiting downstairs, and we drove off. He said, 'Where are we going? What are we doing?' And while I was driving around, Buzzy called a press conference right away to announce that I had resigned. Well, I cooled off after a while, and I came back to the ballpark in the middle of the game. I stayed in the clubhouse. Our manager, Jim Fregosi, came back, and then between innings, groups of three or four players came back . . . they said, forget it, we need you to play, whatever, and so I went back out and sat in a corner of the dugout."

Baylor's enormous passion found a natural home with the Orioles of the late sixties and early seventies. Signed out of high school in 1967, he toured the Oriole minor-league circuit in slightly less than four seasons, arriving on the big team at the end of 1970. A year in Triple A followed before he became a full-time Oriole in 1972. Along the way, he had been named the Appalachian League Player of the Year in 1967, the *Sporting News* minor-league Player of the Year in 1970 and, even more important, had been nurtured and trained by an organization that was expert in bringing finished players from the minors to the major leagues. From the start, the experience for Baylor was almost like being taken into a family.

"I was living with four other guys that first year, made five hundred dollars a month, spent two hundred dollars calling home every day. . . . We lived in a hotel, three hitters and a pitcher. And three beds. The pitcher automatically got one bed and the hitters had a competition for the other two. Whoever had the most hits got a bed. The loser got the cot. . . . We had some good times then. The minor-league director was John Scheurholtz and his assistant was Lou Gorman. Joe Altobelli was manager in Bluefield and then in Stockton. Grich came along in Stockton while he was a student at UCLA, and he was flying back and forth and playing on the weekends. Altobelli moved right along with us into Double A and then to the Little World Series. So all this time we had him taking Grich and myself under his wing, bringing us along. He'd take us out at night, Bakersfield or somewhere—Bob's Big Boy, places like that— and we'd just sit there and talk baseball. . . . He was like a father away from home for Grich and me. We went through all those leagues together. We were ready to play. Grich took over for Davey Johnson. . . ." And, though it was never said explicitly, Baylor was there as the eventual replacement for the irreplaceable Frank Robinson.

If ever there was good working definition of baseball heaven, it was to be young and a Baltimore Oriole between 1970 and 1975. The Orioles, in those years under Earl Weaver, won the division title four times, the league championship twice, the

World Series once—and they did it with a style and a panache that defined the game. They were a mix of superstars, role players, veterans, and rookies. Their campaigns were ongoing clinics in the blended use of pitching, defense, and power. And above all, they were an ensemble. There was a mystique about simply putting on an Oriole uniform in those days that must have matched the feeling of putting on Yankee pinstripes in the twenties. The remarkable thing, according to Baylor, was that this was present not just when he got to the big leagues but was there from the very first day in the minors. "The Orioles had just won the world championship in 1966, Frank Robinson had been the Triple Crown winner—you could just feel the awareness of what was expected of you in the Appalachian League. . . . It was just one of those things where you walked out on the field and knew you were part of the Oriole organization. You had a chance to win every time you showed up. Other teams would always have that little doubt, *maybe* there's a chance to win. . . . 'Maybe,' 'if,' and 'but' are the three biggest words in the vocabulary, but from the lowest-level farm team right to the top, it was like those words never existed."

For Baylor, and nearly everyone else on the team, the engine that drove the Orioles was Frank Robinson. As well as being an inspirational and intimidating player on the field, Robinson off the field was a maestro. He had a uncanny sense of what it took to keep twenty-five individuals focused on the single task of playing winning baseball and yet feeling that they were, somehow, "family." It was never one at the expense of the other.

Robinson, Baylor remembered, could be as tough as anyone he ever met. Once in winter ball, Robinson was managing a team in Puerto Rico, and one of his players was Reggie Jackson. Jackson had just finished a spectacular season in the majors (1969, when he hit forty-seven homers), and was in a mood to bank rather than stoke his competitive fires. He was a superstar, Baylor said, "but he was also playing for one." Reggie, apparently, had a habit then of watching pop-ups as well as home runs. It didn't sit in the least with Robinson. "You'd have this situation," Baylor said, "where four guys in the infield would let Reggie's pop-up fall and he'd still be standing at home plate. So Frank, in front of everybody else, said, 'It'll cost you five hundred next time you do it—or you can go home.' Two weeks later he did it again, and Frank said, 'Okay, you owe me or you're gone.' Reggie said, "I don't need this, I'm going home," and Frank came right back and said, 'Fine, I'll help you pack.' They disappeared for a while, and when they came back, Reggie was with him. Jack came back out and he played for him and he played great. Ended up leading the league in home runs, and he ran everything, I mean everything, out."

Among Oriole teammates, Robinson was instigator, igniter, chief judge, prosecutor, and sole proprietor of a Marx Brothers instrument known as the Kangaroo Court. This burlesque of the Spanish Inquisition was designed to keep baseball and shared good times rolling together. The Court has had its variations and has been advertised since, but the picture it affords of Robinson, Baylor, and the Orioles in the early seventies remains unique.

"The Kangaroo Court started with Frank," Baylor said. "The way it worked was, if you did anything funny in the field—if you got picked off or wound up in the water between bases—you got brought up on charges. You'd wind up with an award. Dumb baserunning, you'd get a bronzed shoe or something. If you gave up a really long home run, you'd get a ball shredded to pieces hung in your locker. Then there was a toilet seat painted red, which we called the 'Red Ass Award.' You'd get this for stuff like blowing your stack and getting kicked out of a ballgame. For a really bad error you'd get a Golden Glove award—a mitt with a hole cut right through the pocket. At the end of a ballgame, you could bring different cases against guys. They had five cases a night. The press was kept on hold till court was over. Everyone had to get their sandwiches and be seated, and Frank was at the center of the court. If guys were hollering and screaming, they were brought up, too. You had to have a witness. If you brought up a guy on charges and you lost, it cost you double whatever the fine on the other guy would have been. Every time someone brought up a charge against Frank, it was thrown out because he was the judge. There were so many guys, Rettenmund and others, who said that what we needed was collusion, but there was no way to beat that system. The thing was, it was always in fun, it was always after a win, never after a loss. We never did it for a loss. You'd bring things up from the day before or the day before that and you would sit there and for ten minutes—even if you had struck out four times and were feeling down on yourself—you'd be laughing so hard you'd forget."

Frank Robinson was traded two years after Baylor first joined the Orioles. But the younger player never forgot. In Robinson, Baylor saw everything a major-league player should be. He played the game as hard as anyone; he studied other players and situations as though he were a chess strategist seeking any advantage from the most arcane to the most obvious in order to win. Even his playing style was not lost on Baylor. As a hitter, Robinson crowded home plate probably more than anyone in his day—he was a power hitter who hit for average and he simply would not be intimidated. In Puerto Rico, Baylor attached himself to Robinson as he had to Altobelli. In his first seasons as an Oriole he would have been content to play less because, as he told Earl Weaver, he thought he would get more picking Robinson's brain than being sent back to the minor leagues to play fulltime. When Baylor ran into Robinson many years later when they were both on the California Angels—Robinson as a coach, Baylor as an expensive free agent—he turned to his friend to help lift him out of one of the worst batting slumps of his career. Robinson had him come to the park every day at four o'clock for several months, and together they worked on an adjustment that allowed Baylor to hit with hands held in a lower position. From that very first season on the Orioles, and throughout his entire career, Baylor has used a single model bat—Frank Robinson's R-161.

Baylor fit smoothly and typically into the Oriole ensemble. As with most Oriole rookies under Earl Weaver, he was gradually rather than suddenly brought to full playing time. Sometimes— as when Weaver benched him in Fenway Park after he had just had a two-home-run, three-for-four game in Milwaukee—he chafed. Sometimes, he needed to defend himself—as when Weaver and hitting coach Jim Frey tried to get Baylor to open his stance more by pointing his front foot toward third base. "I'll give you no more than ten or fifteen home runs this way," he told Weaver, "but I'll hit for a higher average." Weaver backed off. He wanted twenty-five or thirty home runs a year from him. "Then Earl told me I'd be the league MVP within ten years," Baylor said. Among his teammates, and principally at the instigation of the always needling Robinson, Baylor acquired the nickname "The Groove," because of the propensity he had, early on, of getting into almost unstoppable hitting streaks. Baylor's real groove, though, was his place on the team. The transition from minor-leaguer to major-leaguer was as complete as the design of the front office could have hoped for. If he was not Frank Robinson, what did it really matter? He was a player who hit for power, a solid enough average, and who possessed—so unusual in a big man—real speed. In four full seasons with the Orioles, he stole 117 bases. With his sturdy team feeling, his respect for the organization and its traditions, he was the ideal Oriole player. He was due to become one of baseball's first free agents the following season, but that hardly mattered; he had no intention of going anywhere. Baseball, as far as Don Baylor was concerned, began and ended with the Orioles. That is, until April 2, 1976, the day the Orioles traded him to Oakland for Reggie Jackson.

There are veteran reporters from Baltimore who remember the day probably as well as Baylor. What confronted them when they came into the team clubhouse in Miami after the announcement had been made was Baylor, sitting in a corner of the room by himself, weeping. Caution is always called for in labeling any single event in a person's life as transforming but in Baylor's baseball life, this was certainly so. The impact of this decision is still with him. In that moment, coming as it did on the threshold of revolutionary changes about to shake the financial structure of the game, Don Baylor was forever changed. This is how he described it:

"That was the most devastating thing that ever happened to me in baseball . . . such a close-knit family and then to get dropped. . . . You know, you finally hit home runs and do exactly what they ask you to do—the game is just so unfair. . . . I thought I was going to be an Oriole for life. I was one of several guys who were unsigned, but I didn't think much about it. Bumbry was unsigned, but I didn't think much about it. Bumbry was unsigned, Palmer was unsigned, Torrez was unsigned. I had time to play around with it. I do know that whatever happened, I probably would not have left. At any rate, at spring training I was unsigned. I had made forty-five thousand the year before. I had hit .282, hit twenty-five home runs, so I wanted to double my salary, and a week before the season started, they called in Torrez and told him they wanted him . . . and they signed him. So I said, I'll just wait. Two days later, we were involved in a trade—I didn't know what it was—and I had just gotten a base hit or something, and Weaver called me down to the end of the bench and said, 'You've just been traded to Oakland.' . . . Everyone else knew something was going on, and there was a quiet and hush over the whole place and I just went in and . . . and . . . after a while I went in and asked him why. He said we need a left-hand hitter, said we just got Reggie Jackson, and I said, 'But I want to stay here.' He said, 'Well, we already made the deal. I'm sorry. You played good for me and—' It was hard. It became a business from then on."

Over the years, Baylor has acquired the sort of professional mien that has made him seem at times like a member of the Foreign Legion. He has gone where the money was, selling his allegiance and his skill to the highest bidder, which inevitably meant America's richest cowboy in one instance and America's richest producer of obscure theatricals in another.

It is surely true that Baylor has taken advantage of what was there for him to take advantage of. In a way, he was as much a pioneer in baseball free agency as he was in integrating the schools of Austin, Texas. Again, he was not the first in the country, but he was into it early enough so that what he did made it possible for others to follow. The court decision that ended baseball's reserve clause and opened the gates to free agency came only after the end of the 1975 season, and when Baylor was pushed out through that gate with flaming cherubim guarding the way back, he went more in confusion than with ambition. The Orioles did not ship him to Fort Knox. They turned him over to Charley Finley.

At first, Baylor was too hurt and confused to think much about anything. He had an agent, Jerry Kapstein, who understood that what the courts had just done opened the way to previously unimaginable player salaries. But Baylor was confronted with a far more immediate problem. Playing baseball for Finley in 1976 was about as enticing as playing shuffleboard on the *Titanic*. Nine Oakland players were eligible for free agency, and all of them were anti-Finley and looking to get out. The organization had gone into its sputtering crazy death-throes. Everywhere Finley's penny-pinching was manifest, like edicts from Captain Queeg. The telephone in the Oakland dugout—whether on the road or at home—rang off the hook from wherever in America Finley happened to be. The A's manager at the time, Chuck Tanner, who was, in Baylor's words, "the sort of eternal optimist who believed there never was a bad day in baseball," could muster no better resistance than silence. Unfortunately for Baylor, in the midst of his confusion and unhappiness, Finley informed him that he liked him and, regardless of what he did with his other players, wanted to sign him. Baylor was in a quandary. He did not want to get trapped in Oakland, and he simply did not want to be rude to Finley. He consulted with

Kapstein and came up with an alternative—he would give him an offer he could refuse.

"Charley came down to Texas with me, and we went to this place in one of the bank buildings in Austin called the Headliner's Club. . . . I knew how far I could go with Finley because I had talked to Jerry, and knew what figure would scare him off—eight seventy-five wasn't going to scare him off but a million dollars would. So we're having dinner and we finally get around to talking about business. He said, 'You write down on a piece of paper what you think you should get.' He wrote something down and I did the same thing—I wrote a million two for four or five years." Though this was little more than what a utility infielder might expect to make today, Baylor was then sailing into uncharted waters. "I don't know what I would have done if he had said yes," Baylor said. "It was like calling a bluff. I'm sitting there with two twos and two threes, and he's over there with four kings. . . . It was just like Columbus taking a trip. I'd come that far, I wasn't going to turn back. People told me if I go out there as far as I can see maybe I'll fall off the world." But he didn't fall off the world. He fell out of Finley's grasp, and when the free fall ended, he was wealthy and in California, having gone through baseball's first-ever major-league free agent draft.

It seems like decades rather than just years since all this took place. Baylor subsequently settled in and found his place in baseball's Brave New World. California for a time was a good place to be. His old teammate and friend Bobby Grich joined him there, along with Doug DeCinces and Frank Robinson—Orioles in exile. Kapstein's hunch about the direction of player salaries proved to be prophetic, and by 1980, with routine free agent signings dwarfing the pact he won in 1977, Baylor sought, first, to have his contract extended at the same money, and then, when that failed, to win a new contract when his old one ran out in 1982. Along the way, he learned the business of the game probably as well as any player in baseball. He was, in turn, the player representative for the Angels and then for the entire

American League. In his business dealings with management, he learned what he knew anyway—that between management and players, comradeship and sentiment simply did not exist. "One year, I had to call back management and tell them we were going to strike in spring training," Baylor remembered. "Five minutes later, you couldn't take a ball, bat, anything out of the clubhouse. Everything was locked up. They couldn't have cared less about the need for players to stay in shape through any strike." In his travels around the leagues, he saw one example of nastiness after another. Ken Griffey was exiled to the minors one day before he would have been eligible for free agency—a technicality used by management to bind him for another full year. Players who got old, as always, were just dumped. "After all those great years he gave them, look at what the Orioles did with Ken Singleton. Talk about loyalty, what he did—he gets old, and fuck 'im," Baylor said. Over time, like others in the game, Baylor has learned to take care of himself—to invest his money wisely, to make absolutely certain that in exchange for the talent he gave, he would in recompense secure his and his family's future. Whatever passion of hurt he first experienced, Baylor has transformed it by the guiding direction of a first-rate intelligence. He might have ended up without sentiment, but it turns out he is not. He has his wits, his heart, and his game still about him. A century of upright deaconry is a formidable pillar to move.

Over the past few seasons Baylor has lived in a wealthy New Jersey suburb surrounded by mementos of his career, and of the game in general. He has a trophy case with signed bats from other players, historic game balls, and his old uniform jerseys from Baltimore and California. There is a gallery of photographs and prints, all of them framed by Jimmie Reese, many of them remembrances of the work he has done for the Cystic Fibrosis Foundation. Baylor has been the organizer, promoter, and chief inspiration of a group he created called "65 Roses," a fund-raising organization among major-league ballplayers, set up on a chapter-by-chapter basis (twenty-five of twenty-six teams are involved) to aid children with the disease. The name "65 Roses" is a deliberate misenunciation of "cystic fibrosis"—hope in place of misery.

There is, in Don Baylor's conversation and in what he has chosen to surround himself with, ample evidence of what he brings to the field each day. He is a consummate man of baseball. Professionalism, if it has separated him from an Eden where players, managers, owners, and fans were all one, has left him in a world where winning and losing exists within the mortality of brief careers, and never far from the special comradeship of those who experience them together. Baylor is a player's player. He has never lost sight—or touch—with what he first experienced in the game. Tell him that you still see "Orioles" written across his shirt and a quiet joy will light his face. There are, he acknowledges, people in Baltimore who "still like and remember me as one of them." His memories of Earl Weaver are bittersweet, tinged with both enormous respect and a good deal of affection. He admits to special satisfaction in doing well against his old team—he tells a story about going four for four against the Orioles, with Weaver tossing away his clipboard and later warning his infielders that the only defense against Baylor was making sure they played back far enough so they wouldn't get hurt.

He is a student of the game, so much so that an hour or two with him convinces you that he is a manager in the making. He sits on the bench and studies other players constantly; he knows statistics and averages—what batters do best against what pitchers, what percentage moves are contradicted by still other percentages. He has cable hookups in his house and will come home after playing in his own game to watch four or five other teams—because he likes baseball and because, he says, "You can always learn something, because this or that guy might be in our league next week or next month or next year." He even knows the rulebook.

In the special world of the New York Yankees, Baylor has

occupied an ambiguous and difficult position. For years now, he has had no innings in the field. He is a designated hitter exclusively. He continues to be perhaps the game's most notorious streak hitter—a fact, given his age and the propensity of the Yankee general staff to jump at every whim of the Principal Owner, which has precipitated further cuts in his playing time. A June slump (Baylor traditionally does poorly in April and June—"May, July, August, and September have kept me in the big leagues," he says ruefully) led to his being used only against the few left-handed pitchers the Yankees faced. Compounding all of this—and what made the spring of 1985 special for Baylor—was the imminent return of Billy Martin.

Baylor is unsure exactly why, but he has never been on steady ground with Martin. He remembers that one spring Martin passed around a sheet on which he wanted all his players to write down the names of the pitchers they would rather not face. Baylor handed back a blank sheet, and Martin called him into his office. He had to explain that he felt he could hit anyone. On the fourth day of that season, Martin sat him down against Dave Stieb and Baylor asked for an explanation. Martin told him he thought he would appreciate not having to face a right-hander as tough as Stieb. Baylor told Martin to check his stats against Stieb—he had hit .342 against him over his career. Martin had authority, of course, and could do with it what he wanted. But in Baylor's eyes this often had been manifested in ways that startled and upset him. The public hectoring of a sportswriter in the Yankee clubhouse, his denunciations of players to their faces after poor performances, the particular way he undid the nervous system of one starting pitcher by having another warming in the bullpen during the national anthem, all had to leave Baylor questioning not only the ordinary decency of his manager but his baseball judgment as well.

The 1985 season changed nothing. Baylor's playing time diminished even as the Yankees, surprisingly, remained in contention throughout the summer. Only after the Yankees had been beaten by the Blue Jays in a late-season series did he get regular playing time again. By then, Baylor had demanded a trade and Martin had been quoted in the press as saying Baylor "could no longer hit the fast ball or curveball." After the Blue Jays series, Martin had called a team meeting. In it, Baylor told me, "Billy said, 'I hear you want a trade. Well, I've got news for you, you're gonna stay here and suffer just like me.' I played every game after that." Baylor had no plausible explanation for his relationship with Martin other than to say, for himself and many others, "If you got into the penalty box with him, it's like you *stay* in the penalty box."

With all of that, Baylor has been an extraordinary leader on a team of stars. "He is our sergeant-at-arms, our leader," said pitcher Ron Guidry. "If I had a son I'd want him to grow up to be like Don Baylor." Designated hitters, even ones in the penalty box, normally don't affect their teammates that way. But Baylor brings the incomparable style of his performance with him every day. He gives meaning to the definition of what it is to play hard and intelligently. He *is* tough. In 1979, his MVP year with California, when he hit .296, had thirty-six home runs, and led the league in RBIs and runs scored, he played almost the entire season with a broken wrist. Over the years he has been the kind of player who was always one shade shy of spectacular. There was a year he hit thirty-four homers and drove in ninety-nine runs— it was like a signature for his career: one more in each category and he simply would have been regarded differently.

As he waits in the shadows of age and of, again, having to renew his career, he is one of only four players in the history of baseball to have amassed over 250 home runs and 250 stolen bases. In his Yankee years Baylor introduced a semblance of camaraderie where there had been none. The Kangaroo Court apparently travels with him. For the past two seasons, he has been prosecutor—Frank Robinson's old job—and Phil Niekro has been the Chief Justice of the Supreme Court. Beyond the fun of it, Baylor has tried to use the Court as something of an instruction for younger players. Many of the offenses he brings to trial are about fundamentals and correct play in specific situations. First and last, Baylor is a player's player. Whether as a rookie in paradise, a spokesman for other players, or a veteran on the bench, he has always been someone who has been most at ease in the company of other players. Here is a story he tells about his Oriole days; in it is his professional baseball heart:

"I remember in '74 we had a month left, we had thirty-two games to go. We hadn't gotten hot, cold, anything, we had stayed right there—ten back. The Red Sox were in first and the Yankees second. So we all had a meeting, said, 'Okay, this is what we're going to do. We're gonna take full control and responsibility for the game. We're gonna bunt when there are guys on first and second—even if we don't get the sign from Billy Hunter [O's third base coach]. But we have to protect each other when a guy goes out there and actually does it.' So we started doin' it. And all the time we met. Usually every night at Blair's house. We would send the wives home after a game and go to Blair's. And Earl was really baffled. He kept saying, 'What's going on? What's going on? I said for the guy to hit away, guy's bunting, for chrissakes.' But we won ten in a row, and the Red Sox fell out of it. Now it's the Yankees and us. We went 26–6 and won it by two games. In the end, Earl caught on. He said, 'Okay, I know it's twenty-five guys, twenty-five versus one.' But once he realized it, he said, 'Hey, leave 'em alone. They have ability, they're doing the job—let 'em play.'"

All Don Baylor has ever wanted is to play the game.

III

When he was a minor-league player, Dwight Evans had a manager who gave him the nickname of "Dewey." The manager was thus able to keep Evans separate in his mind from two other players he had labeled "Newey" and "Huey."

"I think there was a Louie, too," Evans said. Dewey he has

been for fifteen years—to fans, media, and to some fellow team-mates—but never by choice. "Newey, Huey, and Dewey is right out of Walt Disney," he said. There was resignation more than anything else in his voice. "My name has always been Dwight, but what are you going to do?"

In a way, Evans' whole career—his whole life—has been a struggle for his own identity. The fourth of five children, he spent his early years in Hawaii, where his father worked for a hotel chain in a minor capacity. The family had little money and, apparently, little time for Dwight. He was quiet and shy, he said, traits that have remained with him and, on more than one occasion, have been mistaken for aloofness and even arrogance. If there was any pain for Evans in these early years, he did not acknowledge it. It was only by indirection that you could sense anything more than the pleasure of living outdoors:

"I went to school and then to the beach. Went to the beach and then to school. Went to the beach," he said with a laugh, "and then went some more. It was great. I went to school bare-footed. Loved it. Went to the beach without ever having to go home. I didn't even have to think about shoes because I had calluses on the bottom of my feet, like the soles of shoes."

But when Evans was 9, his family moved back to the mainland, settling in the San Fernando Valley near Los Angeles and near his grandfather, the single most important person in his young life. Evans' grandfather was a dentist and that, it turned out, was more than a casual fact. He wound up living with him rather than his parents.

"There was no divorce," Evans said, "there was no . . . I couldn't live with my folks, that's all . . . there was more than that . . . what I'm trying to say was it wasn't important . . . because I was a quiet, shy kid . . . and my grandfather was a dentist and for five years I wore braces. I was in and out of that chair almost twice a week, you know . . . plus I was going to school. And I was very close to my grandfather. He was a father figure to me."

A measure of the unusual closeness between grandfather and grandson can be measured in Evans' early experiences in baseball. Evans, like many youngsters, went from Little League to the Pony and Colt leagues. His grandfather, not unlike other children's grandfathers, often came to the ballfield to watch. There was a difference, however. Evans' grandfather was dying of cancer.

"He died in '67," Dwight said, "and that really bothered me, because if anyone wanted to see me make the major leagues, it was him. And a lot of times I do play for him, because even when he had cancer . . . and all they had for him at that time was cobalt . . . he would come out to the game and he would have to be under an umbrella. But he watched the game and then he'd take me over to—you remember A&W Root Beers?"

I shook my head.

"You never had an A&W Root Beer and a hamburger? Well, he'd take me over there, and we'd sit and talk about the game . . . he was just extra nice to me."

He also made it possible for Dwight to play baseball. He paid the entry fees for the different leagues, fees that Dwight's parents couldn't afford. But there was more. The grandfather apparently did not want his grandson to feel like he was receiving charity, and so a bargain was struck. Dwight could work to pay him back. Evans did chores at a small ranch owned by his grandfather. The experience in a curious sort of way related to the kind of baseball player he was later to become. "My grandfather had an orange grove, and all kinds of fruit trees," Evans remembered, "and what I'd have to do—he had a tractor—I'd have to plough. I was twelve, thirteen, fourteen years old and I'd have to work. I worked for my entry fee. I was always a hardworking person. I had to buy my own clothes, to go to school. I had to support myself. The food was on the table but I had to work and I think that really helped me out in life. I mean, when I pay for something I know what it is."

Evans was 15 when his grandfather died. He had no inkling

yet that a professional baseball career lay ahead of him. Although he was an obviously gifted athlete even in his Little and Pony League days, he did not foresee a future in sports for himself because, he said, he then weighed only 140 pounds and was not especially tall. When he thought about it, he saw himself as a policeman or fireman because "I didn't see any boredom in jobs like that."

But Evans grew and filled out quickly. In his last year at Chatsworth High School, he was a flanker on the football team and a star third baseman on the baseball team. Scouts began piling calling cards on his mantel. He discovered about this time that a fascination he had always had for throwing and catching a ball added up to something. Somewhere around 18, he realized he was the possessor of what Boston writers later were to refer to as "The Arm," the blessing and curse both of his way to the big leagues, simultaneously a disembodied thing and a gift. At any rate, Evans tended to see his own abilities in limited terms while the scouts who signed him said he was not merely the best prospect in the organization, "but the best prospect in any organization." From the day he set foot in professional baseball, there was affixed next to his name the tag "unlimited potential." For Evans, it was a far more formidable obstacle than any he had known.

Evans' minor-league career, if anything, only whet appetites in the organization even more. A good half-season in '69 was followed by solid seasons in '70 and '71. In 1972, he was the International League's MVP at Louisville. By season's end, he was in Boston and by the following spring, he was the team's regular right fielder.

The inability of Evans to fulfill the impossibly high expectations that had been set for him plagued his early years in the majors. In retrospect, he says, "It was like the first eight years didn't exist." But they surely did. In 1973 he was seriously beaned in a game with the Texas Rangers. He injured his knee severely enough to require surgery in 1977. In 1978 he was beaned again—and in the aftermath suffered dizzy spells and an inner-ear problem that eventually sidelined him for most of the last month of the season.

But there was more. By 1974, the fortunes of the team began to change for the better. Perennial also-rans since their "miracle" pennant of 1967, the Red Sox were contenders again in '74 and winners in '75. When Evans looked, the supporting cast around him included Jim Rice, Fred Lynn, Carlton Fisk, Butch Hobson, Cecil Cooper, and then, when Cooper was traded, George Scott. By his own admission, he was intimidated—and no more clearly than in the way he approached hitting. Though he had great natural power to the opposite field, Evans found himself trying to pull everything when he stepped to the plate.

"I followed Jimmy Rice, Freddie Lynn, Yaz, George Scott—you name 'em—into the cage," he said. "They'd all hit about ten, fifteen, home runs apiece, and then I'd come up. And, of course, I had pride, ego—I tried to do the same thing. . . . I just wound up doing the old routine of bail and whale, trying to pull everything I could."

Evans, meanwhile, seemed to drift through seasons where his performance alternated between spectacular bursts of play and long stretches of offensive ineptitude. No sooner than he would begin to look like the player everyone predicted he would be, he would become slump-bound once again—or injured or so frustrated and unsure of himself that he would change his batting stance so dramatically everyone in New England from the Bay of Fundy to the Greenwich Tool Plaza seemed to know about it. Sparky Anderson, in the wake of Evans' fine play in the 1975 World Series, called him the most underrated player in the game. But by 1980, still struggling to find himself, Evans was benched by Red Sox manager Don Zimmer.

"I probably had three hundred or more stances in those eight years," Evans said. "I'd work on a stance—I was always taking extra hitting—and I'd get it down and have it for two or three weeks, sometimes a month. And I'd do well with it. Then they'd find out the way to pitch to that and I'd have to go to another stance to get out of the last one. I was just wishy-washy in my hitting and my thinking. Instead of grinding it out—that is, staying with one stance—I'd just change. Close. Open. Close. Square off. Move up. Move back. It was a question of losing confidence. And I did, no doubt about it."

When Evans talks about this period today, the most intractable part of it all seemed to be the shadow of potential that was ever at his feet. In his early years, like the long shadows of morning, it was a promise of brightness, but by decade's end it was a midnight specter haunting him with what he had not and seemingly would never achieve. The Boston media, never at ease with him, could not abide his moods or his aloofness. He was criticized for his play, taunted for his changeability, and blamed, in large part, for what the team had failed to achieve on the field. When Zimmer benched him in 1980, he did so believing that Evans was lazy and indifferent. Boston fans, as baffled as anyone, regularly booed him. Symptomatic of the media's attitude toward him was the sort of assertion found in Peter Gammons' recent book on the period, *Beyond the Sixth Game*. "Teammates derided Evans [for being Yaz's sidekick]," Gammons wrote. "[Fred] Lynn used to pretend he was a puppet being dangled by a string, asking teammates 'Who am I?' while Dwight looked on." Only the incident, according to Fred Lynn himself, never happened. "It's just not true," Lynn said. "I heard that was written, read it, and was as shocked as anyone else." "For God's sake, Freddie was my locker buddy," Evans said. "If something like that happened—to my face, no less—don't you think I'd remember it?"

Compounding all of this was a heartbreaking and demanding situation at home. In 1973, Evans' oldest child, Timmy, then 6 months old, was first diagnosed as having neurofibromatosis—a rare disease marked by the formation of multiple, often disfiguring, and sometimes life-threatening benign tumors of the nerve ends. Twenty-five hospital trips and ten major operations followed, but there was no cure for the condition or prognosis for its eventual course. The condition, which can stop as mysteriously as it starts, stabilized by 1977. But only a few years following, the youngest of Evans' three children was also stricken. "Justin had a headache one night, a migraine," Evans said, "and so we took him . . . they did a CAT scan and there was a tumor about the size of a quarter at the base of his brain." Radiation therapy was performed. The child temporarily lost his hair and permanently lost part of his vision because the tumor was located near the optic nerve.

In the course of both children's bouts with illness, Evans says he and his wife, Susan, a childhood sweetheart, became devoutly Christian. Some of the reasons why were in Dwight's description of their son Timmy's last trip to the hospital in 1977:

"You know, he had been there twenty-five times, and now they were going to reconstruct his whole skull and the left side of his face. They were going to cut the optic nerve and reconstruct the whole side of his head. At Mass General, we had the chief neurologist, who's now down in Washington working for the government. He had put together a team of seven doctors, a few had come in from Europe. They had scheduled this ten-hour operation, or longer or worse: they said they might have to sew him back up, put a football helmet on him and try again in six months. If you ever get down on your knees, you understand that my wife and I did. I took him in the afternoon before, into the ward where he was going to be the next morning. The operation was scheduled for the afternoon. I looked at some of those kids lying there moaning in pain, IVs running out of them, their heads just covered with bandages. I was a person that hadn't cried in twelve years. And I still didn't cry. But I was weeping inside . . . the tears just wouldn't come . . . those kids were my son the next day—evening, I mean, because it would be an all--day operation. So Susan and I accepted it. There was nothing else we could do. What could we do? And then, about fifteen minutes later, the head neurologist comes in and tells Susan and me, 'Would you come with me, please.' There were three doctors, and they took us up to this small room and they said that they had been looking at some last-minute X rays. They said, 'We don't know what's happened here, we just know that at this time Tim doesn't need this operation. We just looked at each other and knew it was an answered prayer. . . . That was what got us going. God has done a lot in my life."

Evans' career seemed to get a divine lift, too—but in this case, it came in the decidedly human form of batting coach Walter Hriniak. At midseason in 1980, having signed a new long-term contract the year before, Evans found himself in the worst slump of his career. Eight years and hundreds of stances after he broke into the major leagues, he seemed further than ever from being anything more than a streak hitter with a high-priced gold glove. He was ready to do more than accept what Hriniak had to teach—he was ready to surrender.

"In '80, at the all-star break," he said, "I was hitting a buck seventy, buck seventy-five. I had signed a new contract and thought I was on my way. And all of a sudden, I had this terrible start, and it continued right on to the all-star break. I was trying things and I couldn't hit at all. I had two-thirds of the plate you could throw to; not that I was afraid of the ball, I was just coming off the ball. I started looking into the Charley Lau stuff, and Walter came to me and said, 'Do you want to try this?' And I said, 'I'll try anything right now.' I said, 'I surrender!'"

More than any hitter on the Red Sox, Evans was the one who most thoroughly adopted the Lau style and so the results of his work are easily recognizable: his movements in the batter's box—his "soft" movements—preliminary to the pitch are a few, easy swishes of the bat back and forth; his body rocks forward and backward and gradually he draws back his weight onto his rear foot as he tightens the arc of his preliminary swings and sets the bat back in cocked position off his right shoulder. As he does this, he drags back his left foot, seemingly in stages, heel raised, toe pointing to the ground almost as if he were using it for dowsing. Fully poised and waiting to strike, he is crazily like the caricature of a tango dancer, splayed out, the centrifugal force of his body balanced by the swooping pull of his torso, arms, and shoulders in one direction and his long, extended leg in the other. When he strides into the pitch, however, his balance, like the tango dancer's, is perfect. His body shifts forward but his hands seem to go back at the same time. This weight shift forward is total and complete and it sets him in a position where his bat is, literally, in a position to be launched while his weight, momentarily, is evenly distributed. When he swings into the ball, his head is down, the force of his weight coming forward gradually passes to his front foot, which remains rigid so that the body's full and twisting load of weight can be received; the head remains down as though the effort to see the precise second of the ball striking the bat is an independent act as the hands separate and one hand only brings the bat high over the head as though, in the finishing pose, the hitter-dancer had undergone one last transformation and is now the palace guard who has just finished taking off the head of an offending intruder with his scimitar.

Evans insists he is a mechanical—rather than a natural—hitter. And that it is easy to break down, as he does, each component of the swing so that it can be studied, practiced, assimilated. But this process of endless repetition of "mechanics" is, for Evans especially, something that goes far beyond machine tooling a baseball swing. It is—and has been from the start—a form of mental training, his "psalm."

"We started in Baltimore in 1980," Hriniak remembered. "He had lost his job to Jimmy Dwyer. He was hitting .180 and he was at the end of his rope and he came to me and asked for some help. . . . And what I told him was that the things I was going to show him I wanted him to make a commitment to, sink or swim with them. Because the thing that plagued him in his career was he was always changing things—sometimes one at-bat to the next. Well, the thing was, he stuck with it. From then on. He hasn't changed. He put in hours and hours—flip drills, batting practice—to revamp his whole swing. He adopted Charley's theories more so than anybody on this club. He does everything right out of the book. And that's not an easy thing to do for a person who was in the big leagues for as long as he was and who did things the opposite way."

Certain aspects of the "mental" training were fairly obvious. Simply to pick one batting stance and stay with it—grind it out—involved disciplining himself beyond the grip of periodic disappointment or failure. The ability to "surrender" oneself, an almost mystical component of Eastern training, had immediate and practical results for Evans. Hriniak, like Lau, stressed the importance of hitting "up the middle," straight back at the pitcher. This was a way of training a hitter to use the whole field rather than always to be pulling. For Evans, though, it was also a way of dealing with his own insecurities in the batting cage.

"I started trying to hit the ball hard up the middle, right at the pitcher's screen every time," he said. "For me to get over that one thing, to go up there and hit grounders through the middle while all those guys were hitting the ball out—that was something. You know, they're wondering 'What's this guy trying to do?'—and that has helped me tremendously."

But there is another level entirely to Evans' training, one that goes well beyond confidence-building. The peculiar combination of a willingness to work hard along with the very qualities others had criticized him for—strong dependence on others, an easy readiness to give up his own way of doing things—gave him an extraordinary capacity for discovering in himself a level of performance seemingly beyond the limitations of his own nature. His description of why he works hard is a passable baseball facsimile of reaching Nirvana:

"I work at the game," he said, "to keep the intensity I have to have. The biggest thing is keeping in shape because you can't begin to play without your body. The game is probably ninety to ninety-five percent mental for me. All the stuff I do with Walter—I've probably taken close to one million swings with him in the last six years, and when you do that you get to the point where you don't have to think about what you're doing. I no longer have to think about my hands, or whether I'm coming back far enough or whether my shift is correct. There is nothing in my head then and it's just there."

It is hard to appreciate just how much Evans has accomplished. If his career is measured statistically, it almost appears as if two different players have inhabited his body, one on either side of 1980. Prior to the all-star break of that year, Evans was a career .259 hitter. Going into the 1985 season (when another prolonged early season slump held his average for the year to .263) Evans has hit at a .286 clip. In 1981 he was leading the league in hitting until the strike. He finished the year, leading in home runs and walks. In '82, when he hit .292, he came within two walks of being one of a handful of players in major-league history to reach milestones of 100 walks, 100 runs scored, and 100 RBIs in the same year—a feat he nearly duplicated in 1984 (a league-leading 121 runs scored, 104 RBIs, 32 home runs, and 96 walks). "He's become a terrific all-around player, that's all," said teammate Rich Gedman, "not just a defensive player who hits .250 and has twenty home runs." "He has trouble getting in a groove," veteran first baseman Bill Buckner said, "but when he does, he's better than anybody."

But only part of the story is in the record books and probably not the most important part. It is likely that when he leaves the game he will eventually fade from memory with respectable enough numbers and few votes to include him in the Hall of Fame. Yet he will surely have been one of the era's superb outfielders, among the game's finest right fielders since Roberto Clemente. He has for years been a complete player. His pursuit of a ball in the treacherous sunskies of Fenway is done in a long, loping canter reminiscent of Joe DiMaggio, who defined ease and grace in making difficult plays. To watch the way Evans accelerates to cut down or extend the angle of a hit so that he can retrieve the ball and in his throw immediately convert the potential of an extra base or run scored into the possibility of an out is to watch defensive play raised to the excitement of a dramatic home run.

But there is nothing that so clearly conveys what Evans is about than early morning in Winter Haven. As his friend Carl Yastrzemski had done through all those years, Evans is there before the media and most of his teammates. He changes quickly into uniform trousers and T-shirt and then proceeds to the hitting shed, where Hriniak is waiting for him. The two men say little to each other because each knows what is to be done. Evans stands off to one side and slowly begins a series of practice swings, gradually working until the bat makes a hollow whooshing sound in the heavy morning air. Hriniak in the meantime has moved a large bucket of balls alongside an approximately four-foot-by-four-foot screen behind which he can crouch. Then the flip drill is done.

From his position about ten feet directly in front of Evans, Hriniak flips baseballs toward him, which Dwight swats into the walls of netting enclosing the shed. The Japanese have a drill similar to this, only the batter stands off to the side of the thrower in performing it. Hriniak prefers the straight ahead position because that is the angle a hitter sees pitches coming from in a game.

Initially, nothing seems out of the ordinary as Evans in almost robotlike fashion smashes ball after ball into the nets. But then it gradually dawns upon you that every ball he has hit has gone in the direction of right and right center field. For the next ten minutes all he will do is drive balls, so easily tossed he could do anything with them, in this single direction. Then, on a nod from Hriniak, he hits everything straight out. Ball after ball rockets straight ahead, caroming off the protective screen in front of Hriniak or whistling overhead into the nets behind him. In was in just this manner, years ago, that Hriniak, unable to get his arm back behind his screen fast enough, had an elbow shattered by Joe Rudi. There is no trace of apprehension now as Walter serves ball after ball, ducking behind the screen each time as though he were lobbing hand grenades. After another ten minutes, Evans begins pulling the ball to the left side.

Through the entire drill, few words were exchanged. Occasionally Evans paused to say something like, "Was I lined up?" And Hriniak's response, no less arcane, was: "You need this much." Then after two more swings, the coach added, "That's it, remember it." (Maintaining a vertical line between the shoulder and rear foot, Hriniak said later, was essential in maintaining correct balance on the shift of weight backwards.) At yet another point, Evans stopped the drill entirely because he felt there was something wrong in the way he was dragging his front toe across the dirt as he leaned back into hitting position. This time Hriniak said nothing, preferring to let Evans work out the problem himself. "That's it, that's right," Walter said when Dwight resumed and had taken a few additional swings.

"What I was doing there," Evans explained after his workout, "was edging back rather than getting back smoothly. You know the Lau approach is getting back to go forward, but if you don't get back one hundred percent, you're not going to go forward correctly."

"You step on an egg," Hriniak said.

"Exactly," answered Evans.

I watched this routine many times over many days and the cumulative impression it left was more about the relationship Evans had with Hriniak than about the fine-tuning of a baseball swing. There was no question that Evans, over many years now, had given himself to Hriniak as totally as any adept to his teacher. One day, Evans explained the evolution of his relationship with Hriniak:

"I give Walter a lot of credit. In the beginning, he really forced me. He would get on me, say things like 'What are you gonna do, quit?' That type of thing. And I would have some soul-searching to do and always the answer was: 'This man is right.

You've changed your stance in the past every other week. Are you going to do it again?' 'You want to change,' he'd say, 'go ahead, I'll help you.' But he was really saying. 'Go ahead, quit.' I knew that. A lot of this work is just plain humbling—like today, out in the cage. Today I happened to be swinging probably about as bad as I ever had, even before I started this stance. I wasn't over the ball enough, I wasn't in the right position to go at the ball. You know, the thing was it felt okay to me but he still was able to pick it out. We corrected it and suddenly I started swinging well. We have developed a great understanding. We know each other's dos and don'ts, we know the limits that we can go at each other with . . . you can't put your finger on it, but we know each other very well, is what I'm trying to say."

Evans also accepts the notion that he might one day have to work alone. The measure of what really has occurred over the last five years is this slow gathering of inner strength that is a direct result of shared work. Through it, he has learned that he can work alone. A million swings has taught him, more than anything, how to be his own man.

"It would take a great adjustment if I didn't have Walter," he acknowledged, "but I know I'd survive. One thing Walter has taught me is how to do it myself. Right now, if I didn't have Walter—he is my camera, my videotape. We talk, we put into words what would be on the screen, we have our minds—but still, he is my camera. If I didn't have him I would actually go to videotape, and I know what I'd be looking for. The funny thing is, you can be doing something wrong and not know it—you won't feel it even. But it'll be there and you'll be able to see it. I can do that now."

If Evans were more extroverted by nature, the changes he has undergone in the past seasons would seem more obvious. But because he is not that available, it takes some effort to appreciate what he has really done. The effort, however, is worth it. Years ago, a hitting slump would have precipitated a rush to change things and a reaching out for support. Today Evans says, "I know by doing certain things mechanically, by working hard, I'll come out of that slump. Usually when you go into a slump you start thinking about too many things—it's this, it's that, I'll change this. There may be a number of mechanical things to do but Walt taught me something else. To simplify things. To think of one thing and watch the ball. If I'm in a slump, I know sooner or later I'll come out of it."

As though he had spoken prophetically, the 1985 season put everything Evans had learned to the test. He homered on opening day, leading the Red Sox to a victory over the Yankees, but then he seemed to stall. He slumped as badly as he ever had in his career, staying below .200 for most of the first half. For much of that time, Walt Hriniak, his time taken up by other players, was available only on a limited basis. With a new manager who nervously kept shifting him around in the batting order and who would have benched him had injuries to other outfielders not prevented it, Evans had every reason to jettison what he had learned for something new that might work. In the past he would have done just that. This time he did not. When his hitting returned shortly before the all-star break, he had stayed with what he knew—he had made himself "grind it out." "I lost sleep, that's for sure," he told me later in the season, "but I never thought of changing stances. I made a slight adjustment with my front foot, a hair's difference—hitters are always doing that— but if I gave up on what I'd been doing the last five years, I would have given up on myself." Evans wound up hitting well over .300 for the second half, with 29 home runs, 119 walks, and, in spite of his reduced average, the seventh-best on-base percentage in the league.

It is possible that only a Red Sox pennant will enable Evans to receive the unreserved recognition he has coming in Boston beyond the clubhouse. But in the clubhouse, though Evans is surely a "quiet leader," there is another sentiment. "I've been pretty fortunate," Rich Gedman said. "Dwight's been an incentive to a lot of guys on this club because of what he's struggled through. The very first spring training I had here, I saw the way he worked in the cage—and I've tried to do the same for myself ever since."

Bill Buckner, who has played on championship teams with the Dodgers and who has, for years, had his own approach to hitting, acknowledged that Evans' work habits ultimately induced him to change his own. "He's just an example for everyone," Buckner said. "In fact, he was the one who really got me into working with Walt Hriniak. It was Dwight who got me into different work habits and into a new hitting style this year. It's a tough thing for someone at my age to do but Dwight did it when he was thirty, so I'm doing it now at thirty-five and I wish I could have done it earlier in my career."

But no one knew so well as Hriniak what Evans had been through and what precisely it revealed. "Dwight has been great. Any hitter who goes through two months of hitting .170, you just know how hard it is for him—and the people watching him. I think when you see someone go through something like that and never give up, you gotta admire and respect him for it. It's awful easy to play this game when things are going well but it's very different when things are tough. What Dwight Evans is is a professional. He gives meaning to the word."

"This is my seventeenth spring training," Evans told me months before in Winter Haven, "and it's tough. I have to be an example, that's true. But you can't say it. You can only do it. You have to push yourself a little harder and try to show younger players, hey, you don't sit back—you work harder. You can talk a great game but you have to go out and do it." The example Evans presents to his team is a way of overcoming limitations. In Boston, it is an example to be heeded.

PART FIVE

EPILOGUE

CHAPTER NINE

Till Daylight Fails

Duly were our games
Prolonged in summer till the daylight failed.
—Wordsworth, *The Prelude*

In the beginning of April I packed my car and, with my family joining me for the ride, drove back to the Northeast from Florida. All the way north, we saw the season slowly change so that in a matter of days we seemed to edge backward through a time warp from the ripeness of late spring to the edges of winter. I came north, as baseball players had every year, to see spring begin again. I was reminded, as countless players must have been over the years, of the brevity of seasons, of how the passing of time—no matter how much has happened—always leaves behind the memories of a short season. Spring training, if it is not a paradigm of life, is one of a career in baseball. It is over almost before it begins. Most of us over the age of 40 can remember Willie Mays when he was the boy wonder that Dwight Gooden is now. The passage of time in baseball is both leisurely and cruel in its swiftness. A career, a season, even a single game, is a balancing between the known and the unknown, a mystery in its unfolding, something familiar and permanent in its vanishing.

I was struck, more than anything, by how much spring training really is weighted on the side of mystery. The reason why is easy to understand—it is at the very beginning of things. The season is yet to come. Heaven, the poet says, lies about us in our infancy—and so we are given to this business of looking forward with a passion that gradually merges with reality in summer and fall. Spring is a time to parse the future, to play with the unknown. Twenty-six teams fly twenty-six pennants in their dreams for the season to come. All of us—from vaguely interested amateurs to people who make their living watching baseball—make their pennant-race predictions. And do it, usually, with a sort of pseudoscientific bravura common to insurance agents, gamblers, astrologers, and others in the business of teasing the future out of the present.

Had I not traveled to spring training last season, I would, like anyone else, have surely forgotten the future that was never seen. But I was struck forcefully by just how much a part of the game fortune telling really is. Thinking about it now, it seems certain that expertise—the kind used by scouts, executives, coaches, managers—very much depends on being able to foresee what talent can do. Baseball teams are built this way, pennants won and lost. But this expertise—as Charlie Fox taught me—because it involves trucking in mystery is perilous indeed. The great new Yankee star, Don Mattingly, it should always be rememberd, was a 19th-round draft pick when he turned professional. So was the Royals' star pitcher and World Series MVP, Bret Saberhagen. And there once was a phenom named Clint Hartung. . . .

The rest of us, though we regularly become aware of these blunders in judgment, are rarely chastened. We go after the future just as eagerly, with just as much sense of certainty. Here, for example, are a few of the inevitable predictions for the '85 season made on the eve of play last April:

Sports Illustrated, complete with graphs, computer analyses, and healthy contempt for the usual fortune-cookie approach in these matters, downplayed the traditional division-by-division choices and instead scientifically ranked all twenty-six major-league clubs. Theirs was a "scouting report," not a turning over of tea leaves. First in their order of ranking were the Toronto Blue Jays followed by the Detroit Tigers, Cubs, Padres, and Mets. Next—or 3rd place in the A.L. East—were the Orioles. The Yankees and Red Sox followed immediately. The Phillies were ranked 11th overall (3rd in the N.L. East), the Cardinals 15th overall (4th place). As for the A.L. West, the Angels were ranked 24th (next to last) and the Royals, correctly picked to win, were ranked 9th overall. In capsule summary, the magazine got around to doing what we all do: Jays in the East, winners over the Royals in the West, versus the Cubs, who would beat the Padres for the N.L. flag, in the World Series.

Tom Boswell in *The Washington Post* matched *SI*'s call in the A.L. East, picked the Cubs over the Mets, saw the Phils on the rise—with the Montreal Expos, having "no chance" and the Cards winding up "just too sad to watch."

Peter Gammons in the *Boston Globe* picked the Blue Jays, with the Red Sox right on their heels, followed by the Tigers, Yanks, and Orioles. He picked the Phils in the N.L. East and the Braves in the N.L. West.

New York Times writers Joe Durso and Murray Chass both picked the Yankees for 5th and agreed that the Jays would beat out the Tigers, Red Sox, and Orioles.

Inside Sports had the A's last in the A.L. West and the Cards last in the N.L. East.

Of course, I am hardly above any of this. I picked the Orioles to beat out the Tigers, the Cubs over the Mets, the Dodgers over the Padres, the Twins over the Royals, and, of course, the Cards last. My 16-year-old nephew—addicted to computers and Strat-O-Matic Baseball as well as to the real thing—last year hit four picks out of four, correctly handicapped the playoffs, and got the

Series on the nose. If ever I needed the services of a bookie, I would consult my nephew before anyone. This year, however, he picked the Tigers over the Orioles (he had the Jays 4th), with the Royals, Mets, and Braves winners in the other divisions. No one on earth, to my knowledge, foresaw a Royals' World Championship over the Cardinals, featuring successive three-games-to-one comebacks from the dead to get the job done.

The business of predicting pennant races is, surely, as conventional as throwing rice at weddings. And whatever else it is, it is fun. But being close to the source this past spring, I was acutely reminded of just how much what is known feeds what we do not know about baseball. Baseball surely is the most microscopically and statistically analyzed of our recreations—we go far beyond actuarial tables and tout sheets in weighting what we anticipate with what we know in the present. But a season, a microcosm of time, teases us with the way in which things happen. We seem to have varying degrees of foreknowledge, just enough to sometimes satisfy the need to say "I told you so," but never enough to have seen what actually came to pass.

Most of us could anticipate that during the '85 season Pete Rose would finally break Ty Cobb's hit record, that Tom Seaver and Phil Niekro would reach 300 career wins. But even then, the individual moments of happening were beyond prediction—that Rose, by the discovery of a statistical error, probably surpassed Cobb with no one realizing it, that Tom Seaver would return to New York to win his 300th game in Yankee Stadium, and that Niekro, waiting till the season's final day, would in the process become the oldest man in the history of baseball to throw a complete game shutout (the Yanks defeated the Jays, 8–0), and that he would sail through this memorable game waiting until the final inning before he threw a single knuckleball.

Knowing something only deepens and makes richer or more ironic what eventually happens. Who would have said that when the Blue Jays finally won their division-clinching game over the Yankees, the winning pitcher would be Doyle Alexander, discarded by George Steinbrenner two years before (and still on the hook for his huge salary) as so inefficient he did not want his infielders to risk injury playing behind him? Or that Tom Seaver, like Niekro or Rose, might have had other things in mind than milestone records en route to his moment with the record books. Seaver told me one spring day, "At my age, I know I have only about sixty games left in my arm and so each game I pitch becomes very special for me." Therefore, Seaver's 296th and 304th wins came to have their own meaning for me, too.

Because of my travels, I had a chance to see the season differently. I am certain that the Cubs' falling from grace would not have had the same meaning for me had I remained east of The Superstitions this spring. The Illinois Supreme Court by season's end—a season that saw the entire Cub starting pitching staff jinxed by major injuries—once and for all forbade the construction of lights at Wrigley Field. It fit right in, Dallas Green said publicly, with the bad luck that had burdened the Cubs all year. I did not get the chance to ask him if he had become interested in Jacob Walzer.

The unexpected involvement of the California Angels in the pennant race also made the unknown final weeks of the season more interesting. The closest Jimmie Reese had ever come to a World Series was 1982, when the Angels won their division and then, after winning the first two games of the playoffs, lost three straight to the Milwaukee Brewers. It had been, Reese said, last spring, the worst moment in his baseball career. I became an Angel fan in the closing weeks of the season. I did not see Jimmie Reese when the Angels came east in September—because he was still not traveling with the team. But he was up to a full work schedule at all Angel home games, which meant three or four hours of fungoing—and it was not hard to imagine his disappointment when, in the end, the Angels settled for a second-place finish.

It was impossible, having lived on such leisurely and personal terms with the game in the spring, to have not had far more appreciation for what befell different individuals during the regular season. It was even possible, for example, to see yet another Billy Martin barroom brawl somewhat differently. In all of the turmoil surrounding the Yankees as they cascaded down the home stretch, still in contention, I could not help remembering Martin as I had seen him in the spring. The man *anybody* could approach. "Billy," Clete Boyer said late in the summer, "could run *any* kind of team—a team of stars as well as a team of nobodies." He made his adjustments, he took on whatever came his way—including yet another showdown and firing in the Bradshaws.

The unwinding of a pennant race always has drama built into it. And we were lucky in 1985 to have had not one but four races that went down to the very last weekend. The brief mid-season strike and the late-summer drug trials in Pittsburgh did not deter the season from being the best we have had in years.

Of the teams I happened to follow, certain things did seem inevitable. I was not surprised by the somnolent finish of the Red Sox or by the perfectly inept response of the front office to the non-happenings on the field (two days after a *Globe* article criticizing a "lack of chemistry" on the team, the front office announced—as though in symbiotic relationship with Boston baseball's makers of public opinion—that the problem with the team was "a lack of chemistry"). What this meant (aside from possible collusion with certain members of the media), was a reversal of the old organizational cry "We unfortunately can't fire twenty-six guys, so we're firing the manager." One assumes that burdensome "no trade" clauses as well as limited market appeal will somewhat restrain the hand of the chemists, but given the character of some of the new ownership's past personnel dealings, it is probably good for Red Sox fans to keep in mind that the basic problem, in this laboratory, is an inability to distinguish lead from gold, much less to convert one to the other.

I had a brief conversation with Dwight Evans after the season ended. He was, given the amount of public finger-pointing directed at him, thinking that it might be well for him to play elsewhere. He had thought about some teams where he might better fit in. But he thought about the team he was still on in a way that seemed mightily constructive. "We need to know how to find people and bring them into the organization. I'd like to see us have the ability to teach kids from day one in the minor leagues in a uniform way so that when they came up, they were really familiar with our system. That means scouting, coaching, trading, everything—right up the line. I told Haywood Sullivan that. He's a very proud man, you know, but he agreed with me." Evans paused, then added with a laugh, "You know, I think I might like to eventually be a minor-league director or a director of player development someday."

The unwinding of the Orioles, on the other hand, seemed more surprising. And sadder, because I had had so recently a glimpse of what had worked so well for so long. The Orioles, for the first time since 1967, replaced their manager in mid-season. Pitching coach Ray Miller, at the same time, left to manage Minnesota. The occasion, though it brought back Earl Weaver, was handled poorly. The departing manager, Joe Altobelli, was apparently the last to learn of the managerial decision and had had to wait at the ballpark, twisting slowly in the wind of rumor, till he was told. He left saying he had been "sadly mistaken in the belief that the Orioles were a class organization."

At the same time, the struggling Orioles reached into the bosom of the family for help. They rehired the man who had defined their success on the field for fifteen years. If they were hoping for a reprise of "Orioles' Magic," they could not have chosen more logically. "The thing about Earl," Eddie Murray said, "is that he really can get the best out of twenty-five guys. He knows how to do that, and for sure we need that."

But the Orioles did no better under Weaver (in terms of percentage, the team actually fared slightly better under Altobelli). Still, as one writer put it, "it's fun to walk in here again." And why not? Weaver's grasp of the game was as prodigious as ever, his ability to digest the nine-columned sheets of statistics that prompted his lineup decisions remained unimpaired, and so, too, was his ability to regale anyone in earshot with a conversational élan second to none in the baseball world (he had been fatally miscast as a cleaned-up color man for TV).

Late in the season, the Orioles were hopelessly out of the pennant race. They were in the process of being swept in a weekend series at Yankee Stadium. The day before, Weaver had been thrown out of a game—for the 93rd time in his career. Prior to the last game in the set, Weaver told a couple of Baltimore writers that the day before, when he was ejected, the umpire, Jim Evans, had informed Weaver the "the game has passed you by."

"Who knows," Weaver said, "he may just have been right." He was standing in his baseball skivvies in the middle of his dressing room. "I'll tell you this," he said with a half-growl, half-laugh, "I don't dispute that I've had a helluva lot of fucking fun playing golf. But let me tell you something about that. The first time I got thrown out of a game in the big leagues . . ." He was off. If there had been fifty rather than the five people who were present, Weaver's delivery would not have changed one whit. The secret of any good raconteur is a perfect sense of timing coupled with an uncanny ability to make each listener believe that what is being said is directed to him only. "What happened was Larry Knapp was standing on my toes doing *this*." Weaver pantomimed having his toes crushed into the ground by someone wearing spiked shoes. "He's turning his foot and turning his foot, calling me every name he could think of. And you know what my words to him were? I'm there in agony and I'm tellin' him, I said, 'Old man, the game's passed you by!' That's what I said to him and he's got this nasty little voice goin', sayin', 'You get your fuckin' little shitty ass out of here'—he's tellin' me that, and Christ Almighty I'm hurtin'—he says, 'You won't be here two years, you assholes have two years to laugh and then you're gone, outta the game'—and what am I doin'? I wanna cry but there I am sayin', 'Old man, the game's passed you by, you ain't gonna run me out of the big leagues,' I said, 'because I'm here to stay. Now get the fuck off my toe.'"

When the laughter in the room quieted, Weaver added, "See, Evans used the same words on me yesterday—it's come full circle."

On this particular night, Weaver, frustrated with his team's performance and especially with its inability to contest the Yankees, was in a mood to entertain notions of retirement once again. He had, for the first time since he had returned to uniform, quarreled with his wife—because his team had lost a game. "I just took it out on her," he said, "that's the fuckin' reason I got out in the first place." Weaver thought about his time away from the game more easily now. He had given more than half his adult life to baseball. He had missed birthdays, holidays, graduations, weddings, because all those years he had been, first, a good company man. Now, when something came up in the summer, he would take a day off, he said.

He was still a good company man. And that, perhaps, was the point. Weaver could not do it alone when he was brought back because he had never been able to do it alone in the first place. There had always been the organization behind him. His wizardry, all those years, depended on the smooth working of a many-layered Baltimore operation. More than anything, the 1985 season pointed to seeming weaknesses in the organization. The minor-league system that—almost yearly, it seemed—provided a star pitcher or two, had, for several seasons, been yielding little. Most of the Oriole farm teams had been playing with poor records and few real prospects. Over the previous winter, the front office, for the first time in memory, had gone into the free-agent market in a big way and, midway in the '85 season, sensing a chance to fill a need at second base, picked up the drug-troubled Alan Wiggins from the Padres.

Weaver was not there in the spring. Edward Bennett Williams was. And his impatience and his willingness to change things hung over the Oriole season. The pitching had simply failed. The Oriole organization, in its deliberate, conservative way, would address this problem—or not. A friend in Baltimore, explaining the firing of Joe Altobelli, told me, "Mr. Williams doesn't have much time left to win." But given what I saw this spring, I was reminded of an episode in the book *Zen and the Art of Archery*, where a student archer, after years of study with a Zen master, tries to speed things up. He discovers that by manipulating his thumb in a certain way he can better propel an arrow to the target. The master sees what he has done and refuses to aid him further. The student has misunderstood the very basis of the teaching. It is The Way that produces results and The Way must, therefore, always come first. There was, I knew, only so much Weaver—or any one person—could do about that.

The success of the Yankees in 1985 surely was among the season's biggest surprises. No one had picked them to contend. Most Yankee watchers, myself included, knew they had considerable offensive punch but were burdened with mediocre starting pitching and, with the exception of Dave Righetti, an untried bullpen. In addition, the season began with Rickey Henderson injured, Dave Winfield just back from an injury, and the Red Sox clobbering the Yanks five out of six times. With the inevitable sacking of Yogi Berra and the implausible return of Billy Martin, the reviews for the Producer's latest show were quick in coming. And they were off—about as badly as the original reviews for *Abie's Irish Rose*.

The Yankees, with Henderson at the top of the order and Mattingly hitting either second or third, first destabilized, then destroyed, the opposition. Henderson was better than an ideal lead-off man. He rewrote the book. The key to his success, unlike great lead-off hitters in the past, was not speed alone but a combination of speed and power. He was the sort of base stealer who was a certain threat to take second *and* third. Because of the power behind him in the order, he had to be pitched to. And when he was pitched to, the results were devastating. He hit

.314, a career high 24 home runs, scored 146 runs, and knocked in 72 to go with his 80 stolen bases.

Mattingly, who wound up with 145 RBIs for the year, more than any Yankee since Joe DiMaggio in 1948 (155), not only was able to bring his superlative hitting skills to the plate with runners in scoring position and thunder behind him in the order, but because it was usually Henderson out there, skewering the defenses, he also got an agreeable diet of fastballs to work with. The reason it was impossible to predict what this offensive tandem would do is simple: There had not been one quite like it in the game for decades.

But the real surprise—and secret weapon—was the Yankee bullpen, which not only kept the team in the race till the end but was probably the equal of Toronto's. (The Yankees actually fashioned 49 saves out of their relievers. The Jays had 46.) Some of the credit for this has to go to Martin, some to the staff of coaches, including the patient and skillful Jeff Torborg. But it is the Yankee organization itself—the "baseball people"—which should get their due here. The acquisitions of Brian Fisher and Rich Bordi were just the latest in a series of moves over the years where the Yankees were able, because of superior scouting and clout to back it up, to fleece other organizations of real pitching talent (Righetti, Ron Davis, Jay Howell, and now Brian Fisher were all acquired as minor-leaguers before anyone knew they would be quite so good). With young talent also coming through the Yankee system, the ultimate surprise is that George Steinbrenner's organization is not a jerry-built vaudeville contraption but that it is, in spite of him, first-rate.

Which is not to deny that when it counted, the heavy hand of *shlock* was as decisive as ever. It is likely that Steinbrenner's oafish tirade against Dave Winfield (he called him "Mr. May"— as opposed to "Mr. October," Reggie Jackson), Ken Griffey, and Don Baylor in the midst of the Yankees late-season penultimate series with Toronto, cost the team dearly. They lost five games in a row following the Toronto series, playing as though they were hypnotized, demoralized, and drugged, and even though they staggered back into contention the final weekend, nearly all observers point to that late Toronto series in New York as a sort of climax. It was. The Blue Jays and Yankees took care of the baseball part. The Producer took care of those parts that were Theater of the Absurd.

For Broadway buffs, the portents for this Steinbrenner Production were there throughout the summer. George's penchant for the military, coupled with his unremitting itch to lay a big one on the White Way, had already seen to it that rooting for the Yankees this year would be akin to patriotism (the advertising slogan for the year was "New York's Stars in Stripes are Flying Again"). Early in the campaign, when the Red Sox came to town, Yankee Productions ran a dress rehearsal for what was to come. They plastered the town with a couple of slogans attributed to their soon-to-be-fired manager: "Yogi Says, 'It Ain't Gonna Be No Tea Party.'" And "Yogi Says, 'This Is War.'"

Now, having for years been familiar with the sort of fan violence and mayhem that were a regular part of cultural life at Yankee Stadium when the Producer had a winner, this was a marketing strategy that left one begging for a loser. The Yankees then obliged—though Berra was booted. But later in the summer, when it was clear the Yankees were the only team that had a realistic chance of catching Toronto, the Production team had the hit show it always had been waiting for. Call it a rerun, Steinbrenner-style, of *Yankee Doddle Dandy,* call it by the newly disseminated slogan, "The Yanks Are Coming," whatever. You didn't have to be the ghost of George M. Cohan to know that the September Toronto series would be the baseball equivalent of war between America and a foreign enemy.

Of course it was predictable that, with the Yankees winning, Yankee Stadium would once again turn into a seething hate pit, where the action in the stands exceeded anything that could take place on the field. (This, alas, cannot be exaggerated. Anyone who went to a Yankee–Red Sox game in the mid- to late-seventies understands this perfectly. Opposing players literally took their lives in their hands standing immobile in the outfield. One night years ago I saw Yaz nearly destroyed when one of the Producer's partisans chucked a heavy weighted object past his ear. This year, after a game with the Orioles—which the Yankees won—I waited outside the players' gate with Elrod Hendricks, the Orioles' coach who once played for the Yankees. A howling mob stood behind police barricades, jeering and screaming obscenities at each of the Oriole players who boarded a waiting team bus. This was standard, Hendricks assured me—for Yankee Stadium. He knew no other place where such behavior occurred.)

At any rate, with the race as close as a whisker, the four September dates in New York that Yankee Productions presented as a theatrical version of the Great War had this other dimension beyond baseball. Of course, there were the unison chants concerning the Blue Jays' oral proclivities, the all-out fights in the grandstands that had large numbers of fans on their feet and cheering whenever anything like an injury-inducing blow was struck, and the repeated interruptions of play for objects hurled from the stands at the Blue Jay players.

I am sure that George Steinbrenner was embarrassed by the opening-night booing of the Canadian national anthem, a booing so well joined that it became hard to hear the singer. But even if he failed somehow to understand why it happened, it flowed absolutely from the script he himself had fashioned. If there was any doubt about it, it should have been dispelled when the Yankees, trailing going into the seventh inning of that first game, erupted for five runs, highlighted by a tremendous upper-deck home run by Ron Hassey. The Yankee Stadium organ, by any standard the loudest in the major leagues, erupted with a maximum-decibel rendition of "Over There," the patriotic slambanger from *Yankee Doddle Dandy*. The organ repeated the theme again and again, until, as some of the Yankee players later said, "We wondered what was going on." What was going on was clear enough—victory over the Hun.

Except that the Blue Jays in the next three days turned *Yankee Doodle Dandy* into *Springtime for Steinbrenner*. The Jays professionally disposed of the Yankees and left New York snugly in first place—with the Producer hoisted on the petard of his own advertising. Was he really personally responsible for the vulgar theatrics of the War Show? I asked Don Baylor if he thought George might have had a hand in that seventh-inning musicale accompanying Hassey's gamer. "Sure, he's behind everything," Baylor said. "People are scared to death to make any kind of decision on their own around here for fear of being fired on the spot."

The irony in all this is that George, in the end, provided just the sort of show that in its own corny way was inordinately satisfying to anyone with a sense of poetic justice. The unfortunate part is that it got in the way of some good baseball and besmirched Steinbrenner's own team. The day after the Jays left town, in the wake of Steinbrenner's "Mr. May" salvo, Dave Winfield was sitting with a reporter in the Yankee clubhouse. "The unfortunate thing," he was saying in a tone both subdued and free of anger, "was that, for the first time since I've been here, this has been a real team—with every guy on the roster contributing, helping out. We pulled together this year." He shrugged, and added, "And now this."

The Blue Jays, on the other hand, were a team from the start. They were what I saw in the spring, when winning exhibition games mattered and they were a team, still, when, after years of learning how to lose together, they had finally been able to win together. They came to these decisive games with a sense of professional purpose that was impressive and, in the end, completely convincing. Along with many other observers, I had expected the Yankees, who had been on a roll, to hit the Blue Jays with the force of a freight train. And that was precisely what happened in the initial game of the series. The Jays, it seemed reasonable to assume, were dead Canadian ducks, victims of the first real pennant race they had been in—and, of course, of George's patriotic Pressure Bowl. But they carried their own script with them.

Epy Guerrero had come all the way to New York from the Dominican Republic to see the games. "Want to check up on the boys," he said good-naturedly before the first game but then acknowledged his real purpose in being there. All the scouts in the Toronto organization had been summoned, he said. "In games like these, you see a lot, you see how players perform when it counts most. All of the scouts are here," he said, "because fifty pairs of eyes can see better than five or ten."

The next evening, after the seemingly catastrophic opening-game defeat, Guerrero was not nearly as sanguine as much of the local and national media who had all but written off the Jays.

"The thing about this team is that it is very aggressive," he said. "I don't know why people don't seem to see that. They always play to make things happen. If you beat them, all they will do is turn around and go after you. This will be hard-fought, but I like our chances."

So did the players, the coaches, and the manager who even refused to acknowledge that the team was playing under pressure. In reply to a question about the ghosts of Yankee tradition becoming a factor in the series, Cox, an ex-Yankee himself, snorted, "If Babe Ruth, Lou Gehrig, and Mickey Mantle were in their lineup, I might be shitting in my pants, but I don't see them over there."

Cox's charges resolutely refused to acknowledge that they were playing under pressure, too. This, of course, is standard procedure for modern professional athletes. In baseball, the only cliché more frequently used than "I was just trying to hit it hard somewhere" is "It's just another game."

Damaso Garcia came as close as any ballplayer I've met to actually filling his bladder with something more than hot air:

"I take things one day at a time. Today is today, tomorrow is tomorrow. This is special only because it's Yankee Stadium and there's all that television. But we have to go to Boston after this. You think those games won't be tough? People say these games are special. But the others are, too. I still have to go up there and hit that first pitch and do all the aggressive things I do. . . . Fifty thousand people screaming? That's pressure? Pressure for me is playing in front of three thousand people. . . . I think all of us just play the best we can. That's what we know, that's what we do. If we can go out there and put our names up as people who play the game well, that's all we can ask for. This game is black and white. It's what you do—and no more."

Jesse Barfield did acknowledge that the games were special, that there was pressure. But the middle of a pennant race in front of fifty thousand fans was just where he wanted to be. He was believable in the spring and he was believable now. "This is fun," he said, "this is what baseball is all about." What Barfield did not enjoy was the sense that there was some organized feeling out there against a Canadian team winning the pennant. "It makes you want to win a little more," he said, "and I don't even know the words to 'O Canada.'"

"I do," said the young shortstop Tony Fernandez, who had overheard Barfield. He proceeded to sing the Canadian anthem flawlessly, in a heavy Spanish accent. Fernandez, particularly, given his age and the fact that he had made a crucial error the night before, might have beeen feeling unsettled. He claimed he wasn't. "I love to play with pressure," he said. "I like lots of people in the stands and lots of noise." I wondered about the effect of fifty thousand people on him. "It's fun, it gets me going," he said. "Where I come from, the people make a lot of noise. I tell you, five thousand people where I come from make as much noise as these fifty thousand here. These games make me feel like I'm back home." I don't know if the Blue Jays, as a team, are any more adroit handling the clichés of the trade than other teams, but in the end, under maximum pressure in their autumn race for a divisional title, they were remarkably like the team I saw at ease in the spring. They came within an eyelash of a pennant—and their seven-game loss to the Royals in the play-offs proved only that they were one game short of completing what they had begun in 1977.

As surprising as the Yankees' success was the Tigers' failure during the season. Not only had the champions needed a final game victory to eke out a third-place finish, but the component parts of what sustained them the year before seemed to come apart this year. The bullpen with many arms became the bullpen with one sometimes injured arm. Aurelio Lopez seemed to grow old in a matter of months and, even before the season's end, Doug Bair had been dropped from the squad. Willie Hernandez, alone, was merely mortal.

The Tiger defense, arguably the best in the league the year before, became unquestionably the worst in the league in 1985. The team had committed more errors than anyone and wound up with the poorest fielding percentage in the American League.

"I have no answer for that," Lou Whitaker said one late September day. "I know we tried hard, maybe too hard, maybe being the Detroit Tigers got to us too much this year. You know just because you won you assume you can repeat that just by doing what you did before. You can't. Each time you win, you have to win in a different way."

The Tigers, as ex-champions, were different. The faces, even much of the camaraderie, seemed the same. But they too had been touched by time. Lance Parrish was wearing his britches low ("I still like the ball up," he said, "but let's just say I'm having a little dispute with the front office"); Kirk Gibson, contemplating free agency, was already in the business of revising his positive image for the following year. Alan Trammell was 60 points below his MVP batting average—and out of words. He could not bring himself to talk about the year's turn of fortune.

Sparky Anderson could. He had no explanation for the team's play. There were no excuses. "We just played terrible, that's all." But, Sparky claimed, "I think I've had more fun this year than last." This, he claimed, ensued from the fact that sixteen years in the big leagues had finally taught him how to lose. "You know why? When something happens, it's over. I've won," he said, "I've won championships in both leagues, I don't have nuthin' to prove, but that don't make this year for me. Those championships are in the past. If I need to live in the past, I look 'em up in the record books. Same with losing. We lost this year—and it's over, it's in the past. I have my family, I have my health. . . ." And, Sparky might have added, his contract, too. Management, at year's end, extended his tenure with the team for an additional two years. "I've been to the mountain," Sparky said, drawing on his ubiquitous pipe, "and I'm on the other side." He cared, he said, about his team representing itself well—winning or losing—on the field. This, perhaps, was the only outward acknowledgment that time had been sudden and swift with him in 1985.

The decline of the Tigers, following a pattern set by other pennant winners and world champions in recent years, has stayed with me into the winter. Because I had so recently spent time with them as champions, their fall reminded me as nothing else had that a baseball life—a career, a season—is very short. It is life concentrated and telescoped. Sadaharu Oh, when he retired, told his teammates that life was short but a baseball life was shorter. He urged them, therefore, to make the best use of the time they had.

Baseball is surely a tough membrane, tougher and more elastic than the pollutants in its environment. But it is bounded by time in this peculiar way: beginnings and endings are forced closer together, so that often it becomes hard to distinguish one from the other. Baseball has over it a poignancy of time. The champions appear in the spring and are gone in the fall. Those who come to replace them only a while ago labored in relative obscurity. Where have you gone, Willie Mays; how did you get here, Dwight Gooden?

One March day last spring I watched a baseball game that
surely was about beginnings. Or was it? In retrospect, I thought
it might have been about endings. In any case it underscored for
me, as nothing else, how intimately connected the boundaries of
a baseball life are. It also, for me, happened to represent the
essence of spring baseball—not the free publicity part—but the
part all of us have known in our own experience. For myself, it
had something to do with the High Hard One.

The game I saw was between a pair of community college
teams at Tigertown. I came across the game by accident on a
field behind Joker Marchant Stadium. While this game took
place within yards of one I had just seen between two major-
league teams, it could not have been further from the big
leagues. The Cecil Community College Seahawks, in their
green-and-white uniforms with their gunny sacks of balls and
aluminum bats and shin guards were on one side of the field—
with their parents and friends, who had come all the way from
Maryland with them—and on the other, late in arriving, were
the Florida Southern Jayvees—with their girlfriends. The Cecil
Seahawks were in spring training. They had spent the entire
winter selling raffle tickets and pages in the yearbook to charter
a bus to Florida so they, like any serious ballplayers, could get a
start on the season. And they had made it. Once before they had
traveled as far south as Jacksonville. Now, in 1985, they had
made it all the way to baseball country.

The Seahawks, said their coach, a gentleman named Dick
Brockell, were a serious team. "Last year we were 28–7 overall
and won our conference and have the potential to repeat as
champions." Snow had had them working indoors all winter, a
terrible winter, and they had gotten outside only the day before
they left for Florida. "We stopped off at Saint Francis, Maryland, and Florence, South Carolina. We lost to Saint Francis,
Maryland, 6–5 in the ninth inning, and then we came to Florida
and lost to Saint Leo's in Lakeland, 6–2, and last night we beat
Saint Petersburg, 6–3. We were hoping to play in the big-league

stadium today but they put us on this field instead." The Seahawks, the coach said, had several "prospects," including the pitcher for the afternoon, a freshman named Andy Emmerich. "The scouts," he added, "have been especially high on Emmerich and our catcher, Casey Vaartjes."

Actually, there was a scout present that afternoon. When I asked Brockell if he expected the game to be scouted, he nodded his head ever so slightly in the direction of the backstop and whispered, "That guy over there's from the Brewers." It did not take long to realize that Andy Emmerich and Casey Vaartjes knew it, that their parents and everyone else present at the game knew it, too. I settled myself in next to the Brewer scout, Don Koller, to watch the game.

Koller told me that he knew the Seahawks pretty well, as they played in the region he normally covered. They were a good team for their division, he said, adding that he hadn't seen anyone he thought was a legitimate prospect on the team. Did he expect to see anything that afternoon? "Maybe there's a better game to go to," he said, "but I don't want to get caught short with the front office. I've only been scouting four years and there have been guys doing it for thirty. I get paid to go out and scout—that's what I'm doing."

He sat in a canvas chair behind the backstop, periodically raising a radar gun and a stopwatch to check different players. Every eye in the bleachers and on the bench on the Cecil side of the field kept flicking toward the scout. Occasionally, the coach wandered over and tried to get the scout into some friendly small talk. The scout was pleasant but unwilling to go beyond monosyllables with the coach. At one point, I went to the water fountain, and when I looked up there was a man standing next to me who was a dead ringer for the pitcher, Emmerich—except he was middle-aged. Standing next to him was another middle-aged man who looked enough like Vaartjes for me to draw my own conclusions.

The game did not go well for the Seahawks. They fell behind

early, and it was clear they were in over their heads. The coach came over again and, between idle observations on the weather and the team's upcoming games, told the scout how good Emmerich woud be once he got his spring innings in. The scout merely nodded without committing himself.

"How hard's he throwing?" the coach finally asked.

The scout, who had made a point of switching off the gun when he saw the coach move in, shrugged and said, "Maybe eighty, eighty-one." Brockell knew there was no argument to be made. He looked crestfallen and walked away.

"How hard does a guy have to throw?" I asked later.

"Major-league average is eighty-five," he said.

Andy Emmerich's father came over after his son overthrew one especially swift-looking fastball. The ball hit the backstop but the father didn't seem to care. That was the high hard one and, the father knew, the gun had been on.

"How fast was that last pitch?" he asked the scout point-blank.

"Eighty-three," the scout said.

"Chrissakes, he throws harder than that," the father said without anger. You could almost hear the lump in his throat. Andy Emmerich did not get past the third inning—and the Seahawks got pasted by their larger opponents. To add insult to injury, one of the Florida boys hit a ball to left field that bounced once and somehow went into the opened door of the Cecil Seahawks' bus—ground rule double, knife in the heart.

Emmerich sat away from the rest of his team, a major-league pack of ice on his amateur shoulder, looking as much the picture of defeat and misery as any youngster who has ever experiencd the death of a dream. There was nothing, nothing after baseball. On the father's face was a similar but somewhat sterner look.

The odd thing was that though this was in all respects just what it appeared to be, there was one particle or, more properly, one pitch that crossed the grain of complete failure. Emmerich, in the course of his miserable showing, had thrown one pitch that registered eighty-five miles per hour on Koller's gun. Koller was not going to recommend Emmerich—he did not believe he was a prospect—but he was going to include in his scouting report that the boy had thrown one major-league average fastball, so that another scout in the Brewer organization, somewhere along the line, would be aware that maybe, just maybe, another report might be in order.

I am not sure whether I was witness to the end or the beginning of Emmerich's career. But I do know that Emmerich, along with scores of others I met along the way from The Superstitions to the Everglades, made me realize that the game was secure. But then again, that is common knowledge. Anyone who has ever picked up a ball and a bat, who has felt the ground fly beneath spiked shoes, who has stretched out a gloved hand to spear a baseball hurtling against a backdrop of sky, who has memorized the sensation of a ball striking the sweet part of a bat, knows the game will be part of our lives till daylight fails and there is no one left to turn on the lights.